CREATIVITY TEACHERS

A Cognitive Science Approach

Claire Badger and Jonathan Firth

Routledge
Taylor & Francis Group
LONDON AND NEW YORK

Designed cover image: © InnerDrive

First published 2025
by Routledge
4 Park Square, Milton Park, Abingdon, Oxon OX14 4RN

and by Routledge
605 Third Avenue, New York, NY 10158

Routledge is an imprint of the Taylor & Francis Group, an informa business

© 2025 Claire Badger and Jonathan Firth

The right of Claire Badger and Jonathan Firth to be identified as authors of this work has been asserted in accordance with sections 77 and 78 of the Copyright, Designs and Patents Act 1988.

All rights reserved. No part of this book may be reprinted or reproduced or utilised in any form or by any electronic, mechanical, or other means, now known or hereafter invented, including photocopying and recording, or in any information storage or retrieval system, without permission in writing from the publishers.

Trademark notice: Product or corporate names may be trademarks or registered trademarks, and are used only for identification and explanation without intent to infringe.

British Library Cataloguing-in-Publication Data
A catalogue record for this book is available from the British Library

Library of Congress Cataloging-in-Publication Data
Names: Badger, Claire, author. | Firth, Jonathan, 1975- author.
Title: Creativity for teachers : a cognitive science approach / Claire Badger and Jonathan Firth.
Description: Abingdon, Oxon ; New York, NY : Routledge, 2025. | Series: The teacher CPD academy | Includes bibliographical references and index.
Identifiers: LCCN 2024043636 (print) | LCCN 2024043637 (ebook) | ISBN 9781032719238 (hardback) | ISBN 9781032733180 (paperback) | ISBN 9781032719221 (ebook)
Subjects: LCSH: Creative teaching. | Competency-based education. | Cognitive neuroscience.
Classification: LCC LB1025.3 .B333 2025 (print) | LCC LB1025.3 (ebook) | DDC 371.1--dc23/eng/20250106
LC record available at https://lccn.loc.gov/2024043636
LC ebook record available at https://lccn.loc.gov/2024043637

ISBN: 978-1-032-71923-8 (hbk)
ISBN: 978-1-032-73318-0 (pbk)
ISBN: 978-1-032-71922-1 (ebk)

DOI: 10.4324/9781032719221

Typeset in Interstate
by KnowledgeWorks Global Ltd.

CONTENTS

	About the Authors	ix
	Acknowledgements	x
	Foreword	xi
1	**Creativity as the Cognitive Scientist Views It**	1
2	**Do Schools Kill Creativity?**	12
3	**Building Blocks**	31
4	**Flexible Knowledge**	50
5	**Creativity Across All Subjects**	70
6	**Breaking from the Routine**	94
7	**The Goldilocks Rule of Constraints**	117
8	**Structured Uncertainty**	134
9	**Metacognition and Strategic Creativity**	153
10	**Creativity and Motivation**	173
11	**Creative Projects**	194

12	Assessing Creativity	217
13	Developing Creative Teachers	236
14	Looking Back and Looking Forward	254

References   261
Index   276

ABOUT THE AUTHORS

Dr Claire Badger has been teaching secondary school Chemistry across a range of UK schools for over 18 years. Since 2015, she has been the Assistant Head in charge of teaching and learning at the Godolphin and Latymer School in London where she has been able to develop her interest in the ways in which research from cognitive science can help us all become better teachers and learners. She holds a Masters in Teaching and Learning from UCL's Institute of Education and is a Founding Fellow of the Chartered College of Teaching.

Dr Jonathan Firth is a senior teaching fellow at the University of Strathclyde, and previously worked as a secondary school teacher of Psychology. His research interests include cognition and metacognition, learning theories, and the cognitive basis of skills. He has written several education books, most recently *Metacognition and Study Skills: A Guide for Teachers*, published by Routledge, and *What Teachers Need to Know About Memory*, published by Sage and co-authored by Nasima Riazat. Jonathan also sends a free weekly newsletter on memory and metacognition which can be found at firth.substack.com.

ACKNOWLEDGEMENTS

Both authors would like to thank the series editors and their team at InnerDrive for their support, in particular Bradley Busch for his guidance, patience and reassurance over the writing process, and Janet Voong for her fantastic work with the graphics.

Claire: For me, this book has very much been a collaborative effort, and I'd like to thank the huge number of friends, colleagues and students who have contributed ideas and examples. You are far too numerous to mention individually but I hope you recognise your contributions and will accept my apologies for any unintentional misrepresentations! Specific mentions, however, are owed to Liz, Rachel, Alistair, Izzy and Simon who allowed me to write whilst staying in their lovely homes and provided much valued support and advice. Finally, a special thank you to my friend and colleague John Carroll who has done more than anyone to help this naturally risk-averse person embrace the uncertainty required for creativity to flourish.

Jonathan: I'd like to thank colleagues Paul Wickham and Jane Catlin who worked on the Creativity in Education module at Strathclyde and helped me to refine my ideas, as well as all of the students who participated in that module – it was a pleasure to read your essays! I'd like to thank the schools and universities who have invited me to speak to staff about creativity – the chance to discuss these ideas with practitioners never ceases to be helpful. Finally, I'd like to thank my wife Fiona for her support and forbearance as I worked on yet another book – not to mention editing all my weekly newsletters.

FOREWORD

We are delighted to introduce *Creativity for Teachers: A Cognitive Science Approach* as part of our Teacher CPD Academy series.

Creativity is often viewed as a somewhat enigmatic quality – something that some are born with, while others are not. But this book, authored by Dr Claire Badger and Dr Jonathan Firth, challenges that notion head-on, posing an essential question: Is creativity an inherent trait, or can it be nurtured?

Drawing on the latest research from cognitive science, the authors offer a unique insight into one of the most important topics in education. They reveal that creativity is not a mysterious gift bestowed on a lucky few but rather a skill that can be developed and enhanced in every student.

This book goes beyond theory, providing practical strategies that teachers can implement to cultivate a culture of creativity in their classrooms. Claire and Jonathan offer advice on how to unlock the creative potential within all students, showing that creativity is not just an artistic endeavour, but a fundamental part of learning and thinking.

As with the other titles in our series, there is a module based on this book on our online platform, www.teachercpdacademy.com. This module, alongside other brilliant resources on teaching and learning, is designed to support your continued professional development.

We hope that *Creativity for Teachers: A Cognitive Science Approach* not only challenges preconceived notions but also empowers you to foster and develop creativity in every learner.

Bradley Busch and Edward Watson, Directors of InnerDrive

1 Creativity as the Cognitive Scientist Views It

Creativity Debates and Disagreement

What is your response to the word 'creativity' in education? Many people see creativity as one of the key skills that our young people will need to thrive in the world beyond school. For others the term creativity is vague, woolly and unhelpful – something that does not belong to modern, high-quality, evidence-based education. Perhaps it doesn't seem to sit well with key ideas that inform a modern, cognitive science approach to practice – ideas such as cognitive load or retrieval practice.

For the latter group, it may be a surprise to find out that creativity is an area of research that draws on similar academic traditions to those other cognitive science concepts. Much of the research into creativity has been carried out by psychologists using experimental methods. And those researchers very much acknowledge and draw on familiar principles of cognition – the limitations of working memory, for example, or the importance of knowledge.

For those who see creativity as an important life skill, we agree – to an extent. Creative work is important in many ways. However, developing the capacity to be creative is not so simple. How often do you hear people say things like, *'If children do ___ it will develop their creative skills'*? Quite often, in our experience! Along with other vague statements about boosting skills or preparing learners for their future life and work, the ideas presented are often poorly thought out, representing wishful thinking rather than a clear plan to support students.

DOI: 10.4324/9781032719221-1

When politicians argue that simply adding more time on the arts to the curriculum would pave the way to a highly creative workforce, this is also little more than wishful thinking. The arts are of great value, but as we will see throughout this book, creativity often doesn't transfer from one context to another (see Chapter 6), and in any case, it does not *just* apply to arts subjects (see Chapter 5).

However, there are ways that creativity can be usefully supported and developed in education. As will be explored in this book, creative thinking can be understood in terms of certain processes which are becoming increasingly well understood by cognitive science. Understanding these processes will help us to support and apply creativity effectively in schools, in harmony with and informed by cognitive science.

> ### Pause to reflect
> What is your initial reaction to the concept of creativity in education? In terms of the debate mentioned above, do you fall more on one side or the other? Are you surprised that creativity research draws on similar academic traditions to cognitive science?

Myths and Misconceptions in Education

You may be familiar with popular myths about learning and about the brain, such as the idea that learners only use 10 per cent of their brains. Such 'neuromyths' are widespread despite not being based on research evidence (e.g. Howard-Jones, 2014).

Creativity, too, is subject to widespread myths. For example, Benedek et al. (2021) found that people's everyday ideas about creativity were marked by a tendency to overestimate the role of chance factors, and to underestimate the role of expertise and practice. Most assume that creativity is something that just happens by lucky accident, or by tapping into your 'inner child'. This is notably different from the cognitive science explanation of creativity that we will guide you to explore in this book.

We would argue that tackling myths is an important step in better understanding creativity. There is a major focus in this book on identifying areas where creativity is widely misunderstood, and providing an accessible explanation for the teacher that draws on evidence rather than assumptions. That is to say, we highlight what the myths are, look at the research that tackles them, and consider implications for practice.

Overall, it would be a mistake to dismiss creativity as a concept just because it is sometimes misunderstood, poorly explained, or implemented in flawed ways. We feel that it's much better to grow our professional understanding of the concept, and to begin to share this with students and parents, too.

In depth: Teaching creatively

In preparation for this book, Claire asked several teacher colleagues what creativity meant to them in an educational context. One initial response was that it involved students having 'wild and wacky' ideas!

Overall, aspects that were commonly viewed as creative included:

1. Projects and open-ended tasks
2. Gamifying learning, for example via debates and puzzles
3. Incorporating artistic elements such as posters, presentations, or songs, rather than a traditional written response
4. Extra-curricular activities, clubs and competitions

Taking a cognitive science approach to creativity means scrutinising these kinds of assumptions. Is a song-based response any more creative than an essay, for example, and is it the most appropriate way of developing understanding and flexible use of knowledge and routines? You might wish to return to these examples and consider your responses after reading the rest of the book.

Creativity Too Vague to Be Defined?

One popular myth that is relevant right from the start of this book is the idea that creativity is too vague to be defined. Perhaps you have heard someone say that creativity is a mysterious process – something that just happens, and that can't really be understood or pinned down.

In everyday life, people may believe that each person can or should have their own unique view of creativity, that it's impossible to explore scientifically, or that you can't or shouldn't try to define it. Indeed, it's not just laypeople – some research studies into creativity fail to specifically define the concept they are studying (Bereczki & Kárpáti, 2018, p. 34).

It's also common for people to think that creativity is entirely in the eye of the beholder, and that the quality of art (for example) is completely subjective. For example, in one study, more than half of the participants agreed with the statement that modern art is indistinguishable from children's drawings (Benedek et al., 2021; see Chapter 12).

However, creativity can be and has been defined. Scientists use a specific but broad definition that applies across all possible disciplines and tasks: creativity involves coming up with something new and useful (or *novel* and *valuable*) in a particular social context (e.g. Harrington, 2018; Runco & Jaeger, 2012).

- By *new*, we mean that the individual has had an idea or made a product or object that is novel in some way – it hasn't been done before (or, at least, not by that learner or their peers in that social context). Coming up with an original painting or a game-plan in sport may be new; making a cheese sandwich is not.
- By *useful*, we mean that it has some value in meeting a particular need or solving a problem. This doesn't have to be a practical need – entertainment or aesthetic beauty can also count as needs/uses, so writing a great novel or composing a pop song can be considered useful.

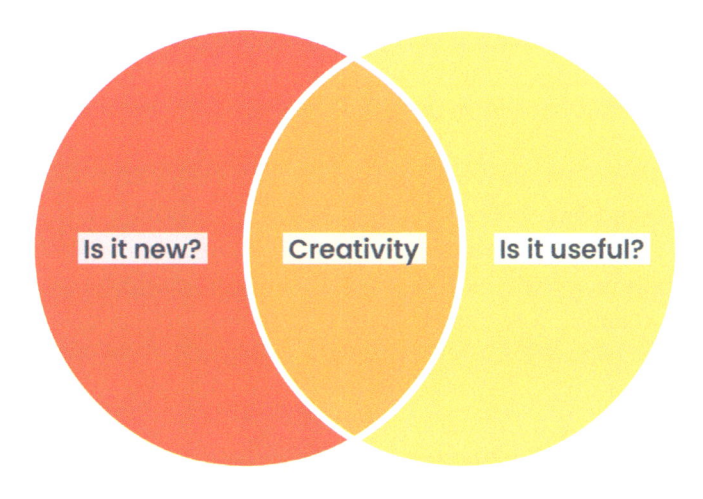

Figure 1.1 The standard definition of creativity

The definition outlined above and in Figure 1.1 is sometimes called the 'standard definition' of creativity (e.g. Runco & Jaeger, 2012), used and shared across academia.

To meet the definition, both criteria – novelty and usefulness – must be met. Labelling the ingredients on a jar of food solves a need but is not new. Throwing together random sentences will create a text that is new but not useful. However, if a student writes an article for a school magazine, this can be seen as both new and useful.

It's worth noting that the above definition doesn't apply just to so-called 'creative subjects'. Scientists who devise a new experiment are thinking creatively, as are engineers who develop a new type of solar panel. Arts-type subjects are not always creative, either; it depends how they are taught and practised. More on this issue in Chapter 5!

It's also worth considering that the standard definition does not just apply to great artistic or scientific breakthroughs. As educators, we (Jonathan and Claire) are more closely concerned with everyday creativity of the kind that our students can engage in, and we imagine that most readers feel similarly. Granted, we hope to prepare students to excel in whatever future field or activity appeals to them. But the emphasis in this book is on the classroom.

To keep track of this distinction, researchers class eminent creative contributions and major breakthroughs as 'Big-C' creativity, and everyday examples as 'little-c' creativity (Kaufman & Beghetto, 2009). The latter involve creating something new and useful on an individual level, for example adapting a recipe or finding an alternative travel route when faced with train strikes.

We will explore and expand on this later in the book, but for now, it's valuable to recognise that creativity *is* possible to define, and what's more, creative processes are within reach of our students. Indeed, they are happening every day in classrooms.

Pause to reflect

How does the standard definition of creativity change your thinking around what we think of as being creative? Can you think of any examples within your own subject where students can 'create' something without it meeting the definition of creative? What about examples of original ideas which would *not* be defined as creative (perhaps because they have done exactly the same thing before)?

Creativity and Cognitive Science

This book takes a cognitive science (or 'science of learning') approach to creativity in education. By this we mean that we will draw on research from fields like neuroscience and (especially) psychology to better understand how creativity works. We hope that this resonates with all practitioners who have seen the value of engaging with other aspects of cognitive science; in recent years, concepts such as memory, attention and metacognition have been more widely applied to the classroom.

We believe that creativity fits with this group of concepts and can be applied in a similar way.

A creative solution is not a routine solution, and its inherent uncertainty may be one reason that people find creativity an uncomfortable concept. There is no guarantee of coming up with an appropriate creative solution to a problem, or a good idea for an essay. However, other evidence-based techniques also have inherent uncertainties; applying an evidence-based memory technique does not guarantee that a student will remember the target information, for example. Drawing on psychological theories and evidence gives us a more secure guide to practice, one that is an improvement on assumptions and tradition (Sawyer, 2006). It provides best bets for the educator. This reasoning applies to creativity.

To look at it from the other side, *failing* to think about creativity and not engaging with the evidence about how to do it well in educational contexts is every bit as uncertain, and neglects any benefits and insights that research evidence can provide. Hoping for the best is not a good approach across other issues such as student literacy. It's much better to soberly assess the challenges and consider what the research evidence can tell us. Such evidence never provides a perfect blueprint, but it is at least a lot better than crossing our fingers.

If you are a teacher who has already started to enhance your classroom practice through the application of cognitive science, this book will help you to take a similar approach to creativity.

Why Is Creativity Important?

The importance of creativity is often assumed, but the reason for this importance is often poorly specified. We feel that it is valuable to be specific about what creativity is for, what kind of situations it can help with, and how it would impact education at different ages.

Perhaps one of the most obvious considerations is that creativity will be useful for life beyond the classroom, including careers. In line with the definition discussed above, there might be many cases where an adult comes up with something new and useful in a particular context. Here are just a few:

- A business idea
- A research insight or invention
- A new way of running a team at work
- A way of managing their own time

Young people also encounter many situations where creative thinking is relevant. They have problems that they need to solve, prompting them to come up with ideas and creations. In academic settings, they may need to think of projects or ideas for stories, talks and essays. In their everyday life, they may be able to apply creativity to hobbies, creative writing, and even to their social lives.

In this context, it is important to consider the role of the teacher and the school. Some educators might argue that in a world increasingly dominated by technology (where the vast sum of human knowledge can be accessed via a quick Google search), the purpose of schools is to develop skills, rather than to fill students' heads with knowledge. The release of ChatGPT and other generative AI tools into the wild and the subsequent debates over the impact that AI will have on education have seen a resurgence of these arguments. It would be easy to assume that knowledge is obsolete, and that creativity can be developed in its absence.

In this book, we will engage fully (but not dogmatically) with this debate. We will outline the vital importance of factual knowledge for coming up with creative ideas and solutions to problems. We also emphasise the limitations of the transferable skill concept – highlighting where creative performance will not easily transfer across subjects, or from the classroom to the workplace. However, we also emphasise that students need to have more than just knowledge. Students can develop a toolbox of creative skills and habits, learning to recombine what they know, and make novel connections. We will explore classroom applications to support students' creative thinking by helping them to develop creative strategies, and to self-regulate this process.

Is Creativity the Same as Problem Solving?

In the previous section we referred to the relevance of creative thinking to help people solve problems. This might make you wonder whether creativity is actually the same thing as problem solving. Couldn't we perhaps conceive of *any* creative task as a process of solving a problem of some sort? If such tasks are no different from the everyday problems that students work on in class, perhaps we don't need to explore research into creativity at all!

Some problems that learners tackle in the classroom, such as how to phrase a sentence, do appear to meet the definition of creativity – the outcome is new and useful. However, other problems may be more routine. It would stretch the definition to say that the 10th problem on a set of 20 examples of multiplying fractions was really *new* – especially if everyone in the class came up with the same solution.

To clarify this issue, creativity researchers make a distinction between convergent and divergent thinking:

- Convergent thinking is when several pieces of information or strategies lead to a single correct solution.
- Divergent thinking is when a single idea or problem leads to multiple possible solutions or ideas. They may vary in value, but there is no one objectively correct solution (see Figure 1.2).

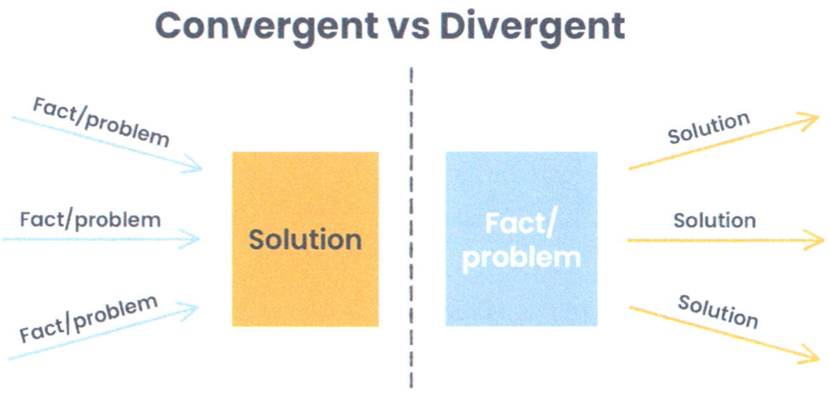

Convergent vs Divergent

Figure 1.2 Convergent and divergent thinking

As may be obvious, divergent thinking is more associated with creativity. This makes sense if you refer back to the definition of creativity. Convergent thinking involves the student using information and strategies to come up with a correct solution – hopefully the same solution as their classmates, and the objectively 'right answer'. It's useful, but it's not novel.

Divergent thinking involves coming up with several possibilities, which the student can then consider and choose among. There may be one starting problem or need, but there are many possible routes forward (again, even crafting a sentence does fit with this way of looking at creativity!). By placing the emphasis less on the problem and more on a way of thinking that students will engage in, the concept of divergent thinking helps to clarify that creativity only applies to some types of classroom problems. We will refer back to this during the book.

There is one caveat to the above explanation – sometimes a routine problem could be tackled in a new way, or, at least, in a way that was new to the student. For example, a routine mathematical problem would generally not involve divergent thinking, but if a student were to come up with an elegant and unusual way of tackling it (one that was not shown to them by their teacher or peers, perhaps), then we could see their response as an example of creative thinking. Basic facts and procedures also act as building blocks for more complex tasks where creativity will be essential (more on this in Chapter 3).

Overall, then, there is certainly an overlap between problem solving and creativity, but the former is a broader term. Only some problems tend to lead to creative solutions. Others have more everyday solutions that don't require divergent thinking. All the same, there are many parallels between the cognitive processes involved in creativity and other types of problem solving. You will see numerous examples throughout this book.

Using This Book

This book is structured as follows. Each chapter contains one or more of the common myths and misconceptions about creativity that were mentioned earlier in this chapter. We then present some of the key theoretical ideas and evidence, helping you to understand *why* the myth is considered to be false, and to explore more evidence-based ways of looking at creativity. These theoretical sections draw heavily on cognitive science, and especially on cognitive psychology.

These earlier parts of the chapters contain many thought-provoking ideas and technical concepts, and we frequently include 'Pause to reflect' questions. The aim of these is for you to think about the material as you read – the questions are designed to be quick, and there is no need to discuss them with colleagues or to write anything down (although you are free to do so if you wish).

Later in each chapter we aim to help you bring the ideas to life in your classroom. In the sections titled 'Applications to Practice', our goal was to build on each chapter's key ideas by presenting a set of techniques and strategies that any teacher can start to use. Of course, the details will depend on your context, but we have tried to make them as clear and specific as possible. To further support you as you think about and apply the ideas, each chapter contains one or more 'in depth' case studies, illustrating and exemplifying creativity in a more specific context.

We finish each chapter with a brief conclusion, as well as two further features:

- Discussion Questions
- Professional Learning Tasks

The goal of these is to allow you to get more from the chapter by engaging with it over a more extended period of time. For example, the discussion questions would be ideas for a teacher learning community or reading group, or simply to review your own understanding at a later point. The tasks invite you to get stuck in, applying the suggested strategies to your own teaching and planning, or otherwise extending your understanding independently. They provide a focus, but you don't need to attempt them all – pick what is most relevant to your context.

Overall, we want you to understand and retain the ideas, and to be able to transfer them to your own setting.

2 Do Schools Kill Creativity?

Popular media present a strange and at times strikingly negative picture of teaching. Pink Floyd told us that we should 'leave them kids alone', while Rage Against the Machine portrays teachers as 'enemies' who promote conformity. In fiction, we meet figures like Dickens' Gradgrind, who strongly opposes imagination, saying that 'Facts alone are wanted in life', and that everything should be measurable and logical.

Some commentators have stated more directly that schools do not work in the best interests of their students' creativity. One of the most well-known examples comes from the TED talk by Sir Ken Robinson, who went as far as to suggest that 'schools kill creativity' (Robinson, 2006).

Teachers, it seems, are all too often seen as oppressive figures, stamping out the spark and originality in their students. Meanwhile, those teachers in books or movies that are shown in a more positive light are often misfits and mavericks. It's easy to see how approaches to education that emphasise mastery of knowledge – and those that do not – can be associated with these simplistic stereotypes.

But is schooling really bad for creativity? Given what was said in the previous chapter, you might not be surprised to hear us push back

DOI: 10.4324/9781032719221-2

against the idea! This chapter will consider where these ideas come from, whether they have any validity, and what we might need to focus on to ensure that schools are supporting rather than hindering creativity.

The Myth

Research by Benedek et al. (2021) found the idea that long-term schooling was harmful to creativity had around 50 per cent approval from an international sample. A related belief that they studied is the idea that creativity is more prominent in childhood than adulthood; Benedek and colleagues also found that 68 per cent of that study's participants agreed with the statement, 'Children are more creative than adults'. This was the third-most endorsed myth overall.

Both of these beliefs seem to be rooted in a similar but flawed idea – that people are 'naturally' creative, rather than it being something that needs to be developed over time. If creativity is perceived as a natural gift, unconnected with the knowledge developed at school, then it's something that young children just *have* – leaving open the risk that schools might take it away. Likewise, it might be perceived that innately creative people won't tend to thrive at school.

The idea that children are creative geniuses is prevalent across the internet. Supporting research that is often mentioned is summarised in another TED talk by business consultant George Land (Land, 2011). Land refers to a study associated with NASA that he carried out with Beth Jarman. Land explains that in the longitudinal study of 1,600 young people, 98 per cent of children scored in the 'highly creative' range when aged 5, but only 30 per cent did so when aged 10, and just 12 per cent at age 15 (surprisingly, no participants dropped out over the ten years of the study!). In comparison, just 2 per cent of a separate sample of adults scored at that level.

A closely connected idea is that only *some* people are creative. If creative thinking is seen as something innate (we are born with it), then differences between students could be explained in similar terms. Why are some students creative, whereas others will always struggle to do anything novel? Students or their parents may see creativity as a gift that only some people harbour, either because they were born that way, or due to early experiences. This might apply particularly in arts subjects that are more strongly associated with creativity. The implications, perhaps, are that only some students have a talent worth nurturing. As you will see, there are good reasons to push back against that view of creativity.

Exploring the Research

Children's creative thinking

The NASA study shared by Land sounds pretty convincing, perhaps because it chimes with the widespread idea that children are naturally creative. However, the details of this study are surprisingly difficult to track down; it doesn't appear to have been published in a peer-reviewed academic journal. This is important, because the methodology and findings have not been scrutinised by experts.

It appears that the study used a divergent thinking test as a test for creativity. As discussed in the previous chapter, divergent thinking is associated with coming up with multiple possibilities, rather than one correct solution. A simple example of a divergent thinking test that might be used on children involves asking them to come up with multiple uses of a paperclip; this example is mentioned in Ken Robinson's TED talk. However, a recent meta-analysis (Said-Metwaly et al., 2021) found no evidence to support the assertion that young children are superior at this task. Instead, the authors concluded that there was an overall upward developmental trend of divergent thinking across grade levels, albeit with a slump around 7th grade (age 12-13).

> **Pause to reflect**
> How many uses of a paperclip can you come up with? Ask the same question to any young children you interact with. To what extent could you describe their ideas as 'creative', i.e. being both new and useful?

Even if there was reliable academic evidence that such divergent thinking measures decrease as children mature, it's worth questioning what this result would mean. There might be a good reason why an older learner would come up with fewer uses for a paperclip – they have more knowledge than a 5-year-old child, and have a better idea of which 'uses' would be impractical or impossible. A more knowledgeable thinker may come up with fewer ideas, but better-quality ones.

Remember, creativity isn't just about coming up with lots of ideas. Returning to the standard definition of creativity (see Chapter 1), a creative idea must be *both* new and useful. The utility aspect is often missed in discussions about schools killing creativity. School provides knowledge which young people need to effectively evaluate whether innovative ideas are in fact useful (Gube & Lajoie, 2020).

A broader problem with the idea that children are highly creative is the way it sees creativity as an ability that a particular person possesses. It is viewed as something they have, and hence it can be 'taken away' by schools. However, if creativity is not seen as an innate trait but rather as a set of thought processes connected to knowledge and experiences, we can begin to see how schools can develop creativity, and do so in ways that will depend on the contexts (Beghetto, 2019). Fortunately, despite the widespread myths about creativity in children, most teachers appear to lean towards the idea that creativity is, in fact, teachable (Bereczki & Kárpáti, 2018).

In schools, beliefs about whether abilities can be changed have implications for how we might seek to support creativity. Notwithstanding the fact that children do differ from each other, it's more in line with an overall cognitive science view of creativity to assume that any learner can develop creative skills via support and practice – even if it's probably also true that they can't all become creative geniuses in any field of their choosing.

Like any cognitive process, the foundations of creativity are laid early, not least through the development of language. Early thinking about concepts and processes also paves the way for more complex thinking. Children are certainly unique and interesting, and they may come up with quirky ideas – often lots of them! That can be enough for adults to view a child as creative.

However, it would be preferable to nurture this originality while also developing the skills and discipline which pave the way for mature creative insights and outputs. In practice, this means that teachers might want to avoid any implication that creativity involves digging deep into our inner child, and instead focus on how we build on the childhood foundations, extending and nurturing their capacities, and connecting early creativity to more mature skills and areas of knowledge.

In depth: Cross-curricular days

Many schools run cross-curricular events, inviting students to draw on what they have learned from all areas of the curriculum in order to tackle an interesting project. The activities might involve students working in groups to come up with a solution to a creative problem. In one school, 12-year-old students were challenged with coming up with an ethical product that would help to solve one of the world's environmental problems.

During the tasks, students were provided with lots of paper and cardboard so they could make a prototype of their product, were taught presentation skills so they could pitch their idea, and were even given some training in video and editing so they could film an advert. Students had a great time, and feedback on the day was really positive. However, many ideas, although innovative and imaginative, simply would not have worked! Some of the products pitched included flying cars, non-stick chewing gum and a perpetual motion machine that quite blatantly violated the first law of thermodynamics. These ideas would not solve any environmental problem. Arguably they were new, but they were not useful.

Fundamentally, the students involved lacked the required knowledge to come up with viable solutions to real problems. Whilst there may have been many worthwhile aspects of their cross-curricular day – there is value in students working together and learning to present an idea to their peers, for example – a more thoughtful and structured programme would be required to develop authentic and practical creative solutions (for more on creative projects, including ones with an authentic legacy, see Chapter 11).

Schools don't kill creativity

As we have seen, the idea that children are naturally creative is on shaky ground. There is also a large body of research which suggests that schools *don't* kill creativity. Maciej Karwowski (2022) offers seven propositions about the relationships between creativity and the ways schools are organised based on meta-analyses, intervention studies and investigations from outside of the creativity literature. Three of these in particular are relevant here:

1) **Creative abilities are drivers of school achievement, not brakes.** Contrary to the popular belief that creative students won't thrive at school, the research shows a positive correlation between academic achievements and creative abilities. Creative abilities are closely interconnected with cognitive processes such as attention or memory, which are helpful for many other aspects of learning.

2) **Creativity processes support learning.** Throughout this book, we will see that knowledge is a building block of creativity – creativity cannot exist without knowledge (in particular, see Chapter 3). Not only does Karwowski's review show that knowledge is essential for creativity, it also provides evidence that creative processes are helpful in building new knowledge and supporting problem solving. Similar arguments have been made for other skills such as critical thinking (Willingham, 2007).

3) **School education supports both academic skills and creativity.** Karwowski argues that schools benefit cognitive processes important to academic achievement, and that because these are correlated with creativity, it cannot be actively harmful to creativity; Karwowski also discusses the idea of a slump in divergent thinking in the teens (see above), suggesting that this is not conclusive and that, indeed, some studies show that creativity increases during school years. However, even if such a slump exists, it could be a developmental change. The paper recognises, however, that schools may be more valuable for convergent

thinking than divergent, and that the bureaucratic nature of schools may make it difficult for creativity to flourish.

> **Pause to reflect**
> Do these three propositions of Karwowski resonate with your experiences in your educational setting? Do any of the propositions surprise you? Are there aspects of how schools are set up that can make it difficult for creativity to flourish?

The promises and perils of creativity in the classroom

Ron Beghetto's 2013 book *Killing Ideas Softly* is subtitled, 'The promise and perils of creativity in the classroom' (Beghetto, 2013). This idea neatly summarises the tensions felt by teachers, and the misconceptions held across society (as discussed at the start of this chapter). Beghetto's book includes the following quote from Mark Runco: 'No doubt teachers respect creativity, in the abstract, but not when faced with a classroom with 30 energetic children' (Runco, 2007, p. 178, cited by Beghetto, 2013, p. 71).

Beghetto's key argument is that in order to develop creativity, we don't need to radically change our approach to teaching or adopt a new curriculum. Instead, we can enhance and develop what we are already doing, making it more effective and more focused on the reality of how creativity works. One way to do this is to consider the different types of creativity that might be shown in the classroom, as opposed to throughout wider society, and the ways in which we might celebrate and support these creative processes – a model of creativity. This is outlined next.

> **Pause to reflect**
> How commonly does creativity occur among your students? Is creativity an everyday sort of thing, or a once-a-term sort of thing, or a once-in-a-lifetime thing?

The 'Four C' model of creativity

As mentioned before (see Chapter 1), researchers have drawn a distinction between everyday and eminent creativity:

- Big-C creativity is the creativity we associate with creative geniuses whose ideas have shaped the world, individuals who have produced something exceptional which is new and useful for society.
- Little-c creativity might not be new and useful for society but is new and useful for that individual at that time; you might not be a famous artist but the sketches you draw whilst on holiday bring you joy at the time and provide happy memories on your return.

Kaufman and Beghetto (2009) argue that these categories are insufficient to describe the various types of creativity seen in society and, in particular, the way that creativity develops across childhood.

For example, they question whether the Big-C category is too narrow. This level of creative genius is clearly very rare. Another issue is that it is usually only ascribed to people posthumously, making it hard to study.

This leaves a little-c category which is very broad, comprising the work of everything from small children to professionals, and again, Kaufman and Beghetto (2009) question whether this makes sense. If an artist has studied for years, regularly presents their work in galleries and makes a living from selling that work, is this really little-c creativity? They might not reach the dizzy heights of a Picasso, but it doesn't seem right to lump this type of creativity together with the amateur holiday sketcher.

And what about the child who is first learning to draw with crayons? If you have children, you may have fond memories of their first sketches which you pinned on the fridge, but these wouldn't be judged as creative (according to the standard definition) by anyone other than a loving parent or carer.

Kaufman and Beghetto (2009) therefore proposed a more detailed model, better accounting for the differing circumstances and outcomes of creativity in children and adults. Their Four C model adds *mini-c* and *Pro-C* creativity to the existing Big-C and little-c categories, with mini-c reflecting the earliest instances of creativity, and Pro-C sitting in between little-c and Big-C, and reflecting professional work like the example of the accomplished artist described above (see Figure 2.1).

	Form of creativity	Example of creative outcome	Example of judge of creativity
Mini-c	Intrapersonal creativity that is part of formal or informal learning and other life experiences.	An insight in a lesson when a student realises the connection between two topics.	The creator.
Little-c	Everyday creativity that is novel and valuable to someone other than the creator.	Combining the ingredients in your fridge in a new way to make dinner.	Family and friends.
Pro-C	Creativity that is novel and useful in the context of a profession.	Scientist working on a new vaccine.	Scientists working in medical and healthcare regulation.
Big-C	Creativity that lasts beyond the lifetime of its creator and is valuable for wider society.	Discovery of the structure of DNA (Watson, Crick, Wilkins and Franklin)	Nobel prize awarding committee.

Figure 2.1 The Four C model of creativity

Mini-c creativity is about constructing personal knowledge and understanding, recognising and valuing these personal insights. It is associated with all learning purposes, and may reflect the earliest stirrings of creativity. It is the child who notices that picking up a crayon and using it to draw on paper can produce interesting patterns, and that they can produce different shading patterns by holding the crayon in a different way. As such, mini-c reflects potential that teachers might seek to nurture, recognising where students may lack the experience or knowledge to fully express their ideas.

But mini-c creativity is not just for kids. This level of thoughts and mental connections, insights or the beginnings of ideas could happen to people at any age, and probably does so on an everyday basis.

While mini-c often represents the beginnings of creative work, it moves into the world of little-c when people start to do something more practical. They may start to play around with an idea, try things out, and experiment – what Kaufman and Beghetto (2009) refer to as 'tinkering'

(p. 7). Typically, this means that the individual will share their ideas with others and get feedback, bringing it into a more social domain.

Kaufman and Beghetto also saw a need to distinguish between everyday little-c creativity and the type of creativity seen in professional expertise; they call the latter Pro-C creativity. As they argue, there is a considerable gulf between an amateur home cook creating a new dish based on experimenting with ingredients they have in the cupboard, and a professional chef whose knowledge and experience of cooking allows them to create a menu for a high-end restaurant. They argue that disciplined preparation is required for the little-c creativity to become Pro-C creativity, usually through some sort of formal or informal apprenticeship. Training to be a chef is one example; training to be a teacher would be another.

A further difference between these categories is the social context in which the creativity occurs, and hence the judgement of what makes something creative. The mini-c level is often kept to oneself, and little-c may be judged by results by those around you. However, the outcomes of the Pro-C and Big-C levels have more formal, established audiences (see Figure 2.1).

> **Pause to reflect**
> What examples from your own life can you think of that fit into the mini-c, little-c and Pro-C categories? Do you demonstrate little-c creativity in one area of your life and Pro-C creativity elsewhere?

Ed-c

Often teachers feel a tension between teaching for creativity and providing the knowledge base that students will need in order to be truly creative, knowledge they will usually gain through following a prescribed syllabus and being assessed on its content. Recognising this tension, Lassig (2021) has suggested the addition of an Ed-c (educational creativity) category to Kaufman and Beghetto's model.

> Ed-c refers to creativity for learning or achievement in formal educational environments. In this form of creativity, individuals' creative processes and outcomes are developed within the external con-

straints of a particular educational body, including limitations posed by task demands, assessment criteria or teachers' instructions.

(Lassig, 2021, p. 1050)

We can therefore insert an additional line into Figure 2.1 above.

	Form of creativity	**Example of creative outcome**	**Example of judge of creativity**
Ed-c	Interpersonal creativity for learning and achievement in formal education.	Digital art series for a visual art asessment.	Teachers or external examiners.

Figure 2.2 Adding Ed-c to the Four C model of creativity

> **Pause to reflect**
> Do you agree that Ed-c adds something important to the Four C model? What examples for Ed-c creativity can you see in your own context?

The concept of Ed-c together with Kaufman and Beghetto's Four C model can help us to tackle the misconception that schools kill the innate creativity shown by children. They help us to re-conceptualise our role as educators as noticing and nurturing mini-c creativity and little-c creativity. They also reflect the role of an accepted knowledge framework to maximise the chances of our young people developing effective Pro-C creativity so they can thrive in a profession, and have an impact on the ever changing world they will be entering into.

Applications to Practice

Creative 'micro moments' in the classroom

Typical classroom exchanges follow an initiation-response-evaluation (IRE) model, a back and forth between teacher and learner that has been used for centuries (Miao & Heining-Boynton, 2011). The teacher asks a student a question, the student responds and the teacher evaluates whether or not their answer is correct. In such exchanges, unexpected or unconventional responses are often quickly dismissed to prevent a derailment of the carefully planned lesson. Beghetto (2013) refers to these as 'creative micro moments' – where a student's mini-c insight is voiced in lessons, sharing it with others. If we dismiss such responses too quickly, then students may be reluctant to contribute such responses in the future and we could indeed be accused of killing their creativity.

Instead, further exploration and feedback on students' everyday insights and outputs can determine whether they are examples of mini-c/little-c creativity or misconceptions that need to be addressed. For example, in an English class, a student might suggest an unusual interpretation of a poem. It may well be that their ideas are misplaced, but rather than dismissing the suggestion out of hand, a teacher could briefly explore the micro moment by finding out how that student came up with their idea. Through further discussion, it may be that the class recognises the value of this interpretation or that the student themselves comes to the realisation that their idea does not really fit with the evidence at hand.

As teachers, we have a valuable role to play in encouraging students to come up with different ideas, but also in guiding them to apply their knowledge to distinguish between good ideas and bad ones. By taking the time to explore where ideas come from, even flawed contributions can provide micro moments from which the class as a whole can learn.

Pause to reflect

Can you think of any times in your teaching where students have come up with unexpected comments? Did you explore their reasoning further or dismiss the idea in order to move on with the rest of the lesson? Having read this section, might you approach the situation differently now?

Tackling 'creative mortification'

As mentioned, mini-c insights often remain inside the thinker's head – at least, unless they choose to share them. Following on from the idea above, it is worth considering the risk that any student takes when they share an idea with their peers and their teacher, and how we can respond to and support them in the risk of sharing (often flawed) ideas.

Beghetto talks about this problem as *creative mortification*: 'a profound creative suppression resulting from a shaming experience ... [which] often occurs after having experienced negative feedback evaluation' (Beghetto, 2013, p. 88).

One simple strategy to tackle creative mortification is to increase the wait time between when you ask a question and when you call on a student to answer. Research has shown that this time is typically only between 0.7 and 1.4 seconds and suggests that increasing this time to 3 seconds can improve the level and quality of students' participation (Rowe, 1986). From a creativity perspective, increasing wait time gives students more time to come up with a thoughtful, creative response rather than blurting out their first ideas. We can also encourage students to jot down their initial ideas on a rough piece of paper or a mini-whiteboard, or give time for students to discuss their initial ideas with a partner.

Teacher feedback could also play a role. Consider options such as the following:

- 'Katie can you tell me ...'
- 'Katie, could you share your initial ideas ...'
- 'Katie, could you start us off ...'
- 'That's an interesting response, could you explain further how you got there?'
- 'Amy, could you build on Katie's answer?'

The later examples frame the ideas more tentatively, and imply that the desired response is not the right answer, but rather a point that can be added to, explored, or built on by other students. This can make it feel more psychologically safe for students to share tentative ideas in the classroom.

Of course, encouraging students to be creative is not about accepting all ideas as equally valid. There are also times when it might not be appropriate to explore a student's insights or misconceptions in front of the whole class. Nevertheless, it is important that students are not afraid to share mini-c insights due to a fear of ridicule.

> **Pause to reflect**
> Have you ever experienced creative mortification yourself?

Playfulness

Creativity in children is often associated with playfulness, and it is worth considering to what extent we encourage students within the context of their schooling to be playful, particularly when they enter upper secondary school.

Playfulness certainly has an association with creativity. Play is often creative, while playing with ideas and options might, in turn, make a person more likely to hit on a novel and useful solution. However, this has led to some academic discussion about whether playfulness is a cause or an effect of creativity! Currently, the consensus appears to be that the two are associated; one can benefit the other, but it is also possible to be playful without being creative and vice versa (Proyer et al., 2019).

Playfulness is often viewed as a disposition (e.g. Fink et al., 2020), which can be problematic – it brings it into the realm of personality traits, seen as relatively stable over the lifespan. This might mean that schooling couldn't really benefit a person's innate playfulness (but couldn't harm it, either).

However, a more nuanced approach to dispositions is that initial tendencies can be supported and built up. Opportunities for playfully toying with ideas, for example, or tinkering with solutions, can be built into educational settings. Touching back on Karwowski's (2022) propositions, we can develop the capacity to do these things effectively, encouraging playfulness and divergent thinking, rather than just convergent thinking tasks.

So, while some students will no doubt be better able than their peers to notice connections and play with possibilities, opportunities and strategies also make a difference (an idea that is also relevant to critical thinking; see Facione, 2015). Playfulness can be prompted and practised. Indeed, play can be a form of practising (Proyer et al., 2019), helping students to try things out in low-stakes contexts. Role-playing social situations in PSHE (personal, social, health and economic teaching) is one example.

When people think, there is the tendency to do things in tried-and-tested ways, following a well-trodden path. Once a particular idea or memory is accessed, it becomes easier to access again in the future – while competing memories become harder to retrieve (Storm et al., 2008). To break away from the predictability this leads to, there needs to be space for playful and funny responses. Ways to encourage these could include:

- Taking a 'no wrong answers' approach to a starter task
- Making space for humour in the classroom
- Exploring hypotheticals
- Acknowledging very 'out there' ideas rather than shutting them down
- Having an open-mindedness to flawed steps along a process, as long as the end result is effective
- Asking students to come up with multiple options and ideas, even if some seem silly (see also the discussion of brainstorming, Chapter 11)
- Advising learners to avoid their first idea or the most obvious connection, and to keep trying to think of alternatives

We will look further at how we can support students to make connections in Chapter 4.

In depth: Categorisation in English

In English, students can struggle to use quotations effectively in their essays, often relying on their teacher to tell them exactly which quotation to use and when.

In order to overcome this, and to help students make their own connections, students can be encouraged to categorise quotations taken from a text out of context. Working in small groups allows for discussion and for students to play with different possibilities. Such tasks consolidate knowledge of the context of each quotation as well as revising the key themes in the text, but it also provides room for playfulness with ideas.

A similar approach could feed into essay planning; students can be given a set of quotations alongside an essay title and decide which would be relevant and which should be discarded.

The categories students come up with can be surprising – in one school, a teacher found a group categorising quotations from *Macbeth* based on whether the characters would survive a zombie apocalypse and another ranking the quotations based on how likely they were to be Taylor Swift lyrics! Even when such responses are not directly *useful*, making space for such tasks encouraged students to look at the quotations through a different lens – it certainly encouraged them to move away from the tried-and-tested path.

Conclusion

It's time for teachers to push back against the myth that schools kill creativity. Contrary to the stereotype of teachers in the popular media, or the idea that schooling in general suppresses individuality, the work that teachers and schools do *supports* creativity, rather than harming it.

In part, this is because schools are essential for developing the skills and knowledge required for the Pro-C (and potentially Big-C) creativity we wish our young people to show in their future lives. Rather than seeing the constraints provided by the school system as inhibiting creativity, the concept of Ed-c can help us to reframe these constraints as providing boundaries within which creativity can flourish. Teaching for creativity can therefore be seen not as something extra that teachers need to be adding onto an already packed curriculum, but as a way of adapting what we already do well.

The practical implications of this include a confidence that academic work supports creativity, but also that there can be value in exploring ideas and making space for playfulness. It can be useful to reflect on how we facilitate or respond to students' mini-c insights; these are the foundations of creative ideas. We can also encourage students to build on these, and to be playful with ideas in our classes in ways that might lead to new and unusual connections.

It is perhaps apparent, however, that some of the foundations of what exactly schools can and should do need further explanation. In the next two chapters we will look in more depth at the role of knowledge in creative thinking, and at how existing knowledge paves the way for new ideas.

Discussion Questions

1) Is creativity an everyday thing? Try to think of some examples of tasks that you already do, and which you might now consider creative (according to the standard definition of creativity).
2) Have you ever come across videos or articles suggesting that schools kill creativity? How would you push back against that idea?
3) Can you think of an example of each of the four different types of creativity proposed by Kaufman and Beghetto (2009)? It might help to draw on a very familiar context.
4) How do you typically respond to students' more unusual ideas and responses in class? Are there approaches that you have found to be useful?
5) What is 'creative mortification'? How might this be avoided in your classroom?
6) In what ways might you support your students to be more playful?

Professional Learning Tasks

Task 1

Watch Ken Robinson's TED talk 'Do Schools Kill Creativity?' and read one or two articles critiquing his ideas (for example those by Alex Quigley, 2023, or Joe Kirby, 2013). To what extent do you agree or disagree with the arguments put forward by these different educators? You could consider setting up a debate about this with students, too – if so, what might you do to support their understanding of the issue?

Task 2

Sketch a graph of how you think your own creativity has changed over time. Now, if possible, compare your graphs to those of family members or colleagues. Do you feel your creativity has decreased over time, which might support the argument that schools kill creativity? (This is also a fascinating exercise to do with students and generates rich discussions around their conception of creativity.)

Task 3

Share the key ideas from the Four C categories with some colleagues. Split a piece of paper into four boxes for the four categories and ask colleagues to add in examples where they have seen the different types of creativity, from either their own experience, observations from teaching or from inspirational figures. Once they have some examples, ask them to identify the prerequisite knowledge base for each.

3 Building Blocks

Many of us associate creativity with great inventions and scientific discoveries – the invention of radio, perhaps, or great artworks, or scientific theories. However, other examples of creativity are a little more mundane.

Consider the wheeled suitcase; did you know that people travelled in space (in the 1960s) and landed on the moon (1969) *before* someone patented the idea of putting wheels on suitcases (in the early 1970s)? It seems extraordinary that although wheels and suitcases had been around for centuries, it took until the second half of the twentieth century for someone to connect these innovations together. This illustrates once again that the creativity of an idea has to be considered within its particular social context, and that the context itself can act to prompt creative thinking (Rhodes, 1961). In prior centuries, travel was a luxury enjoyed by only a privileged few. These upper-class travellers would not have had to carry their own luggage; they had servants for that sort of menial work. It was only when mass tourism took off in the latter half of the twentieth century that the demand for more convenient luggage increased, and hence the wheeled suitcase became a solution to a problem that needed to be solved.

Importantly, though, the example also illustrates that creative ideas can be quite mundane. They may involve the application of relatively simple

32 Creativity for Teachers

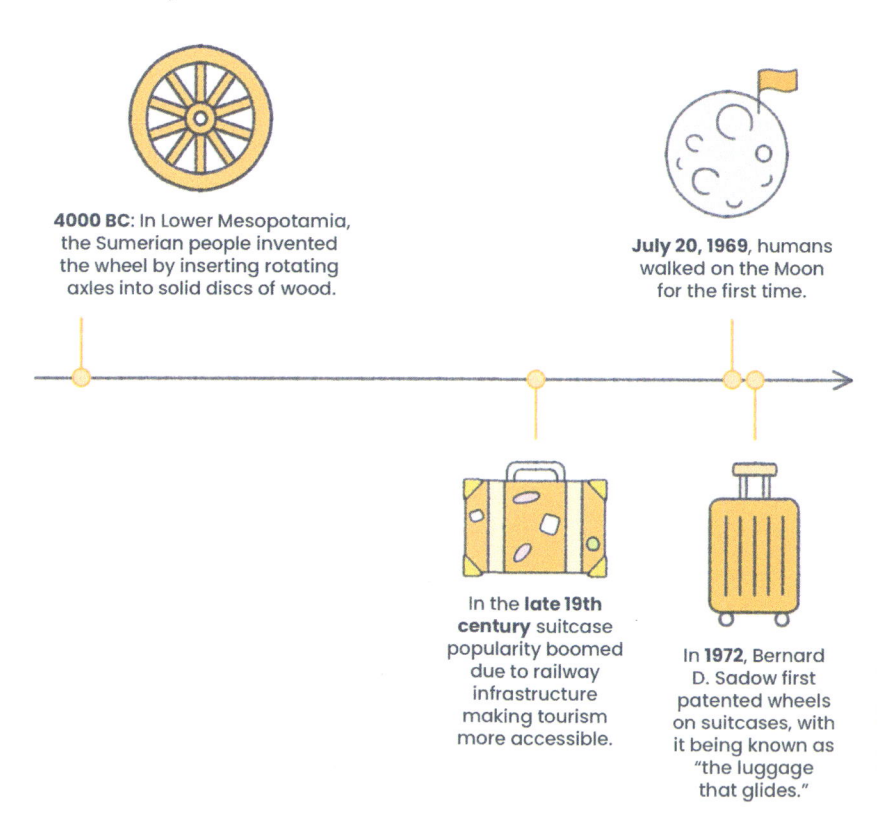

4000 BC: In Lower Mesopotamia, the Sumerian people invented the wheel by inserting rotating axles into solid discs of wood.

July 20, 1969, humans walked on the Moon for the first time.

In the **late 19th century** suitcase popularity boomed due to railway infrastructure making tourism more accessible.

In **1972**, Bernard D. Sadow first patented wheels on suitcases, with it being known as "the luggage that glides."

Figure 3.1 The invention of the wheeled suitcase

ideas around us – such as the wheel. Very often, the building blocks of creativity are things that we (or our students) already know.

When we talk about creativity in schools or elsewhere, it is of course the famous inventions and scientific discoveries that get the most attention. All the same, these instances of creative thinking don't need to be viewed as a mysterious skill. As mentioned in Chapter 1, creativity can be defined, studied and understood. In other words, it can be broken down into more basic elements and processes – building blocks. When we look at it this way, the emphasis is less on great ideas by special people, and more on how we can support any learner to think creatively. And as we will see, this is based more on what we already know than on vague skills or capacities.

The Myth

You may have heard people say that creativity is one of the key *twenty-first-century skills* (e.g. Geisinger, 2016) – skills that learners need to thrive in today's world. And while it's true that creativity is very relevant to our learners and to their future beyond schooling, the twenty-first-century skills view can mislead us into thinking that creativity is *just* a skill, disconnected with what students know and learn from the world around them, or from the content of the curriculum.

Looking at creativity as a thinking skill could mean placing an emphasis on the cognitive processes it involves and trying to understand them. This fits well with the cognitive science approach taken throughout this book. However, problems arise when the conception of creativity as a skill becomes detached from knowledge. At that point, it may be unthinkingly assumed that someone is *just creative*, regardless, for example, of their level of expertise. This is a myth.

Today, researchers largely agree that it is impossible to treat creativity as a skill without also considering the knowledge to which it links. Indeed, it's impossible to be creative without having sufficient relevant knowledge (including knowledge of relationships and procedures, not just facts) – knowledge that is relevant to the creative task or problem at hand (Bransford et al., 2000; Baer, 2017).

How would you create something new in music without knowing musical scales, for example? Or devise a new computer program without knowing coding languages and techniques, or, indeed, knowing something about computer users? How would you invent a wheeled suitcase if you didn't know about suitcases or wheels?

These simple examples help to show why the idea of creativity as a stand-alone skill is considered to be a myth. They emphasise that while creativity does involve a set of cognitive processes, it can't be separated from what we know – a person's existing skills and knowledge.

Exploring the Research

Fundamentals of creativity

If creativity is not a mysterious skill, then what are its basic elements, and how can it be supported among our students? How do creative ideas and problem solving connect to the basic knowledge which so often forms the focus of lesson planning?

The answer may surprise you – the facts and simple routines from an area of knowledge form the basis of creativity, rather than sitting separately from it (Baer, 2017). The more a learner knows, the easier it will be for them to come up with a new idea, or the solution to any kind of problem. Clearly, many important examples of (Big-C) creativity involve major, once-in-a-lifetime ideas. But it's not just about that. Think back to the standard definition of creativity – anything new and useful can be seen as creative, including everyday and small-scale 'little c' creativity.

A key idea in this chapter is that just like with the development of the wheeled suitcase, students can use their existing knowledge, strategies and ideas to come up with something creative (Nijstad et al., 2002). They don't need to be a genius, and they don't need to produce something earthshakingly brilliant. Sometimes, it will be just a matter of teachers providing the right problem, and prompting students to use their knowledge.

The cognitive science of knowledge

From a cognitive science perspective, all of the fundamental knowledge discussed above (including a learner's understandings, routines, previously formed associations, and so forth) is stored in long-term memory. A key implication is that what is stored in memory is essential to creativity.

We have to ensure that students are provided with opportunities to take in this knowledge, that they retain it (tackling forgetting), and that they can retrieve it when needed. Some memories are more accessible than others. What they do when they study and practise will make a difference to how well consolidated their learning is, but also how accessible it is and how flexibly it can be used (Bjork & Bjork, 2023).

The flip-side of this is that learners with a level of knowledge that is impoverished or hard to access (whether overall, or connected to a specific curriculum area) will have a much harder time thinking creatively. Rather than inhibiting learners from being creative, this means that schools can and do play a key role in supporting it (again, we do not *kill* creativity – see Chapter 2). Schools provide their learners with knowledge and skills that provide the foundations of thinking. The learner who can think better and has more ideas to manipulate is better able to think creatively.

That's not quite the whole story, of course. Throughout the rest of this chapter and the book as a whole, we will explore how this knowledge can be developed in ways that facilitate and support creative thinking. After all, students won't come up with anything creative if that knowledge sits inertly in their long-term memory. But it remains critical to emphasise that a student can't think creatively (or engage in any other kind of complex thinking) if they don't have anything to think about.

> **Pause to reflect**
> What key knowledge or fundamental procedures are especially relevant to your curriculum area or context? Functions in coding? Art techniques? How to assemble lab equipment? Musical scales?

An analogy: building blocks

To develop the above idea via an analogy, creativity can be seen as putting existing building blocks together in a new and useful way. If you don't have those building blocks in the first place (or if you have a smaller and less diverse range than other people do), then you will be less able to come up with creative solutions and outputs.

Imagine a child (or indeed an adult) playing with Lego. How many fun and interesting models could they make if they were only given five identical bricks? And what about if they have a hundred bricks, all of different kinds? Or ten thousand? It's easy to see that the better, more creative and more successful models would depend on having enough bricks to play with!

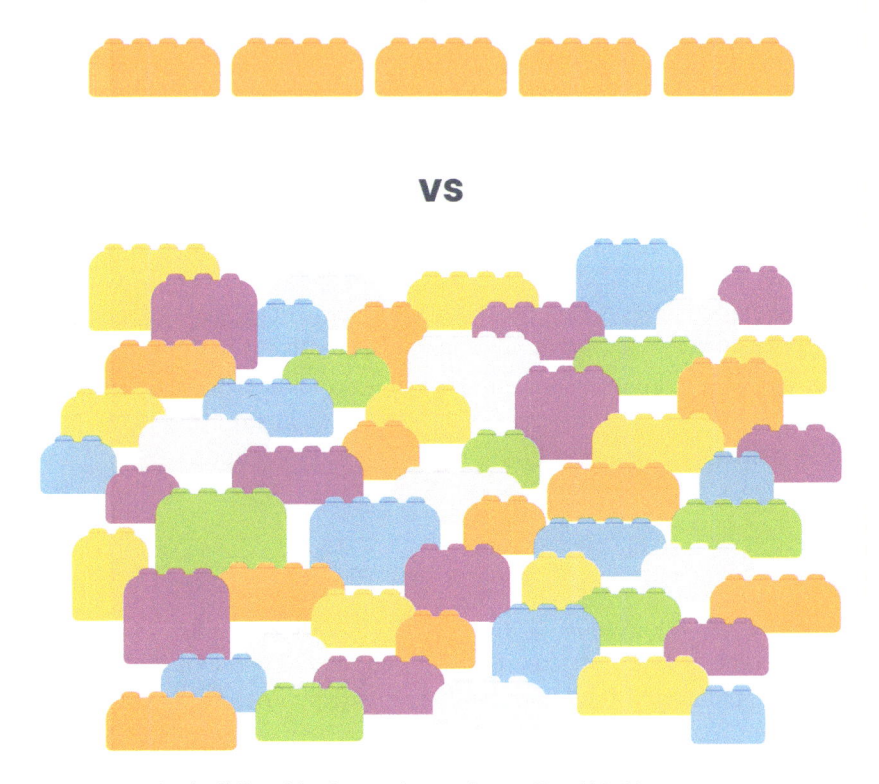

Figure 3.2 The building blocks analogy of creative thinking

The analogy here, of course, is that the learning of knowledge and simple routines provides the learner with more 'building blocks' that they can then use for creative thinking – for building something new. Creativity involves combining such elements together in novel and useful ways.

Hopefully this analogy shows the importance of having key foundations in place. Factual knowledge and ideas, basic skills and routines, vocabulary – all of these things are essential to creativity. Knowledge must not be neglected in education, or any efforts towards creativity will fail. Teachers should at the very least check that certain basics are in place before expecting students to tackle creative tasks. Without enough 'building blocks', it will be hard or impossible to produce successful creative responses to a task. Or, at least, the solutions that are available to the learner will be more limited and constrained. We can't think about things if we don't know they exist.

A connected point is that increasing the quantity of 'building blocks' – i.e. boosting a student's foundational knowledge – will make creative solutions more likely. Therefore, efforts to increase creativity need not (always) focus on creativity at all. It is also valuable to work on students' underlying knowledge, and their facility with basic procedures and routines. In other words, an important but counterintuitive way to boost creativity is to focus on developing knowledge.

These points indicate another area where the cognitive science of creativity fits well with other ways that we apply cognitive science to education. Knowledge is powerful. The more that learners know about a topic, the more successful they will be at a range of things, including getting answers right, solving problems and taking in new knowledge. Creative ideation simply adds to that list.

Pause to reflect
Think about how some forms of creativity might depend on students' literacy skills – using punctuation, crafting effective sentences, building vocabulary, and so forth. How does this fit with the building blocks analogy? What, in this case, are the blocks?

> ### In depth: Creative writing
>
> Creativity depends on knowledge. It would be hard to create something new if you didn't know anything, right? Further, this knowledge gets more complex and more intricately structured as expertise increases. It underpins our ability to think about complex problems.
>
> One example of this is how a student engages in creative writing. Children don't write using familiar genres and styles – they write whatever comes into their head, chaining one idea to the next (Bereiter & Scardamalia, 1987). With increased knowledge, writers come to engage in particular types of story, using their experience to craft characters and set up tension. Even very successful creative writers don't tend to invent entirely new styles of story, but instead use their knowledge of genres, tropes, and settings. They use their existing knowledge to create something new. They are, of course, also using their fundamental language competence in grammar, vocabulary, and so on.
>
> As another example, scientists (and remember that science is also creative!) have to build on existing theoretical knowledge, understand where gaps lie, and use familiar tools and methods to make progress. Their knowledge of science facts and processes is key to designing new experiments or creating new theories. None of this would be possible without foundational knowledge.
>
> Chapter 4 will look further at how learners can make connections among their existing knowledge, and at how this knowledge is structured together and organised in the mind.

Skills vs. knowledge

As was briefly mentioned in Chapter 1, creativity can be promoted purely as a skill. This can cause some educators to celebrate it as a part of a modern or progressive curriculum, and to assume that developing the skill of creativity among students is an important goal. It's now time to analyse this idea in more depth.

The idea of being skills-focused, especially when those skills are labelled as twenty-first-century skills, no doubt sounds good to policy makers. Likewise, using the term 'higher-order skill' for processes like creativity and analysis may mislead people into believing that these should be emphasised *instead* of knowledge.

However, cognitive researchers have frequently cautioned that we cannot display creativity (or other complex skills, such as critical thinking) without a sound foundation of knowledge. Students need to have something to think about. Just as we can't become educated simply by using Google, we need to have enough knowledge to form novel and useful combinations of ideas, and to evaluate whether they would work. As Rotherham and Willingham (2010, p. 18) put it: 'Educators and policymakers must ensure that content is not exchanged for an ephemeral pursuit of skills.'

For example, consider what goes into coming up with a creative idea for a lesson, or even for a specific homework task. It's not the case that this involves just being creative. Teachers who do this are drawing on their knowledge of several things: the curriculum, pedagogy, policies, the students in their class, prior experience and feedback on previous homework, what colleagues are doing, and so on. Creativity doesn't just involve recalling this knowledge, but it is informed by it at every stage. The same applies to any domain.

A focus on skills in the curriculum is sometimes associated with Bloom's famous taxonomy of skills. However, the perspective from cognitive science suggests that we can't attain higher-order skills without taking care of the basics. This was recognised by the authors of the taxonomy; as Anderson et al. (2001, p. 60) say in their revision of Bloom's taxonomy, 'all objectives are some combination of the Knowledge and Cognitive Process dimensions'. That is to say, everything that we might want young people to learn involves both knowledge, and doing something with that knowledge.

So ... Is creativity a thinking skill?

Certainly, creativity is listed as a higher-order skill on Bloom's taxonomy (see Anderson et al., 2001), meaning that it is seen as a process that someone does with knowledge, rather than being a form of knowledge itself. This fits what has been discussed so far in this chapter – knowledge forms the building blocks that we use for creative thinking.

What's more, knowledge and skills are intertwined and mutually supporting. Bransford et al. (2000, p. 23) put this as well as anyone: 'attempts to teach thinking skills without a strong base of factual knowledge do not promote problem-solving ability or support transfer to new situations'.

All of this means that viewing creativity as a generic thinking skill doesn't make sense. What's more, practising what we have learned in the context of flexible tasks can help to secure new knowledge. As Bransford et al. (2000) add: 'Students' abilities to acquire organised sets of facts and skills are actually enhanced when they are connected to meaningful problem-solving activities, and when students are helped to understand why, when, and how those facts and skills are relevant' (p. 23). This fits well with Karwowski's (2022) propositions (see Chapter 2) – schools can support both academic excellence *and* creativity in tandem.

However, these points also show that it is flawed to suggest that education should only concern itself with knowledge. Fundamental though knowledge is, learners also need to develop the flexible and adaptive use of knowledge, practising strategies to do so. It should not sit inertly in memory (Perkins & Salomon, 1988; Whitehead, 1929).

Overall, then, knowledge is the foundation of any complex thinking – a learner needs to have rich, interconnected concept knowledge. They also need to be able to *do* something with that knowledge. The two cannot be separated without losing something important along the way. Cognitive science approaches to creativity therefore help to show how contrasting skills and knowledge is a false dichotomy. Each affects the other. This more nuanced approach is reflected in the rest of this book.

> **Pause to reflect**
> Before picking up this book, had you come across the skills vs. knowledge debate? On which side of the argument did you tend to fall? How has your thinking changed since reading this chapter?

Applications to Practice

The previous section highlighted the importance of knowledge within creative thinking, as well as ensuring that learners are equipped to use that knowledge in new and useful ways. We will now explore some practical ways of applying these ideas to your learning context.

Making the most of memory

What has been said about students' knowledge, and the fact that it is based in their long-term memory, leads to a fundamental but counterintuitive way to develop students' creativity – by developing this knowledge!

Clearly there is much more to creativity than practising information, as we will see throughout the book, but it is important not to neglect the fundamentals when preparing for a task. If a student's building blocks of creativity depend on relevant knowledge, then we can help to support their success at creative tasks by practising and deepening this knowledge.

There are several evidence-based strategies that help information to be learned – retained in long-term memory, ready to be used when needed (Soderstrom & Bjork, 2015). These include:

- Spacing out practice: engaging in practice of facts and skills after a delay.
- Retrieval practice: quizzes, flashcards, mini-whiteboards and 'closed book' tasks that force students to dredge up information from memory.
- Combining spacing and retrieval, e.g. via delayed quizzes, periodic reviews, and consolidation via homework that is set days or weeks after initial learning.
- Engaging in 'deep processing' – meaningful tasks, such as where students categorise information, ask questions about it, or elaborate.
- Dual coding – tasks that involve multiple modalities, such as both a verbal explanation and a diagram.

A related consideration is that learners may have relevant knowledge, but this might not be fresh in their minds when they tackle a creative task or problem. Reviews and other forms of consolidation can help to boost accessibility. For example, prior to a creative writing task, the teacher might wish to plan some practice of sentence structure and punctuation, or to go over relevant facts and processes that the students might use during the task itself. This is not about emphasising short-term retention. Rather, it recognises that items in long-term memory become less accessible over time – especially if we don't use them. The good news is that evidence-based techniques such as the ones listed above can both boost the durability of memories *and* make them easier to retrieve.

A full discussion of memory and its applications is beyond the scope of this book, but there are many good resources on the subject (see Task 3 at the end of this chapter for suggestions).

> ### In depth: Drawing as a mnemonic strategy
> Research by Wammes et al. (2016) looked specifically at the role of drawing as a memory strategy. Their primary methodology was to read a list of words and ask participants to either write or draw the item named. In a series of experiments they found that drawing (rather than writing) had a powerful mnemonic effect, and one that cannot be explained purely by other well-understood cognitive factors, such as processing the ideas more meaningfully. They suggested that drawing promotes the integration of the verbal meaning of a memory trace with its visual and motor representations. This has become known as the 'drawing effect', and is a further evidence-based way to boost knowledge in long-term memory.

What if ...?

Questions based around 'What if ...?' invite learners to take their existing knowledge and start to look at it in new ways. Doing so may also enhance that knowledge – it encourages students to think about what they know, meaning that they must retrieve information from memory (perhaps after a delay), examine it, and ask questions about it – all factors that help to consolidate memory (see previous section).

Asking 'What if?' is also fundamentally creative. It recruits divergent thinking, as there is rarely a definitive answer – instead, students are expected to consider multiple associations or possibilities based on a single fact or problem. Philosophers such as Charles Sanders Peirce recognised this as a process that differs from logical deduction, and which involves coming up with possible ideas or hypotheses, each worthy of further investigation (Douven, 2021).

Cognitive flexibility and thinking of multiple uses for familiar objects are recognised aspects of creative thinking, and accordingly, they appear in mainstream tests of creativity (see Chapter 12).

When tackling problems or issues with older students, Beghetto (2017a) suggests framing a 'What if ...?' question in this way: 'What other ways might we view this problem? Is this the actual problem or a symptom of a deeper problem? How might we think differently about this problem?' (p. 189). For younger learners, it might involve coming up with multiple questions about what something is, why it is so, or what to do next. Learners of any age could be asked to consider why something is done the way it currently is, and what would happen if it were different:

- What if we didn't put full stops after sentences?
- What would happen if nobody went to school?
- What if the country didn't have any laws?
- What would the world be like if the dinosaurs had never died out?

More specifically, whether in science, the expressive arts, or social science essays, students might be asked to consider popular techniques, and then to consider what would happen if they *didn't* use those techniques. After all, innovation generally involves breaking from the norm!

The idea of using knowledge flexibly and making new creative connections will be explored further in the next chapter.

> **Pause to reflect**
> What popular techniques in your teaching subject, field or practice might you ask students to reconsider? Would this be a thought experiment, or would they benefit from trying the alternative(s) out more directly?

Knowing what you know

Knowledge is essential, but it also helps students to have more awareness of what they know (and what they don't). This is a key part of what researchers call *metacognition*.

Metacognition is defined as thinking about thinking, so it includes a student thinking about what they know, about what they are learning, or about how to learn. Metacognition therefore includes the way that learners manage their creativity, and how they think about and apply their own knowledge in creative situations, and we will return to this issue (see Chapter 9). But on a more basic level, students need to have a metacognitive awareness of what they know, and where they need to improve.

Metacognition supports transfer of knowledge to new situations and tasks (Bransford et al., 2000; EEF, 2018), as it involves the learner thinking about what knowledge they have, how relevant it is, and how to use it. It involves:

- Knowing what they know, and when it is relevant
- Having a fairly accurate picture of their own strengths and weaknesses at tasks, including creative tasks

In the classroom, metacognition is not just about ability, or even age. Learners can be *prompted* to engage in metacognition, and sometimes this means reminding them not to engage in routine activities – for example, to question which strategy they should choose (prompting playfulness is another example – see Chapter 2). A metacognitive learner is better at choosing strategies and using their existing knowledge well. Self-assessment can help to boost metacognition, as learners become more aware of what they have forgotten (and need to practise). Again, therefore, these fundamental ways of supporting students' knowledge link together.

Seeking novelty and usefulness

The definition that has been discussed earlier in this book (see Chapter 1) states that creativity involves coming up with something new and useful in a social context. Another classroom strategy to support the building blocks of creativity is to analyse your tasks and activities with this in mind. What does being new and useful look like in the social context of your classroom?

Often, this won't be obvious – and as the Four C model (see Chapter 2) suggests, there may be a lot more everyday creativity going on than many people would assume. Clearly, original presentations, essays, artworks, poems, project plans and other pieces of work done by students are new (and useful). But on an even smaller scale, examples they think of, their observations and the specific way they construct notes may reflect mini-c creativity.

Consider the following instances of creative thinking:

- Any time a student writes an essay, they are creating something new and useful.
- An idea for a project in any discipline is creative.
- Coming up with a novel example of a concept is creative.

Creativity therefore plays a role in a huge number of classroom activities, and just as vast a range of situations outside of the classroom.

Bear in mind that originality (the 'new' part of the definition) is relative in the classroom; to the teacher, the work might resemble something that dozens of students have done before, but it may be new to this particular student or class (maybe very similar examples and projects were shared last year!). Usefulness is perhaps more straightforward – anything that is connected with and advances the student's classroom learning is useful.

In terms of pedagogy, applying this in the classroom begins with identifying some of the ways that students can be creative, for example by looking over lesson plans and course plans, or reflecting on recent lessons. Then, where appropriate, more opportunities can be built in. This should not be at the expense of the building blocks of the curriculum, but rather in ways that allow students to practise what they know in new ways.

> **Pause to reflect**
> What examples can you think of from your teaching where students have come up with something new and useful to them, but which is not necessarily new to you or useful in a broader societal context?

Conclusion

This chapter has considered the role of knowledge in creativity. We have seen that knowledge is fundamental to thinking creatively, even though this may feel counterintuitive. The really exciting aspect of this is that knowledge and expertise can always improve. Creativity isn't out of reach for our students. What's more, these building blocks are at work every day, and in every lesson.

Baer (2017) suggested that people are probably more creative and less creative than they think. This chapter helps to highlight why creativity is both simple but also complex, and easily misunderstood. It is, as Sternberg and Lubart (1996, p. 681) put it, the 'extraordinary result of ordinary processes'.

However, this leads to another key idea – knowledge alone, although essential to creative thinking, is not enough. In as far as creativity can be viewed as a skill, it is because students must *do things with their knowledge* – use it in service of new problems, at times deliberating carefully and opting not to follow routines that are so well practised they have become automatic.

Thus, the building blocks of creativity need to be applied with some flexibility. This depends partly on the extent of a person's knowledge – an expert has better-structured knowledge than a novice, as we will see – but also on several other factors that will be discussed in this book, including dispositions, strategies, and metacognitive awareness of the learner. A creative expert doesn't *just* have more knowledge – they are also aware of what they know, and how to use it. They think flexibly and have some control over the creative process, rather than just allowing (or hoping for) it to happen.

The first step in moving from knowledge to creativity is to think more about how basic building blocks, in the form of facts and knowledge, can somehow come together to create something new. How do learners combine what they know in new and useful ways? This will be the focus of the next chapter.

Discussion Questions

1) What does the term 'building block' mean to you? Can you give some examples of fundamental knowledge, routines and skills in your subject?
2) Following the example of the wheeled suitcase, can you think of any other examples of when two existing ideas have been combined to form something new? Perhaps there are examples from your hobbies or from your teaching specialities.
3) What memory consolidation techniques do you already use, and what new ones are you keen to try?
4) How might you talk to students about the idea that creativity depends on fundamental knowledge and routines?
5) Reflecting on the idea of asking 'What if …?' questions, what specific ideas do you have for how this could work in your classroom? What if they don't work as well as you had hoped?

Professional Learning Tasks

Task 1

Following on from some of the applications above, take a few minutes to analyse one of your recent lessons. What opportunities were there for students to think creatively? What did they do that was new (to them), and useful? Would you make any changes if teaching the lesson again?

Task 2

In this chapter, we have explored the idea of creativity as a skill or process, but as one that can be supported in very specific ways, and which is based on a foundation of knowledge. Consider which of the following options would be a better way of supporting creative thinking among students:

1) Teaching geography facts followed by more teaching of the same geography facts
2) Doing a creative project in geography followed by another creative project in geography
3) Teaching geography facts followed by a creative project that draws on and applies these facts

These are simplistic examples, but perhaps you can see a parallel with teaching in your own context – note down your thoughts.

Task 3

As mentioned in the 'Applications to Practice' section above, there are many resources that provide an evidence-based explanation of memory, and how it applies to the classroom. Visit your school/college library's professional learning section, and look for *Powerful Teaching* by Agarwal and Bain (2019), *How Learning Happens* by Kirschner and Hendrick (2020), or *What Teachers Need to Know about Memory* by Firth and Riazat (2023). Find the parts of these books that are most relevant to you, and begin to identify more ways of building secure and lasting knowledge among your students.

4 Flexible Knowledge

During his voyage on HMS *Beagle*, Charles Darwin made careful observations, noticing variations in the animal specimens he found. Famously, the finches on the Galápagos Islands had different beak shapes depending on their food sources. It was already well understood at the time that animals could be organised into families and into a broader taxonomy based on relatedness, but Darwin's observations led him to consider how species evolve within their environments over long periods of time.

Darwin knew how farmers and breeders can select individual animals, such as horses or hens, to pass on certain traits. He had also been influenced by ideas current in geology at the time; it was increasingly being recognised that Earth was millions of years old, not thousands. This allowed gradual changes to the landscape over long periods of time, and Darwin drew parallels with changes to species.

Another influence on Darwin was the work of Thomas Malthus on the population of cities. Malthus was aware that if populations kept rising unchecked, there would be terrible overcrowding. This idea influenced Darwin; he came to see that this could happen in the natural world, too. Combining these ideas, Darwin developed and later published his theory of evolution by natural selection, which explained how species change over long periods of time due to traits that favoured some individuals over others.

As we have seen so far in this book, new creative ideas don't just come out of nowhere. Whether we are talking about school students or great scientists, they are based on what the creator knows. Charles Darwin's theory of evolution by natural selection fits well with the view of creativity – as a scientist, he already had all the building blocks to come up with his theory of evolution. He also developed his ideas on evolution over time, and we have a good insight into the knowledge and scholarship that influenced him.

However, this is not the whole story. What was it that allowed Darwin to put these together and come up with something new? One assumption might be that Darwin was just a genius. This fits with a popular conception of creativity – one that sees it as arising from a flash of genius that is hard for normal people to understand (see also Chapter 9).

In the previous chapter, we explored the idea that creative ideas don't come from nowhere; they involve the application of knowledge in context. In this chapter, we will look in more detail at how that process works. How do people take that existing knowledge and use it to come up with ideas, or make something new and useful?

The Myth

We previously discussed the flawed idea that children are naturally creative until school strips this away (see Chapter 2), and touched on a problematic implication of that myth – that some learners 'have' creativity, and others do not. Such a view portrays creativity as analogous to a reservoir within particular students, something that they can somehow dip into whenever they need to do creative tasks.

The idea of some people being inherently or naturally creative is a version of the nature-nurture debate; perhaps unsurprisingly, people have strong beliefs on the issue. Your students (and perhaps their parents) may assume that some people are naturally gifted and others are not. This might apply particularly in arts subjects that they associate more strongly with creativity (see Chapter 5).

While cognitive science *does* recognise that pre-existing differences between students play a role in outcomes, these differences are frequently exaggerated in people's minds. And whether differences are due to 'nature' or something else, any aptitude a student brings to their learning appears to speed up the learning of knowledge and routines rather than rendering the 'nurture' side unimportant (Simonton, 2012).

In schools, beliefs about whether some children are naturally more creative have implications for issues such as subject choices. Children do of course differ from each other, but it's more in line with an overall cognitive science approach to creativity to assume that *any* learner can develop creative skills with the right guidance (even if it's probably also true that they can't all become creative geniuses in any field of their choosing).

Overall, the idea of some people being naturally creative is just one of many popular myths about how creativity works. It is clear that a lot of practice is necessary for anybody to become highly creative, and that this practice has to be done in an effective way (Ericsson, 2017). Just as creativity is not just about 'Big-C' ideas, it's also not something that only applies to a few special people. It's important to challenge the assumption that creativity will rarely or never be encountered, and that whether someone is good at creative tasks or not is a matter of luck.

Tackling this means putting more of an emphasis on the process of creativity – it's more about what students do with their 'building blocks' of knowledge than who we are.

Pause to reflect
What is your view on how we support all students to fulfil their potential to become creative thinkers?

Exploring the Research

Existing knowledge

We have already established the role of long-term memory in coming up with creative ideas – this is where all of a thinker's knowledge is stored, and therefore provides the building blocks for coming up with new creative ideas and solutions (see Chapter 3). Still, creativity is not the same as retrieving what you already know, or even applying it. Retrieval from memory must be involved, but this by itself does not create anything new (though it might be useful).

Benedek et al. (2023) tried to make sense of this by exploring the process of memory retrieval. According to their research, memory plays a role throughout creativity, but very dynamically, as the creator thinks of and recalls different ideas at different stages. They recall different types of knowledge, too – personal 'episodic' memories as well as semantic knowledge. We can see these memories as feeding into and supporting the development of a new creative idea or solution.

Making connections

Sternberg and Lubart (1999) argue that an act is creative if it involves making something new or finding an original recombination of existing elements, provided that the end result is useful in some way. This is a version of the standard definition of creativity, but one that emphasises that the novelty will often feature *recombinations* of existing knowledge.

This means that coming up with a valuable new idea very often involves putting together familiar elements taken from other places – just like Darwin did. We re-use what we know, and in line with an analogy we shared previously (the Lego bricks), novelty can involve assembling several different components to make something new.

The role of connections and putting existing ideas to new uses was also recognised by Enlightenment philosophers. For example, the French writer Voltaire is often associated with the quote that originality is *'nothing but judicious imitation'*. Although apocryphal, this phrase highlights the idea that new work is often largely based on elements from older ones, polished up and put into a new framework.

Indeed, most movies, articles, projects or artworks don't produce something that has never been done before, but they take already recognisable ideas, actions and characters and weave them together in a way that is new and exciting. Researchers draw on their store of knowledge and of methodology when they write a new research paper, while a novelist might craft a murder mystery using familiar concepts such as a sleuth, a victim, clues, interviews with suspects, and a denouement. A work has to be at least recognisable to be considered a part of a genre or artistic field at all!

Flexible thinking

The process of using existing knowledge to think creatively also involves a certain flexibility. There is a willingness among creators to rethink and re-use existing ideas, and to view them in a new light if necessary. These thinking processes have also been studied in cognitive science research as part of our understanding of where ideas come from.

For example, Nijstad et al. (2010) argue that the process of coming up with new ideas depends, among other things, on *cognitive flexibility*. Cognitive flexibility means thinking in non-routine ways, and includes a person's capacity to playfully reconsider existing knowledge and ideas – to rethink and re-imagine (see also Chapter 2). It is at work, for example, when someone realises that a book could also be used as a doorstop.

Viewing creativity in terms of repurposing or re-evaluating knowledge is somewhat counterintuitive. After all, we define creativity as novelty, and tend to focus on examples of creativity which are especially surprising and unusual. As such, this idea doesn't sit well with common beliefs about creativity. However, it is perhaps easier to see that at least some of the people we think of as naturally creative are in fact just better at thinking flexibly, and recognising the opportunities to repurpose familiar ideas and objects.

Pause to reflect
What do you make of the idea of cognitive flexibility, and using old ideas in new ways? How relevant is this to your teaching?

In depth: The Remote Associates Test
The Remote Associates Test (RAT) was devised in the 1960s by Sarnoff Mednick as a way to test how well people can come up with connections and associations. Participants are provided with a list of three words, and tasked with coming up with another word that links them all together. For example, when given the words *cake*, *Swiss* and *cottage*, a word that would connect them all together would be 'cheese' (cheesecake, Swiss cheese, cottage cheese).

Here are some further examples:
1. Thin – cream – skate
2. Ranger – preserve – tropical
3. Pine – crab – sauce

The examples highlight the role of cultural and linguistic background, and therefore of knowledge – many UK residents would struggle to see *forest* as the common idea in the second example above, as the term 'forest preserve' (rather than reserve) is used mainly in the USA.

All the same, the RAT is a simple exercise in making connections that could easily be adapted to classes. It would make an excellent quick starter. Any three or more related terms – perhaps drawn from classes that took place days or weeks earlier – could be used. Sometimes, it will suffice for teachers to point out connections, but asking students to make connections for themselves will provide practice of the processes described in this chapter.

(By the way, the solutions for the three examples above are: ice; forest; apple.)

Classroom-relevant combinations

Returning to a question raised earlier in this book, is creativity an everyday sort of thing, or a once-a-term sort of thing, or a once-in-a-lifetime thing? Recall the point in Chapter 2 that we can look at everyday 'little-c' creativity, and also consider 'mini-c' creativity. This works in a similar way when it comes to connections and using ideas in new ways. These processes don't have to involve 'Big-C' insights. For a child, it could involve thinking of a 'new' use for an object in a game (even if this is very similar to what many children have thought of before).

The idea of recombinations of elements does apply to bigger breakthroughs too, of course, such as Darwin's theory and other new ideas of science. Most of our students are not going to make huge scientific breakthroughs, but they may combine ideas into other novel outputs, such as:

- A persuasive essay that draws on existing knowledge
- A new musical piece that they compose
- A new recipe

This idea illustrates why it's so important to have a base of factual knowledge and skills in your field. In these and hundreds of other educationally relevant examples, students need to know the basics in order to create anything worthwhile. The more they have and the better they are at developing and recombining this base of factual knowledge, the more creative their thinking will be.

It also helps to highlight that the difference between mature creative work and the 'mini-c' creative play seen among children is less about the process of thinking, and more about the knowledge involved. Being cognitively flexible and playful in your thinking is valuable at any age (see Chapter 2). A professional just has more extensive and well-structured knowledge to play with.

In depth: Music

The idea of creativity involving connections and combinations may be more intuitive in some fields than in others. For example, in music, it is straightforward to see how prior knowledge is recombined.

When composing a piece of music, it is clear that a musician will draw on fundamental building blocks such as scales and musical notes, and their knowledge of musical genres will also be important. In some cases, repurposing knowledge might involve taking a musical phrase or theme and putting it into a different context, changing the tempo, or otherwise varying it from the original.

These creators are using existing building blocks to make something new. The specific notes and combinations might not be entirely new, but neither are they directly recalled from memory – instead, the musician playfully experiments with these, repurposes them, and combines them in unusual ways.

None of this involves being as random as possible. Instead, the work proceeds with an understanding of the original, and an awareness of the intended outcome – the effect on a listener, for example.

Links to creativity as a skill

Both processes mentioned above – making connections among existing knowledge and flexibly re-using ideas – are part of how creativity arises from knowledge. Understanding these processes and how they contribute to new ideas helps to shed more light on the debate raised in the previous chapter.

In particular, the emphasis on creativity as connections and recombinations should help you to see why viewing creativity entirely as a skill, disconnected from knowledge, doesn't really make sense (see the discussion of this idea in Chapter 3). As creativity is about making new combinations and associations among *existing* ideas, it has to involve things we already know. Retaining facts in long-term memory is therefore a prerequisite for creative thinking (and other 'higher-order' skills), and all the better if prior learning is well understood and easily remembered – this will facilitate the elements being put together in novel ways.

The example at the start of this chapter indicates how important it is to connect together existing knowledge; Darwin's idea was new, but drew heavily on his existing knowledge. The wheeled suitcase example in the previous chapter, too, demonstrated using an old idea in a new way.

Overall, the concept of using old ideas in new ways adds to the 'building blocks' analogy we discussed earlier in the book. This emphasised the importance of having enough relevant knowledge, but making connections may not depend just on the *amount* of knowledge a learner has. How much more creative a model could a person build with a million blocks to play with, rather than 100,000? Perhaps not all that much more! At some point, the way that the items are organised could be just as important. Can you even find the 'building blocks', for example, and do you understand the subtle differences between them?

This leads to the issue of how knowledge is structured in memory.

Boosting creative thinking

As Anderson put it in 1984, 'Knowledge is not a "basket of facts"' (p. 5). That is to say, a learner has to be able to use that knowledge; there may be diminishing returns to adding more and more. What's more, it's a misconception to view knowledge purely in terms of its amount. Just as important is how this information is linked together and structured.

A focus on how knowledge is interconnected has been a major theme across cognitive science. New information is not taken into human long-term memory like saving to a computer hard drive. Instead, it is combined and connected to what is already known (Fiorella & Mayer, 2015; Wittrock, 1974). For creativity, our capacity to come up with new ideas doesn't just depend on the amount of existing knowledge, but on how well we can use that knowledge to analyse a new problem (or problems) to be solved.

Flexible Knowledge 59

Episodic memory   Semantic knowledge

New idea

Figure 4.1 Incoming information is connected to what we already know

In long-term memory, information is structured into *schemas*. A schema is a set of ideas about a particular concept or situation, and may include relevant facts and details, recall of past experiences, emotions, and much more. For example, a student may have a schema about dogs, about travelling by plane, about parties, and so on. The story conventions and genres used in creative writing are also examples of schemas.

These schemas can subdivide as a learner's knowledge becomes more sophisticated, and they begin to appreciate subtle distinctions that they were previously unaware of. For example, a child may know that there is a type of insect called a beetle, but as they get older they learn that there are many different types of beetles. Experts categorise into even finer sub-categories (an entomologist, for example, knows that there are hundreds of species of beetle).

These categories help people to understand the world around them, making it easier to engage in everyday thinking (Rosch, 1978). Having information structured into schemas helps it to be more quickly accessed, and can also allow the learner to fill in gaps and to make inferences. Further, it affects how easily new information is taken in, and supports thinking about new ideas in complex ways.

Schemas therefore help to explain something that cognitive scientists have long recognised – that experts differ from novices not just in the amount that they know, but also in how it is organised (de Jong et al., 2024). Novices think in less flexible ways. They may be able to recall factual knowledge, but they are not very good at doing things with that knowledge (Bransford et al., 2000). An expert, in contrast, is fast and accurate in a given domain, and able to analyse new challenges and problems (Ericsson, 2017), and usually flexible in their thinking, too.

There may come a point, therefore, where learning more and more information is not the best strategy; having more knowledge doesn't always lead to better creativity. The processes discussed above help to explain this; it depends what the learner does with it, and how well it is structured in memory. Indeed, as we will explore in a later chapter (see

Chapter 6), it is possible to develop expert knowledge without any of the cognitive flexibility and openness to new connections that we have discussed so far.

It is worth emphasising that as we go through the book, we are never moving away from the proposition that well-learned and flexible knowledge in long-term memory is essential to creative thinking. However, there can be more to getting the most out of that information than simply adding to it.

> **Pause to reflect**
> How familiar are you with the concepts mentioned in the previous section on cognitive science, e.g. schemas and long-term memory? Can you think of how these concepts link to your curriculum area(s)?

Applications to Practice

So far, we have seen that creative thinking is not just about knowledge, but also depends on how effectively and flexibly that knowledge is used. It should be obvious from the points so far that just telling students to 'think hard' or to 'be as creative as possible' will be of little help in coming up with creative ideas. So, what will? The rest of this chapter will focus on some practical classroom strategies.

Reminders

Information might be well stored in long-term memory, but this doesn't mean that it is easily accessible. This means that your students might have relevant knowledge but simply fail to recognise it or think about it in the situation.

When exactly should material be reviewed? It is common practice to engage in some form of self-assessment and consolidation during a lesson, or soon after. However, this does not take account of forgetting.

Forgetting proceeds rapidly after something is studied. Even well-learned material can become rusty – how easily can you recall the address of your childhood school(s), for example?

To address this issue, it can be beneficial to plan reminders and refresher tasks ahead of or at the outset of a creative task such as a project or essay. For example, a quiz could be used to remind students of what they have covered over the previous days and weeks.

A specific way to do this might involve setting a practice test. Rather than its more common use for testing or revision, a test could be set with the specific aim of reminding students about ideas and concepts that could play a role in an upcoming creativity-focused lesson. A consolidation homework activity could also be used.

Such tasks will prompt retrieval from memory, making it easier for connections to come to mind during the lesson; any connection is going to occur more readily when the items in memory are more accessible.

When planning, you may have particular connections in mind, and use this strategy to prepare students for later parts of the lesson. At other times, there may be advantages to serendipitous connections, and allowing students to come up with ideas for themselves – ideas that you might not have thought of in advance. To facilitate this, try throwing in a few facts and concepts from different topics. You could also directly ask students to make links between the items on the test (see the next strategy, below).

Seeking out connections

To prompt more thinking about connections, try displaying a set of items or concepts to students (these could be the answers to quiz questions, or key terms from a recent topic), then asking them to make connections. What do X and Y have in common?

This is similar to the RAT task (see 'In depth' box, above), though you could extend it in various ways. For example, you don't need to limit it to single words. Sets of terms, factual statements or processes could be used, as could images, or even longer texts.

Putting items or problems side by side helps students to see meaningful differences between them and is an example of *interleaving* (more about this in Chapter 6). This approach can also be used to support assessment. Rather than asking students to write a full essay to assess their understanding of a topic, two essay questions could be placed side by side and students could be asked to identify which concepts might be applicable to both and where arguments would differ.

The idea of finding connections could also be extended in various ways. For example, a discussion could arise from a categorising or sorting activity – perhaps students don't agree on the common factor, such as the underlying theme across a series of poems in English. Larger sets of items could be sorted into categories, and students could then be asked to justify or write about their choices.

Comparing and contrasting multiple examples at the same time encourages deeper thinking. As such, all of these activities can help support students to think flexibly, and to develop well-organised schemas. As ever, though, it is important to think carefully about the difficulty level of such activities, whether students have enough prior knowledge, and how much time should be devoted to it.

Note taking

There are various forms of note taking that can contribute to combining ideas creatively. While it is of course important that students' notes are well organised so that they can find important information in their notes, there can be a cost to being too rigid and structured – it will limit the ease with which the mind spots interesting new connections.

As a visual support for the process of making connections, a mind map (or 'concept map') can be used to encourage new associations. Here, notes are put together into a cluster or spider-shaped diagram, with a central idea as its hub. You could ask students to draw lines between terms to show connections that they find or that you provide, each time labelling what the connection is.

Mind maps are sometimes recommended as an aid to memory, but drawing these maps tends to be time-consuming, making it somewhat inefficient compared to other ways of taking notes or revising facts. However, they may at times be helpful for triggering non-obvious connections, and developing possibilities that might have been quickly discarded if they weren't down on paper.

To get the benefit of retrieval practice as part of the mapping process (see Chapter 3), we like the suggestion of Caviglioli (2019) that students are first asked to recall from memory relevant facts and ideas, writing these on Post-It notes. They then organise these into a diagram, focusing on how the ideas link together into a structure.

You can also suggest to students that older notebooks are worth revisiting periodically, for example when designing experiments or projects. They may underestimate how much they have forgotten, and reading through old notes might cause them to come across a half-developed idea that would go on to spark a new connection.

Prompts and sparks

Taking the previous idea one step further in terms of randomness, you could build up a set of varied prompts on slips of paper or index cards from across your subject area. These could include words, quotes, historical photos, musical phrases, media characters, or whatever is appropriate to your subject. The more varied the better.

These could be displayed to a class/group of students, or prepared in some other way for them to access, such as on a worksheet, or even a deck which they would draw from. Then, as with the 'Seeking out connections' strategy (see above), students could be challenged to come up with a common link between two or more items. They could also be asked to think of unusual uses for an item, encouraging cognitive flexibility.

Younger students will enjoy such tasks as they have game-like elements. They can be a fun and motivating way to start a session, taking up only a short amount of time. Bear in mind, though, that it's not just about fun; the task practises creative processes, and also prompts retrieval from memory. Students are forced to recall the item and what it means, and the task will also provide an opportunity for some formative assessment of key ideas.

It's helpful to point out to students that what they are doing (making links) is part of creative thinking, and that it is useful to practise. If you are lucky, students will come up with some fascinating new connections, but it's important to emphasise to them that this takes practice. All of this helps to develop their metacognitive awareness of creativity – recognising what it is, that it takes effort, but also that it is accessible to all learners. As discussed in Chapter 2, it's valuable to make them comfortable sharing tentative ideas, and tasks like this one could help.

Students could also be encouraged to find their own prompts and sparks, perhaps to come up with ideas when engaged in writing tasks. You could also draw parallels with how prompts are used in some fields, such as creative writing prompts that are widely available, or the 'Oblique Strategies' created by musician Brian Eno together with Peter Schmidt (a set of cards with prompt phrases aimed to 'break creative deadlock' during music writing, but which could be used for other creative projects too).

In depth: Halogen displacement reactions

Halogen displacement reactions are used in Chemistry to show the trend in reactivity for the halogen elements. Students often find this a tricky concept, but there are many parallels with metal displacement reactions – a topic which most students grasp much more quickly.

Rather than simply telling students about the parallels directly, some schools use activities which help students to make this connection themselves. Steps for this can include:

- Checking for requisite prior knowledge/using reminders
- Setting students the task of coming up with as many ideas as possible for how the trend in reactivity for the halogens could be investigated
- Comparing ideas in groups
- A plenary by the teacher
- A follow-up practical

There are advantages to having students jot down their ideas individually at first; in an open discussion, conversations can be dominated by the first (or loudest!) ideas shared.

In this and similar tasks, the teacher may also choose to carefully feed in ideas, comments, reminders of prior knowledge, and so on. These help students to make connections. For example, students could be asked about possible parallels with metal reactivity, or to think about similar reactions they have seen.

This approach to teaching a topic recruits creative thinking, supporting students to start making connections in their science work, as well as making them more comfortable with uncertainty. The process of exploring the ideas in this way can also consolidate and deepen their scientific knowledge, as it promotes connections with other topics.

Conclusion

In this chapter, we have explored how creative thinking brings an element of novelty by rethinking or recombining existing knowledge. Retrieval of knowledge is necessary, but not sufficient. It's also important to use existing knowledge in new ways.

To return to a point raised earlier, creativity is not just about a few geniuses – great scientists, inventors or artists. Granted, these people had more expertise than the average. But all the same, just as creativity is based on common building blocks, there are processes such as connections and flexible thinking that feature in the classroom, just as much as they do in eminent creativity. There are great similarities in how students make creative connections and how famous creators and experts do so.

We hope you also recognise from the discussion and examples in this chapter that these processes can and do happen every day, supporting what was said in the previous two chapters. As such, creativity in the classroom will be less about finding 'great ideas' and more about the habits and processes involved in thinking flexibly, and in ways that characterise well-organised, well-connected schemas. This is true throughout the different developmental levels of creativity, from mini-c upwards, and it is the complexity of the building blocks that varies.

These points have also further emphasised that creativity is not a stand-alone skill, but rather depends on well-learned knowledge. It will be easier to make the 'aha!' connections once you have already established at least the beginnings of expertise in your area. Creativity is not *just* a skill – but there are key ways in which creative thinkers use their knowledge that can't be taken for granted.

The following chapter will start to look at how this plays out across the curriculum, considering the role of creativity across different academic subjects and disciplines.

Discussion Questions

1) The chapter starts with the example of Charles Darwin. Think of other famous scientists, artists or other creators – are you aware of what influenced them? Were there popular ideas at the time, rivals, new technology, or particular social problems that they were trying to solve?

2) Reflect on the idea of creativity being a process that everyone can engage in. Do we sometimes, in education or elsewhere, communicate the idea that only some students are 'creative types'? Or do parents and students themselves tend to believe this? If so, how can that be challenged?

3) Consider the idea of creativity as involving connections and repurposing material. What, in your field, are the most important links and connections that students make? Are there some that they especially struggle with?

4) In your practice, is there a way that you could establish a set of random prompt cards, or other stimuli that might spark learners' creativity? Could previous pieces of work be used in some way? What would be the best format?

5) One example of a schema given in the chapter is a student's knowledge of stories and genres. Can you think of any further examples?

Professional Learning Tasks

Task 1

Where in your subject or phase can you make connections between different topics, perhaps across different years? How might you adapt your teaching to support students to make these connections themselves? How will you ensure they have the requisite prior knowledge to make these connections? Make a list of possible starter tasks or plenary activities.

Task 2

A quick Google search for 'Remote Associates Test' will bring up lots of examples you can try with a group of students or colleagues. Are some word combinations harder for some groups of people than others? Can you link this to any cultural or language differences between different groups of people? What does this tell you about the importance of background knowledge for creative thinking?

Task 3

Have a try at writing a concept map or mind map to represent a schema – a concept that is important for your students to know about. Connect in key facts, processes and ideas. As you do so, think about the potential benefits of visual notes. Do they make it easier for you to see connections? How could you adapt this to your practice?

5 Creativity Across All Subjects

A personal reflection from Claire

I spoke to lots of people in the process of writing this book and several expressed surprise that someone with a scientific background was writing about creativity – surely a teacher with an arts background would be better suited to such a project? As it happens, I do have some involvement in the arts. I studied Music at A-level, spent a lot of my time at university singing in various choirs and still sing regularly with an amateur choir in London. However, singing is probably an area of my life where I am at my least creative; I go along to rehearsals and sing the notes written on the page (mostly correctly …). There may be some creativity from our musical director in how he interprets the pieces we are singing, but personally I don't feel I am producing anything new. That is not to say that the experience isn't useful for me; it's a hugely important part of my life. It's just not particularly creative.

My experiences as a research scientist when I completed my PhD in Chemistry on the other hand did require me to be enormously creative. I was carrying out lab experiments and it felt at times as though I was never going to be able to get the equipment to produce any useful data. Finding new ways to adapt the experiments involved a lot of creative thinking (as well as a great deal of perseverance).

Nowadays, I would say I'm most creative in my role in school. I like to think I've reached the level of Pro-C creativity here where I can find new and useful ways to help both students and teachers use the findings from educational research to improve their practice. This book is part of that work and I hope shows that even a scientist can write about creativity.

The Myth

In everyday discourse and in the media, creativity is often mentioned in association with subjects such as art, music and drama. These are often termed the 'creative subjects' (try Googling that term to see what you find!). Policy makers, too, often talk about arts subjects in a way that implies both that these subjects are always or inherently creative, and/or that they are the only subjects that involve creativity.

Conflating creativity with artistic fields can lead to the misconception that creativity does not play a part in subjects such as science and maths, when it absolutely does! Creative thinking takes place in science, maths, languages, and any other field you can think of. None of this is an argument against the value of arts subjects. Rather, given what has been said so far about the building blocks of creativity, it would be erroneous to view it as the sole preserve of these subjects.

If you teach a subject outside of the arts, you might be quicker to dismiss the idea that creativity is unimportant in your own teaching (and there is some evidence that this 'arts bias' myth is less prevalent amongst teachers than amongst the general population; Patston et al., 2018). However, even if this seems obviously flawed to you, don't forget that students and their parents often hold these misconceptions. The idea is worth tackling at a whole-school level. In addition, while arts subjects can and should be championed, it's best for such advocacy to avoid flawed and simplistic arguments along the lines of 'children need these subjects in order to develop creativity'. Likewise, it doesn't make sense to suggest that we can develop a creative workforce by providing a curriculum with more arts subjects at school, despite policy makers often suggesting this.

Exploring the Research

Creativity is not just for the arts

The definition of creativity introduced in Chapter 1 helps us to dispel the myth that creativity is just for the arts. Recall that being creative involves coming up with something new and useful in a particular social context (Harrington, 2018; Runco & Jaeger, 2012). Therefore, creativity is by definition not limited to certain subjects or activities – an idea or output could be new and useful in engineering just as much as in music.

It's also more than possible to engage in the creative subjects in an entirely non-creative way. Consider Claire's experiences singing in an amateur choir as shared above. Other examples could include craft projects where you simply follow instructions written by someone else, for example painting by numbers or following a cross-stitch pattern – these could be described as useful, but they are not novel or innovative.

How well something fits the definition can to an extent depend on which creativity level (from the Four Cs) we mean. Something that might not be creative on a Big-C level can still be seen as creative within a *different* social context; a student teaching themselves coding would be creative on a little-c level even if their coding is not at the level of a professional computer scientist.

Teachers' views

At the authors' request, in August 2023, TeacherTapp posed the following statements and asked users to respond on a 5-point Likert scale.

1) Creativity is an essential component of my subject (secondary) or phase (primary).
2) It is an important part of my role to develop my students' creative thinking skills.
3) I have the skills and knowledge to effectively develop creative thinking in my students.

Creativity Across All Subjects 73

The questions were answered by over 8,000 teachers and the overall results are shown in Figure 5.1, below.

TeacherTapp Survey Data
August 2023

[Horizontal stacked bar chart showing three statements rated across categories: Strongly agree, Agree, Neither agree nor disagree, Disagree, Strongly disagree, Not relevant/cannot answer.

- Creativity is an essential component of my subject (secondary) or phase (primary)
- It is an important part of my role to develop my students' creative thinking skills
- I have the skills and knowledge to effectively develop creative thinking in my students]

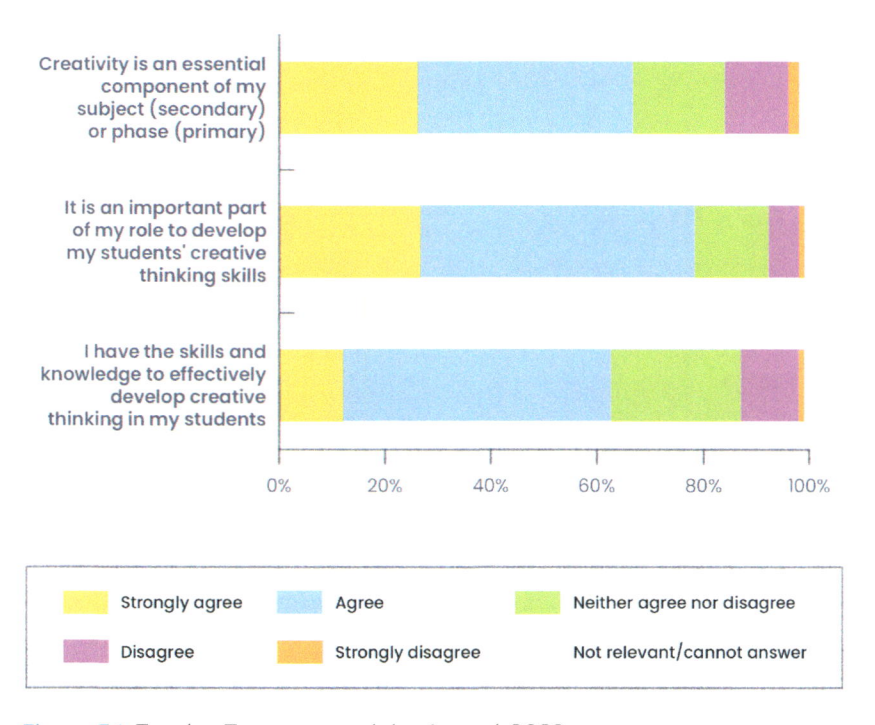

Figure 5.1 TeacherTapp survey data, August 2023

It is gratifying to see that the majority of teachers feel that creativity is an essential component of their teaching and that developing students' creative thinking skills is an important part of their role. There was less agreement as to whether teachers felt they had the knowledge and skills to do this – something we hope that this book can begin to address.

74 *Creativity for Teachers*

However, the subject breakdown is particularly interesting in the context of the myth discussed above (see Figure 5.2).

Creativity is an essential component of my subject or phase

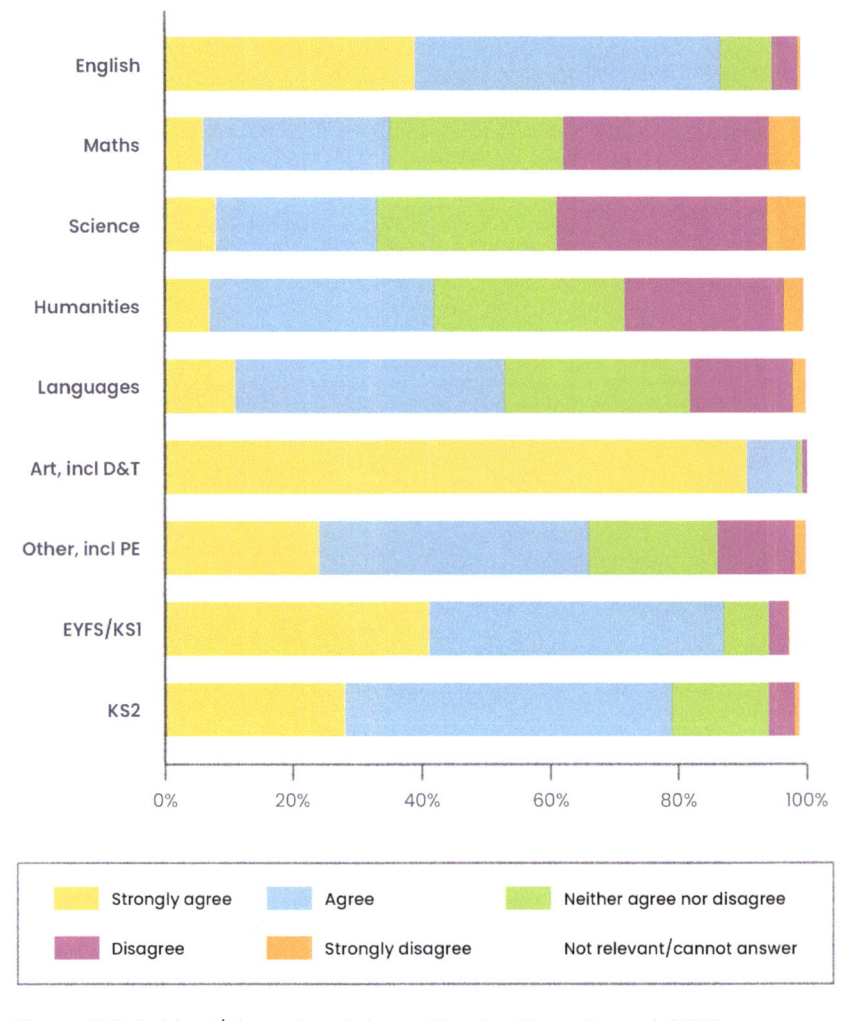

[Bar chart showing responses by subject: English, Maths, Science, Humanities, Languages, Art incl D&T, Other incl PE, EYFS/KS1, KS2. Categories: Strongly agree, Agree, Neither agree nor disagree, Disagree, Strongly disagree, Not relevant/cannot answer.]

Figure 5.2 Subject/phase breakdown, TeacherTapp, August 2023

From the results in Figure 5.2, we can see that the high overall endorsement of the essential nature of creativity is influenced by the opinions of Art, English and primary teachers. Over 90 per cent of Art teachers strongly agreed that creativity is an essential component of their subject whereas the figure drops to less than 10 per cent for humanities, science and maths. Similar subject breakdowns were seen for the other two questions.

At least among the teachers surveyed by TeacherTapp, then, there is a degree of endorsement of the myth discussed earlier (the responses from primary teachers may to an extent also reflect the association between creativity and childhood – see Chapter 2).

In August 2024, another question on creativity was posed: How important do you believe it is for students to learn creativity and problem-solving skills in lessons?

As before, there was a difference across phases and subjects, although this was less stark than the earlier data, perhaps because of the inclusion of problem solving alongside creativity. Within early primary, 67 per cent felt this was highly important, for Art & Design Technology it was 85 per cent, whereas for science and Maths it was 37 per cent and 48 per cent respectively. Overall, differences again appeared, with some more likely than others to see creativity as integral to their teaching.

Pause to reflect
What answers would you give to the statements in the TeacherTapp survey? Do your answers change when you consider your subject more broadly or your subject in the context of teaching? Or when you consider the definition of creativity introduced in Chapter 1?

Creativity – domain-general or domain-specific?

Creativity researchers talk about particular 'domains' of knowledge, as well as micro-domains. A domain corresponds fairly closely to a curriculum subject such as Geography or Psychology or Engineering, while broader areas like science are sometimes called 'general thematic areas' (Baer & Kaufman, 2005; van Broekhoven et al., 2020).

Within the literature, there is debate over whether creativity is a domain-general or domain-specific skill – that is to say, can someone's capacity to be creative apply to everything they do, in the same way that the ability to read is useful across the curriculum? Or is it subject-specific, like the ability to test pH which is mainly useful in Chemistry?

This has implications for educators – if creativity is domain-general then we should be able to teach general creative thinking skills decoupled from any specific subject area and can assume these skills will be transferable to any subject.

It's also not obvious. The fact that we use the word 'analyse' across the curriculum doesn't mean that the activity involved is actually the same. Is analysing characters and themes in a text in English really the same thing as analysing data in Biology or analysing the causes of events in History? Being good at one of these certainly does not guarantee facility with all three.

Arguments for the domain generality of creativity tend to focus on psychometric and personality data with the implication that some people are naturally disposed to being creative. A person with a creative outlook, it might be argued, is going to be creative at whatever they turn their hand to.

Arguments for the domain specificity of creativity stem from the fact that creativity cannot exist in the absence of knowledge. This can be seen in the analysis example above – the reason why the Biology scholar might struggle to analyse the History examples is that they won't have as much relevant knowledge about the events and their context as a historian would.

Domains and creativity – examples

We can delve deeper into the idea of domain specificity by studying the complex behaviour of experts. For example, chess masters appear to require from 50,000 to 100,000 hours of practice to attain the highest levels in the game. They need to have encoded a huge number of moves, patterns and sequences to long-term memory (Chase & Simon, 1973). Doing so allows them to guide their future moves flexibly and creatively, at times creating novel combinations based on that stored bank of knowledge. It takes years to build the knowledge base to reach Pro-C levels of creativity; no matter what your levels of generic creative thinking skills such as open-mindedness, you are highly unlikely to be able to do this in more than one domain.

Chase and Simon also found that chess masters could remember the positions of pieces on a chessboard much more accurately than novices could. They retained up to 20 pieces in memory even after only seeing the board for a few seconds, while novices could only remember four or five. However, when a board was shown with random positions, rather than positions from a real game, their recall was no better than that of the novices (Chase & Simon, 1973). The chess masters' experience only counted when the configuration of pieces was meaningful to them, and fitted with their prior knowledge of games and strategies. This shows that even phenomenal expertise doesn't necessarily help with unrelated tasks. Their chess ability did not develop a domain-general cognitive skill.

In their paper 'Could Steven Spielberg manage the Yankees', Kaufman and Baer (2002) discuss how the evidence for creativity general factors tends to come from studies of creative personalities which often rely on self-report data. In their opinion, these self-report measures are flawed as measures of creativity. Rather than providing evidence for domain-general creativity, they instead show how people conceptualise creativity – self-confidence, ambition and openness to experience may *appear* to be domain-general but are in fact specific; you can be open to experiences in one domain and not in another.

In depth: STE(A)M education

The importance of learners engaged in so-called creative subjects is championed across all stages of childhood. Parents are urged to buy their young children 'creative toys' such as toy drum kits and painting kits. Schools are lauded if they offer a wide variety of opportunities for students to be involved in Art, Music and Drama. The implication is that if children do more artistic subjects, they will become generally more creative in ways that will affect their performance across the board.

An example of this is the concept of STE(A)M. It is a movement that inserts the letter 'A' for Art into STEM (Science, Technology, Engineering and Mathematics). The rationale for doing so is that a focus on arts will make STEM students more creative ... and that creativity is greatly needed in fields like Biochemistry and Mechanical Engineering.

In doing so, it brings a welcome emphasis on creativity to these fields. It might also be seen as a defence against an unwelcome narrowing of the curriculum by giving a rationale for more teaching of the arts.

However, there are at least two problems to the logic. First, as already mentioned, people can think creatively in all fields. Given that creativity is just as integral to STEM as it is to Art, the argument for doing Art in order to get better at science subjects looks a lot weaker.

Secondly, is it really the case that doing a lot of artistic subjects will actually make learners better at STEM? As we've seen, scientists do need to be creative, but creativity in those subjects requires domain-specific knowledge.

Overall, improving creative skills in one domain by studying another is not as straightforward as might be typically portrayed.

Evidence for the domain specificity of creativity tends to come from studies of the creative products produced across different domains; these studies have found little correlation between creativity ratings of artefacts produced by people across different domains. Kaufman and Baer (2002, p. 5) conclude that 'people's implicit conceptions of creativity may often contain general creativity-relevant factors [but] the actual cognitive mechanisms underlying creative performance … are domain specific'.

The domain-general vs. domain-specific debate

Baer and Kaufman have attempted to reconcile these two debates with their Amusement Park Theoretical (APT) metaphor (Baer & Kaufman, 2005). This has four levels, incorporating the domains and thematic areas mentioned earlier:

- Initial requirements
- General thematic areas
- Domains
- Micro-domains

Initial requirements are essential: to go to an amusement park you must have transportation and a ticket; to be creative you need a certain baseline level of knowledge, motivation and an appropriate environment. This could include a disposition to be curious, playful, and so on (more on this later).

Next are general thematic areas – you can decide to go to a water park or a zoo in the same way you can decide to work within the arts or sciences. More specific still are domains – you need to decide which specific amusement park to visit, or whether to work in physics, chemistry or engineering within the sciences. Finally, micro-domains represent specific tasks associated with each domain – once you've decided to go to Legoland do you choose to go on the roller coaster or the teacups?

From a creativity perspective, this means that creative strategies will look different in different domains or sub-domains, with some being more general than others. For example, within the domain of Chemistry, one might work in an organic synthesis lab or in a group modelling the chemistry of the atmosphere. A creative strategy for the synthetic chemist might be trying out different solvents for a purification step; for the modeller, a creative strategy could be to find a different way of representing the reactions in your model which can be coded more efficiently. The APT model integrates both domain generality and domain specificity; initial requirements are very general but specificity increases down the levels.

	Theme park	**Education**
Initial requirements	Transportation + ticket	Intelligence + motivation + environment
General thematic areas	Waterpark or zoo	Arts or Science
Domains	Specific amusement park	Subject within science (i.e., Chemistry)
Micro-domains	Ride the rollercoaster or teacups	Organic synthesis or chemistry of the atmosphere

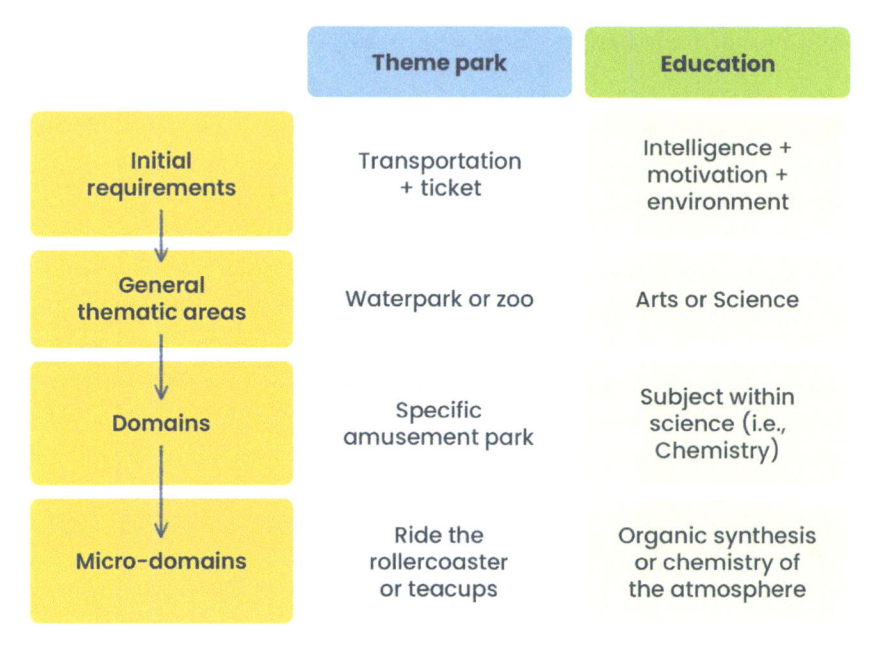

Figure 5.3 The Amusement Park Theoretical model

Pause to reflect
To what extent do you feel the Amusement Park Theoretical model provides a useful way to conceptualise both domain-general and domain-specific aspects of creativity? Can you think of any examples of micro-domains relevant to your teaching?

While Baer and Kaufman (2005) believe that both domain-general and domain-specific processes are happening at different levels, Plucker and Beghetto (2004) argue that, for educators, the distinction is largely irrelevant. For them, only the extreme ends of this spectrum are problematic:

- A person who continually deals with domain-general techniques can end up with only a superficial understanding of a problem.
- Fixed and inflexible ways of thinking can result from too great a focus in one domain.

There are plenty of examples from the world of business where domain-specific expertise left people blind to creative ideas: Blackberry failing to invest in touch-screen technology and being overtaken by the Apple iPhone; the video rental company Blockbuster deciding not to buy Netflix in 2000; and Kodak failing to invest in digital photography despite the fact that the technology was invented by one of its engineers. Plucker and Beghetto (2004) conclude: 'Specificity downplays the importance of outside perspectives, generality overemphasises the importance of all other information and the hybrid position values perspectives from other domains but acknowledges the value of expertise and task commitment' (p. 161).

The implications of Plucker and Beghetto's (2004) work for schools are that educators should ensure students are exposed to a wide range of contexts where they might apply their creativity, and that flexible thinking should be valued both inside and outside of education. In other words, the emphasis is more on developing flexibility and a willingness to think creatively than on developing highly specific skills in micro-domains.

The overconfidence cycle

In *Think Again*, Adam Grant (2021) also champions the value of flexible thinking. He argues that it is all too easy for us to get stuck in 'overconfidence cycles' where we seek validation for our ideas and are prone to confirmation bias. In contrast, in a rethinking cycle, we are doubtful and question our assumptions, leading us to be curious and discover new ways of thinking.

The rethinking cycle

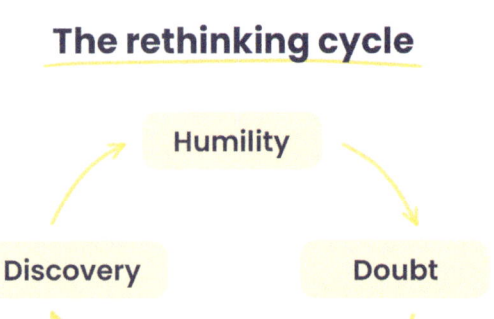

- Humility
- Doubt
- Curiosity
- Discovery

The overconfidence cycle

- Pride
- Conviction
- Confirmation & desirability biases
- Validation

Figure 5.4 Rethinking and overconfidence cycles, adapted from Grant (2021)

Pause to reflect

Can you think of any times where you, or your students, have got stuck in an overconfidence cycle? How might the concept of rethinking help you to avoid this in the future?

Grant talks about the importance of

> confident humility: having faith in our capacity while appreciating that we may not have the right solution or even be addressing the right problem. That gives us enough doubt to reexamine our old knowledge and enough confidence to pursue new insights.
>
> (Grant, 2021, p. 47)

Confidence without humility breeds blind arrogance, and humility without confidence yields debilitating doubt.

Confident humility may provide another way to reconcile the domain-general/specific debate. To be creative we need to be secure enough in our domain-specific knowledge to be confident, but humble enough to know that there are other possibilities and alternatives out there which might require us to utilise more general creative skills such as open-mindedness.

Differences between students across subjects

We have seen that creativity can apply to many different domains. But what about the students themselves – is it possible that more creative students are drawn to study arts subjects, for example?

Students (and their teachers and parents) often have stereotypical views of what arts and science students are like. They may see arts students as more accepting of uncertainty and willing to play with different possibilities, whereas science students could be seen as more disciplined and logical. Some of these stereotypes are often ingrained at an early age. However, this needn't mean that the students who favour different subjects actually think differently.

In a study looking at German university students, van Broekhoven et al. (2020) found evidence that openness, creative self-efficacy and divergent thinking were general prerequisites for creativity. This matches with the ideas discussed above of creativity having some domain-general characteristics. However, this research also found some small, but statistically significant differences across domains, particularly when it came to the qualities of creative products. For example, although both arts and science students strongly associated originality with creativity, this association was greater amongst arts students compared with science students.

There are, of course, some differences in the creative work done across domains. Studies of the relationship between age and achievement have shown that Big-C creativity begins in one's 20s, peaks around 40 and then drops off. However, the drop-off is sharper for arts and, within sciences, contributions tend to start later and peak later (Simonton, 1997, cited by Kaufman & Beghetto, 2009). This is probably partly due to the large expertise base that scientists need to develop before they can contribute something new and useful for wider society, while artists may be more likely to start building their own expertise base earlier.

Thus, it is unsurprising that we might find it difficult to recognise creativity in the science subjects in school-aged children and it may seem easier for these students to display creativity in the arts. For example, they can create paintings and compositions that could be considered creative beyond simply the requirements for an externally assessed examination. However, something can be creative if it is new and useful within the social context of education – this is the concept of Ed-c introduced in Chapter 2. So a student composition completed in a school music lesson could be creative on an Ed-c level even if it is unlikely to be performed outside of the student's classroom. Other examples of how creativity can be shown in an educational context include:

- Solving a complex maths problem that brings together lots of different topics
- Creating a video explanation of the processes needed for gene editing for your Biology class
- Taking part in a Spanish oral exam without having pre-learnt a script
- Writing an essay exploring the gothic themes in Dracula, taking an evidenced view that differs from teachers or peers
- Students collaborating to produce a group presentation on the features of coastal dunes in Geography

Applications to Practice

The debates discussed above suggest that we should consider developing creativity in our young people from both a domain-general and a domain-specific perspective. Although there may be merit in running sessions for students looking at creativity on a general level outside of mainstream academic lessons, it would be erroneous to think that the knowledge and understanding developed in such sessions would transfer without explicit recourse to evidence-based strategies, some of which may be specific to particular subjects. The problem of transfer will be discussed further in Chapter 6; here we will consider how creativity can be championed and developed in all school subjects.

Creativity in school subjects

At a school level, it is common for students to associate Maths and science with having just one right answer, whereas the opposite is true in English. Both extremes are of course incorrect but these naive misconceptions go some way to explaining why creativity becomes associated with the arts. We should support students to see the value of open-mindedness and embracing different perspectives in all subjects, not just within Art, English and History where the application of these ideas is more immediately obvious.

One potential way of overcoming these naive conceptions is to introduce students to the definition of creativity discussed in Chapter 1: to be creative something needs to be both new and useful in a particular social context. Breaking this down into the different levels of creativity introduced in Chapter 2 is a way to show students that creativity is as applicable to science as it is to the arts, and is also applicable to the way in which these subjects are viewed in schools, the concept of Ed-c.

> **Pause to reflect**
> Within your own subject specialism, what examples of mini-c, little-c, Ed-c, Pro-C and Big-C creativity can you come up with? How do you think your students would respond to this activity?

Overcoming student preconceptions

Some students associate science and Maths with just having one right answer and correspondingly do not see the relevance of creativity. One way to overcome this naivety in a Maths or science classroom is to make use of goal-free problems.

Typically, in these subjects, students are given a specific goal to attain, e.g. find angle ABC in a geometry problem. In a goal-free problem, students are provided with the same initial parameters but given more general instructions such as 'find as many angles as you can'. Not only will such problems encourage students to try different approaches and move beyond the conception that there is only one right answer in Maths, evidence from cognitive science research suggests that such problems result in deeper learning (Sweller & Levine, 1982). However, goal-free problems need to be introduced with care to avoid students moving down the wrong path and embedding misconceptions. Lovell (2020) suggests that 'for a goal-free approach to be successful it must include: restricted actions, rapid feedback and reliable results' (p 136).

Within the arts subjects, overcoming students' naive conceptions might involve supporting students to build their technical knowledge before allowing them to embark on a more open-ended task. And, potentially more importantly, explaining to them why this technical knowledge base is essential for creativity. Or it could involve placing some clear constraints on the creative product – we will talk more about the role of constraints in creativity in Chapter 7.

Within subjects such as History or analysis of literature or musical composition, rather than the 'anything goes' naive conception of these subjects, students need to realise that although multiple interpretations are possible, these interpretations must be supported by evidence. There is such a thing as a wrong answer in English, and speculation without a firm evidence base belongs in the realms of historical fiction, not History itself.

Pause to reflect
In your experience, could sciences and Maths benefit from taking a wider perspective and arts or social sciences a narrower one? What might this look like in your classroom?

In depth: Theory of Knowledge
Theory of Knowledge (TOK) is a compulsory component of the International Baccalaureate Diploma Programme (IBDP). TOK asks students to reflect on the nature of knowledge, and on how we know what we claim to know. Within TOK there are five areas of knowledge – Maths, Arts, History, Natural Sciences and Human Sciences. One way in which students are required to look at these different areas of knowledge is to consider how knowledge has developed over time. Looking at subjects from a historical perspective helps students to see the role that both prior knowledge and creativity play in these different disciplines. For example, when looking at past, now proven incorrect, theories in science such as the geocentric model of the solar system, students begin to recognise that previous theories may have provided a perfectly acceptable explanation of phenomena at the time but, as further evidence was uncovered, these old theories needed to be replaced. The scientists who came up with the new theories had to be creative in order to break away from previously accepted ways of thinking.

Creative learning habits

Although there are clearly differences in how creativity manifests itself across different school subjects, there do seem to be some initial requirements for creativity, as mentioned earlier. These could include dispositions associated with developing creativity – the kind of thing that would be important to support within a school culture.

While there is an academic debate about the extent to which dispositions are innate (whether they are best seen as intrinsic *traits* or as learned *habits*), we can certainly modify the opportunities available for students to show these, and how they are responded to. Consider traits and habits like playfulness, risk-taking, reflectiveness and tenaciousness – is there space for these in the classroom? It's worth considering how we can build a school culture that is supportive of such traits.

The model of creativity developed by the Centre for Real-World Learning at the University of Winchester (Spencer et al., 2012) is a useful way of breaking down the dispositions that are relevant to creativity, and linking them to concrete classroom practices. The model has five core 'creative habits', each composed of three sub-habits. Specific teaching strategies that can be used to develop these creative habits are discussed in Lucas and Spencer's book *Teaching Creative Thinking* (2017).

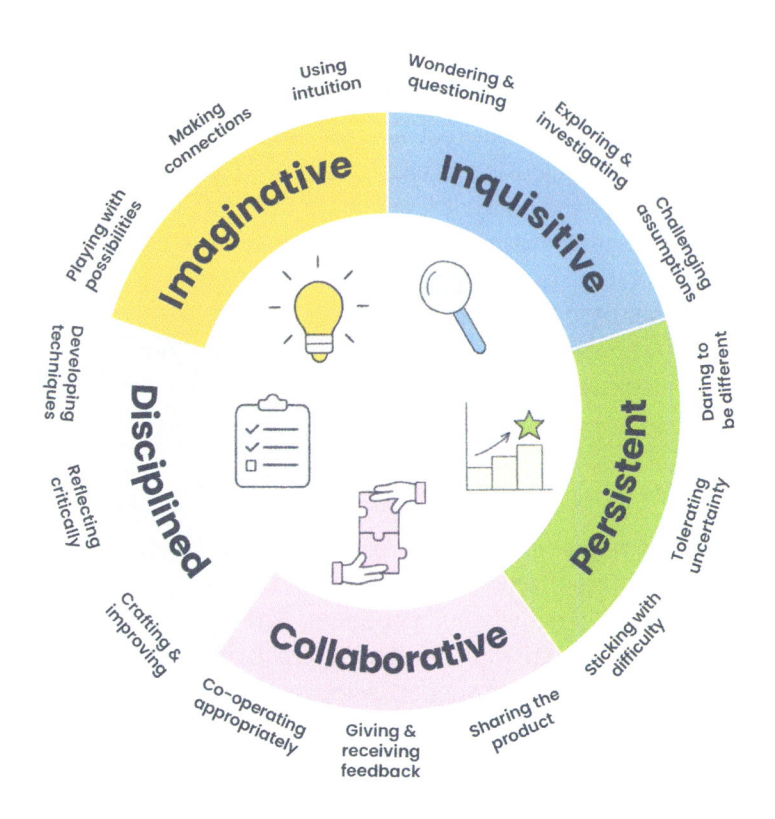

Figure 5.5 Creative learning habits, adapted from Lucas and Spencer, 2017

Breaking down the idea of a creative disposition into these habits and sub-habits can be valuable in supporting both staff and students. It can help students move away from superficial connections between creativity and the arts, and to see instead where they have the *initial requirements* that could pave the way for more domain-specific skills – when they are persevering with a difficult maths problem and trying an alternative approach, for example.

It's worth noting that even though habits such as persistence and inquisitiveness sound quite domain-general, the exact manifestation of these (and their sub-habits) may look different in different domains. Exploring and investigating in science will not look the same as exploring and investigating in an English lesson. Motivation to be creative will also play a role (see Chapter 10). It may be valuable for groups of teachers to discuss how these habits play a role in their subject(s), and across a variety of different contexts and topics.

In depth: Using the creative learning habits

The creative learning habits can be used to reflect on the extent to which, as teachers, we are teaching *for* creativity, i.e. using specific pedagogical practices that promote creative thinking in young people. These habits can be used both as a personal reflection tool and as an observation tool when observing other lessons.

An economics teacher used the habit diagram to reflect on their own practice. They recognised that they often found opportunities for students to be disciplined and persistent but probably did less to encourage students to be more imaginative and inquisitive. Every secondary school teacher will be familiar with the cry of 'do we need to know this for the exam?' or 'would that get a mark in an exam?' and it can be really difficult to challenge these comments in class. The teacher found that a few small tweaks to the questions they asked in class helped shift students' desire for the 'right' answer and encouraged them to become more inquisitive. For example:

- *Why* is that the right answer?
- What might a common *wrong* answer be?
- That answer might have been allowed by an examiner but can you write a *better, more accurate* answer?

The teacher then used the habits as a lens to observe the lesson of a modern languages colleague. It was clear to the observer that students were really confident speaking in the target language and were able to both give and receive feedback. However, they showed little inquisitiveness; it was noticeable that they were trying to construct sentences by direct translation from English to German, causing problems with formal and informal terms of address. In a feedback discussion, it was recognised that the teacher could encourage the students to wonder and question more by asking them to explain their reasoning.

Conclusion

In this chapter we have shown that far from being associated just with arts subjects, creativity plays a role across all subject domains.

There seem to be some overarching habits and dispositions associated with creativity, and these are sometimes viewed as initial requirements for creativity, relevant regardless of the domain. However, this does not mean that creativity is best taught as a generic skill in stand-alone lessons with the hope that it will magically transfer to different subjects. Given that creativity relies on a firm knowledge base, and that domains and sub-domains have specific procedures, there are many aspects of creativity that are domain-specific. Creativity can and typically should be embedded into the curriculum, rather than standing alone.

All the same, dispositions to be creative, or creative learning habits, are characteristics that are relevant across school subjects. Using a shared language for these habits can help to build a culture where creativity is celebrated across a school, despite the differences in content and essential knowledge.

Over the next few chapters, we will look at some pedagogical principles that apply in a similar way – the specifics will depend on the subject, but the general principles hold across a great many learning situations. These will help you to think about what creativity will look like in your classroom, no matter your phase or subject, and the pedagogy needed to support it.

Discussion Questions

1) Were you surprised by the survey answers on how essential creativity is across different subjects? How do you think your colleagues would respond?
2) What do you make of the STE(A)M concept? Is it helpful for either science or the arts?
3) Do people tend to associate creativity with the arts where you work, and if so, what could be done to make schools and other institutions recognise that it applies to science, Maths, and elsewhere?

4) Can you link the four stages of the Amusement Park Theoretical model to your area of expertise?

5) In what ways might you overcome students' naive conceptions that 'anything goes' in arts and humanities whereas 'there is only one right answer' in Maths and science?

6) Do any of the five creative learning habits suggested by Lucas and Spencer (2017) stand out to you as areas where you would like to place more focus?

Professional Learning Tasks

Task 1

Ask staff in your department or school to complete the TeacherTapp survey questions. How do the results compare to the TeacherTapp data? Repeating the survey after some professional development on creativity could provide a method for showing progress in this area.

Task 2

In collaboration with colleagues across a range of subjects in your school, create a table with examples of mini-c, little-c, Ed-c, Pro-C and Big-C creativity in different subjects. What similarities and differences can you see in the types of creativity across these different subjects? Does it appear as though it is easier to develop creativity in schools in some subjects more than others?

Task 3

Have a look at the information about Theory of Knowledge provided by the International Baccalaureate Organisation (IBO). If you work in an IB school, or know someone who does, then it is worth having a look at the detailed study guide which includes thought-provoking questions about the nature of knowledge in different subjects. Could you make more use of historical examples to show how knowledge has developed in your subject over time to counter some of your students' naive conceptions and show them what it means to be creative in different contexts?

Task 4

David Epstein's book *Range* (2019) digs into the research on the potential power of being a generalist (as opposed to a specialist). Epstein draws on Robin Hogarth's distinction between kind and wicked learning environments. Kind learning environments are highly predictable and the feedback you receive is quick and accurate. Wicked learning environments on the other hand are much more complex, information is missing and feedback can be delayed, absent or even misleading. Do some further research on these different types of environments. Where do specialists thrive? When are there advantages to being a generalist? Which type of environment do you think your current students will be facing during their careers? What should we be doing in school now to support them with their future endeavours?

6 Breaking from the Routine

When was the last time you changed your commute? You might have experimented with some different options when you first moved to your present role or home, but if you're like the majority of us, you soon fixed on a preferred route that has become habitual, and which you follow daily without much thought. You may, in fact, be missing out on more efficient routes as a result.

People's flexibility to adapt their routine commute was studied at the time of a London underground strike in 2014 (Larcom et al., 2017) which forced some commuters to experiment with their route. The researchers were able to anonymously track commuters using the electronic payment system, comparing their behaviour during and after the strike. The strike did not affect the whole of the underground network, providing the researchers with a natural control group. They found that whilst the majority of commuters returned to their original routes once the strike was over, around 5 per cent did not – as a result of the strike, they had found more efficient ways to travel, particularly in areas where the stylised nature of the tube map meant it was less representative of the actual geographical area or where lines travelled at different speeds. The researchers concluded that 'people might get stuck with suboptimal decisions because of underexperimentation' – although today, the use of online journey planners may counteract this problem.

We can get stuck in routine ways of thinking at other times, too. Being creative by definition is not about doing something repetitive or routine, so it is interesting to consider when and why people break away from well-practised behaviours (one example, playfulness, was discussed in Chapter 2). The example above reminds us of the strong tendency to stay consistent and avoid experimentation – even though many of the commuters could be amazingly creative in other aspects of their lives. This question of how and when creativity transfers from one domain to another (and when it doesn't) will be explored in this chapter.

The Myth

We have already addressed the limitations of the idea that creativity is a stand-alone skill, unconnected with knowledge. While creativity does involve cognitive processes such as making connections and thinking flexibly, we have seen that a foundation of knowledge is indispensable to this, and therefore to having meaningful creative ideas (see Chapters 3 and 4).

A myth that follows directly from the idea of creativity as a stand-alone skill, and is often bundled together, is the notion that it is a *transferable* skill. Usually, this is taken to mean that engaging in any creative activity (sometimes defined narrowly as arts activities) develops in learners the ability to apply similar creative skills in other classes/subjects, in the workplace, or in their everyday life. We have seen a version of this in the idea, discussed in the previous chapter, that being taught general creativity skills, or learning arts subjects, would make you better at STEM (see Chapter 5).

Policy makers might therefore suggest that all we need to do is get students to do lots of creative learning at school (by which they usually mean lots of art, music, and so forth), in order for those students to enter the workplace ready to excel at higher-order skills across the board. However, to quote Perkins and Salomon (1988, p. 23), this view of how thinking skills will automatically transfer from one context to another is 'inordinately optimistic'.

Would spending time painting watercolours or practising the piano actually make someone more creative in their lab work, when devising a new drug, or in exploring a set of astronomy data? Given that it draws on two myths – one about creativity as unconnected to knowledge, and one about it applying only to some domains – it's easy to see why this idea could be challenged. From what we have seen so far in this book, creative thinking in science depends a lot more on your knowledge of science facts than it does on practising artistic pursuits.

In fact, these are not the only problems faced by assumptions about creativity as a transferable skill. It is in fact quite hard to transfer *any* skills and knowledge from one context to another. It is hard even in familiar contexts, such as from one school subject to another, and harder still when the new context appears superficially quite different (Barnett & Ceci, 2002; Haskell, 2001). Creativity is no exception. This doesn't mean that it's impossible, or that nothing useful can *ever* be transferred from prior learning. However, it does mean that some attention needs to be paid to identifying what the different activities have in common, and to supporting students in the process of applying their previous learning (Perkins & Salomon, 1992).

Exploring the Research

We have all heard of transferable skills, but what exactly is transfer, and how does it work? This concept has been quite widely studied over the decades, even if rather neglected in education! Transfer involves *using what has been learned in a new context*. Haskell (2001, p. xiii) describes transfer as 'the very foundation of learning, thinking, and problem solving'.

Transfer is important. Every learning situation, and every workplace, requires that people apply what they have learned previously, from maths to literacy to science. Indeed, without a student profiting in some way from what has been learned in a class, and being able to use it in some way in the future (or otherwise having an impact on their behaviour), we might very well ask what the point of going to school was in the first place!

Examples of transfer might include:

- Learning to write an essay introduction in History, and then applying similar principles in a Psychology essay
- Learning lab safety rules at school and using them in the workplace
- Using arithmetic when working out which mobile phone will cost more over two years

Given that it involves using prior learning, transfer is certainly relevant to creativity, too. A key question here is whether engaging in and practising creative tasks in school makes people more creative at future creative tasks. And we have already seen some factors that could pose a barrier to this. For example, do people have enough knowledge to succeed at the future tasks?

In fact, it's not just creativity – there is broad agreement that transfer is hard to achieve, or at least, it should not be taken for granted (Haskell, 2001; Perkins & Salomon, 1992). This means that students often *fail* to apply knowledge and skills learned in one context to other situations, even when the relevance of the learning seems quite obvious to us as teachers.

Three views of transfer

Perkins and Salomon (1988) discuss three main views of transfer:

1) That transfer is easy and automatic. This is associated with Piaget's views, and with an emphasis on repetitive practice of skills and knowledge with no consideration of how to support later application of these. The researchers flippantly refer to this as the 'Bo Peep' theory – essentially, that if we leave it alone, everything will be fine.

2) That transfer is essentially impossible. This is associated with the views of social anthropologists Lave and Wenger (1991), who argue that learning is bound up to a unique social situation from which it cannot be extracted. E. D. Hirsch (2008) was also pessimistic about the possibility of transfer of strategies and skills.

3) That transfer is difficult, but possible in the right circumstances. This is the view taken by Perkins and Salomon, and also aligns with research by Bransford et al. (2000) and some other cognitive psychologists.

In depth: Sport skill

Matthew Syed, a world-class table tennis player turned journalist and writer, opens his book *Bounce* (Syed, 2011) with a story of playing tennis against Michael Stich, a retired tennis player who won Wimbledon in 1991. Since table tennis is played on a smaller scale than tennis and requires extremely quick reflexes, Syed expected to be able to return Stich's serve with ease, but was quickly disabused of this notion.

This example shows that expertise built up in one sport won't necessarily transfer well to another. Sport stars' expertise will be limited to a relatively narrow skill set. A top athlete may be fit and fast, but will probably fail to beat even a mid-level professional who specialises in another sport.

So, are there circumstances that can facilitate transfer? In Chapter 3, we looked at the basic building blocks required to develop creative thinking, including the vital importance of knowledge. But as we've also seen (e.g. Chapter 4), there are strategies that students can use so that they can best profit from this learning. We don't want their knowledge to sit inertly, or only be useful in very similar situations to the original task. Instead, we can find ways to help them use their knowledge flexibly, and to make creative connections between ideas.

The above summary is closely in line with how cognitive science views expertise. Experts are not just people who have accumulated factual knowledge. They have also learned how to *use* this knowledge flexibly and creatively. Repetitive practice of facts or simple skills can actually undermine a learner's ability to use this flexibly in future (e.g. Feltovich et al., 1997; Gube & Lajoie, 2020).

The example in the next section features a task that is widely used in cognitive science research, and which shows that even having recently practised a relevant solution doesn't always lead to transfer.

Why transfer is important (and difficult)

Researchers Mary Gick and Keith Holyoak (1983) showed people a story of a general trying to march his armies towards a fort that was within a medieval town. The town had narrow streets, and the army was too large to march down any of the streets *en masse*. However, marching down a narrower line of soldiers would be too weak an attack, leading to defeat!

The solution was to split the army and march it down several streets simultaneously, so that they arrived at the same end-point all at once. The researchers called the underlying idea that led to solving the problem a 'convergence schema' (see Chapter 4 for more about schemas).

The researchers then showed a superficially different problem, but one that also drew on the convergence schema. In this case, the problem concerned operating on a tumour using a laser. A single strong laser was dangerous, and would injure the patient, but a weaker laser would fail to destroy the tumour. The solution was to fire several weak lasers from different angles, so that they all met at the same central point – at the tumour, destroying it.

Can you see the similarity between the two problems? The underlying deep structure is the same across both problems, and yet the majority of research participants failed to see the connection between them. In other words, transfer did not occur.

Transfer is necessary for creativity in general. Creative thinking involves novelty, and therefore is (by definition) never about repeating a set of moves or a pattern of thinking exactly. In addition, transfer is necessary for the knowledge developed in one setting to impact on future problems – ones which might be similar but yet look superficially different.

What these points suggest together is that while prior knowledge is necessary, it's not always sufficient. Just as we saw in the chapter on connections (Chapter 4), a creative thinker needs to move beyond repetition of their knowledge in familiar contexts and come to apply it in novel, unpredictable ways.

Overall, then, transfer can be seen as a key cognitive process underpinning creative thinking. A learner needs to be able to use what they have learned in new ways, not to just repeat it in the same context. As with other examples of transfer in learning, they may fail to realise that their prior knowledge is relevant.

Pause to reflect
Students often fail to notice the relevance of their prior knowledge in the classroom. What strategies have you used – or observed in other teachers – to help draw their attention to this? How might these teaching techniques help to scaffold transfer?

Routine and adaptive expertise

As mentioned earlier in this chapter, the idea of using knowledge flexibly for new problems sits well with how cognitive science views expertise. Experts – or at least, *some* experts – are very good at using their knowledge flexibly. Their expertise is not just about how much they know, but about how well they can use their knowledge.

To simplify this, it is useful to think about two key types of expertise, each associated with quite different outcomes in terms of transfer and creativity: routine and adaptive expertise in a particular topic or domain (Bransford et al., 2000; Gube & Lajoie, 2020; Hatano & Inagaki, 1986).

- Some expertise can be described as *routine*. Routine expertise occurs where experts have honed their skills to become increasingly efficient at a specific set of tasks. They get very good at quickly doing a set of tasks or accessing knowledge in familiar contexts. This doesn't mean that the work is always the same, but problems are sufficiently similar to be easily recognised. Many sub-skills become automatic, and therefore operate much more quickly and with less focused attention needed. Examples might include how a chef chops vegetables, or how a teacher manages entry and exit in their classroom.

- Other expertise can be described as *adaptive*. Adaptive expertise is characterised by interconnected, flexible knowledge, and allows these experts to respond more effectively to novel problems. Here, the nature of the practice undertaken pushes the expert to constantly adapt to varied circumstances, using their skills in unfamiliar ways. An example is someone who must give speeches in many contexts, or how a teacher delivers a lesson.

When building routine expertise, a certain level of automaticity is acquired. This frees up cognitive resources, making the expert more efficient in their thinking and actions. This expertise is, of course, based on long-term memory, and its well-learned nature makes the use of the limited space in working memory accordingly more efficient.

However, the faster processing associated with routine expertise comes at a cost. It is often acquired at the expense of creativity and adaptability. Routine expertise also doesn't transfer very well to other tasks. It is highly domain-specific.

Hopefully you can see the connections to creativity. Routine expertise is good for predictable skills, but is not associated with (much) novelty. In contrast, adaptive expertise may pave the way towards creative thinking, at least within fairly simple circumstances. It means taking well-learned facts and skills and applying them to new tasks, and in ways that differ from the ways we previously practised.

Adaptive expertise is best developed by engaging in practice that is varied and unpredictable, pushing learners out of their comfort zone and having them try to use that stored knowledge in new ways. Variation helps because the situation of use is unpredictable (Bjork, 1994). By making the practice situation and the later use situation more similar (in that both of them are varied and non-routine), it becomes easier for students to transfer their knowledge and skills at a later point in time.

> **Pause to reflect**
> Some tasks which require routine expertise are already undertaken by computers, and this is only likely to increase in future. What are the implications for our students, and for supporting young people to develop adaptive expertise?

Routine expertise and the curriculum

What we have seen about expertise so far in this chapter has a direct link to the curriculum. Hatano and Inagaki (1986) are clear that expertise is not just for adults – a child can become expert at a particular skill, and that expertise can be either routine or adaptive. However, just as with an adult, that depends on what kind of practice they undertake.

Therefore, let's think about how skills are typically mastered in the school curriculum. Often, lots of practice of similar tasks is done. This allows certain basic skills to become automatic, speeding up performance. Think of simple arithmetic, for example, or reading or spelling.

However, there is a downside to the automatic aspects of thinking that this entails – it can be a barrier to using knowledge flexibly and creatively. It is possible, as Holyoak (1991, p. 312) put it, to be 'able to solve familiar types of problems quickly and accurately [and yet] have only modest capabilities in dealing with novel types of problems'.

For example, students completing a worksheet in maths all of which requires a similar application of Pythagoras' theorem can't be said to be creating anything new, and would struggle to transfer what they have learned to anything other than easily recognisable problems.

Another example is the use of 'formula triangles' to help students with calculation problems. The student who has learned to successfully use a formula triangle to calculate speed, distance and time in basic physics problems, and has done many practice problems, can be said to have acquired routine expertise. They may be quick and fairly accurate at doing these problems, but their ability to transfer this to other settings is questionable, for example problems where a simple triangle cannot be used to represent a mathematical formula.

Indeed, many teachers will have noticed that difficulties can arise when a problem is reframed, and students don't recognise what strategy they should use. For example, perhaps they have to analyse a visual example of a problem, or use the principles of speed, distance and time when discussing a sports move. These examples require students to use their knowledge flexibly. Not only does practising a lot of similar problems fail to improve students' performance at such tasks, it can actually make them worse at it.

There's no doubt that it's important to master the basics. However, ways of doing this that focus on repetition of very familiar problems tend to develop routine rather than adaptive expertise.

While routine expertise is of course useful in many circumstances (it is still expertise, and therefore better than being a novice!), the predictable circumstances that lead to routine expertise don't facilitate transfer, or support the learner to use their knowledge in creative ways.

Pause to reflect

Do you agree that practice tasks in education are often quite repetitive? Have you ever come across a situation where lots of practice failed to transfer to an unfamiliar problem?

Adaptive expertise and the curriculum

The points above, as well as the experiment by Gick and Holyoak, serve to highlight an important principle – transfer is hard when the new problem is different from what has been practised (Barnett & Ceci, 2002). It's easy enough to transfer to a problem that looks superficially similar, and repetitive practice supports this. But it doesn't support the flexibility associated with adaptive expertise. To put it another way, repetitive practice leads to learners becoming better at doing very predictable things.

There is an alternative – practice that is varied, and forces learners to be flexible. Researchers in memory have recognised that *varied* practice is better for long-term retention and transfer (Bjork & Bjork, 2023). That is, the more varied the practice, the better learners will be at remembering and using information when they later need it.

Variation can take many forms. As educators, we can vary the social context of a task, how recently it was practised, how formal or informal the task is, and so on. Variation could also include using techniques that add complexity and deeper processing.

Varied practice helps to develop adaptive expertise. It helps to develop experts who are better at using what they know in new contexts and unpredictable circumstances – they can transfer what they knew to new problems, and use it in novel situations. In other words, it is more strongly associated with creative thinking.

In summary:

- *Repetitive practice* helps to develop *routine expertise* and entails *low* levels of creative thinking.
- *Varied practice* helps to develop *adaptive expertise* and entails *higher* levels of creative thinking.

The experts differ in other ways, too. Often, adaptive expertise is associated with a deeper understanding of problems. Routine expertise can be quite superficial. This links back to how long-term memory is structured (see Chapter 4). People with adaptive expertise have knowledge which is strongly interconnected in schemas. They don't just know isolated facts. This makes their knowledge more flexible when there is a superficial change to a problem.

However, adaptive expertise only goes so far – it doesn't make learners good at every comparable task. You might remember that in Chapter 5, we mentioned the researchers Chase and Simon (1973) and their study of expert chess players. Their participants had domain-specific knowledge and skills. Not only did this not make them good at every type of game or puzzle, they weren't even better at remembering unfamiliar/impossible chess-boards. This helps to show that transfer is challenging in areas where people have not built up expertise – even if the task looks superficially similar or uses the same memory systems.

In depth: Deeper understanding

An early experiment carried out by Scholckow and Judd (cited by Bransford et al., 2000) showed the importance of a learner's understanding of a problem.

The researchers looked at how accurately learners could throw darts at an underwater target. The task was difficult because refraction of light caused the target to appear in a different place than it actually was. Two groups were studied; one was given an explanation of the scientific principles behind refraction, and one was not. With practice, both groups successfully threw darts at the target. But what was especially interesting was what happened when the target moved. The group that had just practised the task became much worse, but those who had received the explanation – who understood the task – adapted more quickly.

This suggests that understanding is important for adaptive expertise. Routine practice without understanding will make it hard for students to transfer their learning when they encounter problems that are superficially different.

A further example of how limited conceptual understanding can affect students' transfer is explained by Mccrea (2023) on his *Evidence Snacks* blog. Mccrea explains that when first introducing a new topic or concept, showing students multiple different examples, as well as *non-examples*, can help students to draw out the relevant features of that particular concept. For example, students who are taught the definition of a triangle as a three-sided shape and are then shown only examples 1–3 in the figure below may not realise that shape 4 is also a triangle (students may well refer to this as an 'upside down' triangle!). Equally, without it being made clear that the three sides must connect together, they may incorrectly categorise shape 5 as a triangle.

Figure 6.1 Examples and non-examples of triangles

Pause to reflect

Think about the use of examples in your subject. Could you use more non-examples? Are there cases where adding in non-examples might lead to misconceptions rather than develop deeper understanding?

Applications to Practice

We will now think about how you can apply the ideas discussed in this chapter so far. How can we try to develop adaptive expertise among our students, for example, and provide experiences that promote transfer and creative thinking?

Boosting variation

As mentioned earlier, one of the key things that leads to routine expertise is engaging in practice that is very repetitive. In contrast, we can find ways to increase the level of variation that our students experience. Placing an emphasis on varied practice, particularly after essential knowledge and skills are in place (though possibly even before that time), will help them to transfer what they have learned to new situations, including novel, creative problems.

Many study sessions involve repeating the same kinds of tasks in the same context – for example, lists of similar questions or exercises. And even when the tasks are different, there's a fair chance that they are all done in the same classroom, at a similar time of day, and surrounded by the same classmates.

To support the development of adaptive expertise we need to reduce this kind of predictability, or move away from it entirely, increasing variation to support our students' understanding and the flexibility with which they can transfer knowledge. Some things that can be varied in lessons include:

- Having students work with different partners/groups, and perhaps even students from other years
- Varying the context in terms of the level of formality/seriousness of the task
- Varying the location – learning outside, for example

- Varying the level of application, by moving from basic facts to a more applied task
- Varying the presentation and appearance of the task itself, in terms of its format; for example, you could try setting a familiar written task orally.

As discussed elsewhere in this book (e.g. see Chapter 4), creativity is not just about how much a student knows, but also how they can use it. Knowledge is essential, but so is having flexible, interconnected knowledge that helps students to tackle novel tasks and come up with creative responses. To support this, we need to move away from predictable practice.

> ### In depth: Comparing questions in Maths
>
> The Gick and Holyoak research discussed earlier in this chapter shows that novices often focus on the surface features of a problem and fail to see the underlying deep structure. This can lead them to choose incorrect problem-solving strategies. One way to overcome this is to directly compare problems with similar surface features but different deeper structure side by side – Craig Barton calls these SSDD problems (Barton, 2024). Barton uses the following example:
>
> 1. A can of pop has a height of 120mm and a base diameter of 86mm. How much pop does the can hold?
> 2. A can of pop has a height of 120mm and a base diameter of 86mm. How much aluminium was used to make the can?
>
> Both of these questions have the same surface features – they are about the same can of pop and ask 'how much' – but the underlying mathematical principles are very different. In question 1 a volume calculation is required, whereas in question 2, the calculation is of the surface area. Comparing these questions side by side helps students to identify the differences in the question and hence choose the appropriate solution strategy.
>
> This teaching strategy is also a form of interleaving, discussed further below.

Concreteness fading

As the example of the darts throwing shows (see 'In depth', above), deep understanding helps students with transfer. Bruner (1966) suggested that this understanding is based on an abstract or *symbolic* representation – one that links to many situations, not just one task or problem. A concrete example, in contrast, tends to be more specific. For example, the movement of one ball rolling down a hill is a concrete example, but mass and momentum are abstract concepts, with principles that can be transferred to millions of situations.

To transfer what they have learned to new, unpredictable contexts – including creative tasks – students need to develop that abstract representation. However, we also know that specific concrete examples are really useful for learners, helping them to grasp complex new ideas. So, given that teachers often depend on these concrete examples to clarify teaching points, how do we develop abstract understandings, and support transfer?

According to Fyfe and Nathan (2019), this can be done by working gradually towards a more abstract understanding, 'fading' out the surface features of the concrete example and focusing more and more on the deeper, schema-based idea that underlies it. By doing so, this abstract representation becomes easier to understand, and can later be transferred. They explain that practice should move through three main steps:

- A more concrete form, such as the example of a ball rolling down a hill.
- A symbolised, usually pictorial form, where the key ideas of the concrete problem are represented. For example, this could be a diagram showing the ball and a simplified slope, and arrows to indicate forces.
- A decontextualised and abstract form that captures the underlying idea, for example the physics principles of a ball rolling down a hill could be expressed in mathematics and symbols, or using language (the language of Newton's laws of motion, for example).

This concreteness fading has been shown to be useful with young children's maths, and is superior to doing things in the opposite order – leading with the abstract notation, and then providing concrete examples later (Fyfe et al., 2015).

Many new ideas in your own classroom could similarly be explored through a progression of concrete, pictorial and then abstract tasks. Concreteness fading helps to scaffold the move towards a more decontextualised understanding that also helps learners to make connections between what they have learned and new situations (Fyfe & Nathan, 2019). In a way, it leads them by the hand from superficial aspects of learning to the really important ideas.

By helping with transfer, concreteness fading can boost creativity. It makes it easier for your students to make connections across ideas and across topics.

> **Pause to reflect**
> In your own experience and observations, do teachers tend to start with concrete examples and move towards abstract ideas? Or vice versa – do they tend to start with the principles and give examples later?

Interleaving for variation and understanding

Given that both varied practice and deep understanding help to develop adaptive expertise, it would be great if there was a technique that boosted both, wouldn't it? Well, one such technique is known as *interleaving*. Interleaved practice is 'varied' in the sense that students see items or problems that are mixed up with contrasting ones, and by seeing items that fit a concept as well as others which are subtly different (examples and non-examples), learners deepen their understanding of what fits in a category and what does not.

For example, Eglington and Kang presented learners with examples of chemical molecules of different types (Eglington & Kang, 2017). Compared to a group who were shown multiple examples of the same type of molecule, the researchers found that participants who had seen different types of molecule mixed together were better able to correctly identify previously unseen examples. That is, transfer was better.

Blocking

Interleaving

Figure 6.2 Blocking vs. interleaving

Interleaving appears to enhance learning as it allows learners to discern similarities and differences between examples. It has been found to help them avoid mixing up problems that look superficially similar in subjects like Maths (Rohrer et al., 2015). It helps learners distinguish between concepts on a schema level, and boosts transfer to new examples, not just memory for previously studied ones (Firth et al., 2021). However, it's important that specific examples are contrasted close together (e.g. one straight after another). With a longer delay between contrasting examples, it's less likely that students will notice the key difference(s) between them (Birnbaum et al., 2013).

To apply interleaving, try following this series of steps:

1) Identify concepts that students find hard to understand, or where they often make errors.

2) Think about what examples or tasks would be a useful stimulus for practice. Typically, these examples will be very brief, e.g. words, images, very short texts, short tasks, or questions.

3) Analyse current practice materials and think about whether blocked practice is being used. If so, you could consider changing this.

4) Where relevant, modify the order of presentation, so that the examples are interleaved.

5) Ensure that the emphasis is on comparing and contrasting subtle differences, and that the contrast happens immediately or soon after (not in separate lessons).

6) As the students get better at the task, shift the contrast to be more subtle and challenging to recognise. The type of task or the type of example could be varied. This will increase the difficulty, so only do it when the students appear secure in what they have learned so far.

Overall, interleaving is a desirable difficulty. It boosts retention and transfer by helping students to notice meaningful differences between items or problems.

In depth: Geographical landforms

In Geography, students need to be able to recognise landforms from photos, simplified diagrams and from contour patterns on maps. This provides a good example of how a concrete example, such as a photo of a specific valley, differs from an underlying principle, such as glaciation or U-shaped valleys. It is also an area of the curriculum where some students tend to focus too much on superficial features of a problem.

When teaching glaciation and the features of glaciated landscapes, teachers could apply concreteness fading by showing multiple examples of valleys before getting students to try to identify some common patterns across different geographical locations. This would lead well into a discussion of why these structures form.

A Geography teacher could also interleave examples. In doing so, it would be best to ensure that the examples were superficially similar; looking at examples side by side (or in close succession) would draw students' attention to subtle differences, such as the spread of sporadic rocks, or the vegetation cover or human use of the land. However, it would be a mistake to interleave examples from a completely different Geography topic, such as urban land use – students wouldn't benefit from this, as there would be no subtle differences between features for them to discern. The mixing up of unrelated topics could even cause confusion.

Bridging

You might recall that in the classic experiment by Gick and Holyoak (the one with the general and his army), researchers found that many participants didn't transfer the strategy they'd learned unless this was directly pointed out to them.

Similarly, we can explicitly point out links between one subject or topic and another, helping to guide the connections that students make. Researchers call this 'bridging' (Perkins & Salomon, 1992). It involves directly drawing a learner's attention to what they learned before, and asking them to reflect on it, and can be seen as a form of scaffolding.

Perkins and Salomon (1992) give the example of a teacher asking students to come up with an exam strategy, drawing on their previous performance.

Bridging is rather different from concreteness fading (see above) as it is more deliberate and less gradual. It asks students to think about superficially different things, and what they have in common. There are a lot of similarities here to the Remote Associates Test (RAT) (see Chapter 4), where students were asked to think about one factor that three words had in common, as both involve making connections.

Where your students struggle with this strategy at first, the difficulty may just be too high – they can't build that long a mental bridge between the two ideas. This can be managed with hints, with the chance to retrieve relevant information in advance, or via an intermediate step.

Conclusion

To return to the example at the start of this chapter, it's all too easy to fall into the trap of mindlessly repeating what's familiar. A student can be rather like a commuter travelling to work and never stopping to think that there might be a better way; many learners just repeat well-practised habits and routines. What's worse, they may be completely thrown if they encounter an unfamiliar-looking problem.

There are ways around this, but a challenge is that, in general, it's very difficult to transfer knowledge from one situation to another. This is particularly true across domains. For example, doing a lot of artistic activities would be no guarantee of making people creative at science (see also Chapter 5). This helps to show that while practice can lead to expertise, it doesn't always lead to transferability of what is learned, especially when the practice activities are very predictable.

A useful way to think about this comes from Hatano and Inagaki's concept of routine and adaptive expertise. As they see it, highly repetitive practice can lead to a form of expertise where students (even children) can get really good at that particular task, but lack flexibility. This is routine expertise. Adaptive expertise, on the other hand, is more flexible, and supports the learner to tackle new problems. As such, it is essential for creativity.

Clearly, expertise can't be divided into two clear-cut groups, and most individuals will engage in practice that is at times varied, and at times repetitive. As with all cognitive processes, the reality in the real world is messy. All the same, this distinction helps to focus our attention on the kind of classroom processes that might promote adaptive expertise in the classroom, and thereby support our learners to think more creatively.

Practising in varied ways can help, but as we have seen, it is not the whole story. The practice needs to boost deep understanding, developing the underlying schemas and categories that the student is supposed to be learning, especially when these become abstract enough to transfer to multiple new situations. Strategies such as interleaving, concreteness fading and bridging can really help here. When students start to make subtle distinctions between categories and recognise the deep structure of a problem, they are better equipped to make creative links.

Some of what has been discussed in this chapter will push learners out of their comfort zone, at least at times. Over the next two chapters, we will explore the surprising role of constraints in supporting creative thinking, as well as the idea of structured uncertainty – a specific way of making practice more demanding and more effective in order to boost creative thinking.

Discussion Questions

1) Were you surprised to find out that many researchers consider transfer of learning to be difficult or impossible? How well does that fit with what education policies say about transferable skills?
2) Hatano and Inagaki said that routine expertise develops when practice is very repetitive. Is this likely to be a problem in classrooms, in your experience? What about in students' homework and independent learning?
3) Are you concerned that tasks which involve routine expertise may be done by AI or computers in future? What would that mean for your students? Are there any implications for the curriculum, or for teaching creativity?
4) What would adaptive expertise look like for students in your subject/specialist area?

5) Interleaving and variation are considered desirable difficulties, in that they make practice harder but also more effective (Bjork & Bjork, 2023). What other desirable difficulties have you heard of? Have you tried them out?

Professional Learning Tasks

Task 1

Pick a topic or area of the curriculum, and follow the steps outlined for interleaving, above (see 'Applications to Practice'). Make sure that you are focusing on an area where students currently experience some confusion or where you feel their understanding needs to be deeper.

Task 2

It is relatively straightforward to increase variation in a list of tasks or problems – you can simply shuffle the order (this is also a form of interleaving). Take some time to think of other ways to vary lessons (especially if you don't use sets of written problems in your teaching). How can you do this in a way that is manageable, and pushes students out of their comfort zone without upsetting them? Make some notes, and begin to try out some options in class.

Task 3

Think about developing adaptive expertise among your students. Do you have students/former students who displayed this? Make a list of tasks and strategies you might use to encourage and scaffold this in future. Discuss them with a colleague.

Task 4

What examples can you think of in your subject or phase where students focus on superficial features of a problem or task and fail to see the underlying structure? Pick an example, and explain it in a short verbal description, and/or a diagram. Could you then share it with the students themselves? Perhaps you could also share your thoughts about this problem in a professional blog post or a talk at a conference. You can explore some of the references in this chapter to help.

7 The Goldilocks Rule of Constraints

Tim Harford opens his book *Messy* (Harford, 2016) with the story of Keith Jarrett's 1975 performance at the Cologne Opera House. Jarrett was an American pianist and was about to perform a sell-out improvised jazz concert. He had sent ahead very precise specifications for the piano he required but the opera house had instead provided a much smaller, out-of-tune instrument with some notes that didn't work and pedals that stuck. Despite his initial refusal to play, Jarrett was eventually persuaded to go ahead with the concert and, much to his surprise, the result was the performance of a lifetime. The constraints placed on Jarrett by the 'unplayable' piano forced him to be more creative and the result was a multi-million-selling album.

Creativity is often associated with complete freedom of choice and intuitively it would seem that in order to be creative you should be free to wander at will with no constraints. However, as the above example shows, putting constraints on creative work can increase creativity.

The relationship between constraints and creativity is not straightforward, though, and it is also possible to impose too many constraints, thereby making creativity less likely. This chapter seeks to help teachers to decide what constraints we should place on students, and when, to best support the creative process.

The Myth

In the research into creativity myths by Benedek et al. (2021) that we discussed previously (see Chapter 2), the idea that creativity involves total freedom was the second most widely endorsed myth about creativity.

It's easy to see why. Creativity means doing something new, so the idea of being totally open and free makes intuitive sense. It is also appealing to the educator to tell students to 'be as creative as you like', or 'have some wild ideas' (see Chapter 1).

However, researchers consider the benefits of unlimited freedom to be a myth. Despite the appeal, freedom from constraints is actually quite problematic for the creative process. Consider how hard it can be to complete a piece of writing when faced with a blank page!

Teachers may be wary of hampering the creative process by putting any limits in place, but in practice, this is probably making creative tasks much harder and less productive than they need to be.

Exploring the Research

Problem space

Solving a creative problem involves what researchers call the 'problem space'. This space can be broader or narrower. A really wide problem space means a vast number of options – and that can make thinking slower and more difficult. Having no constraints at all means that the problem space is huge, and students may feel overwhelmed, unable to start a task.

Counterintuitively, narrowing the problem space by adding in some constraints can lead to better ideas. Rather than stifling creative thinking, a constraint can give a student a place to start, and help them to evaluate the solutions they come up with. For the teacher, this means that rather than avoiding giving guidance or telling students to be as expansive as possible, you might put in place certain limits, conditions or rules. These impose limits to thinking, helping students to come up with more or better ideas (Tromp & Baer, 2022).

Tromp and Baer give an example of this from creative writing:

> When students are asked to write a short story about anything they want, many find it difficult to get started, let alone get creative. However, when they are asked to write a story focused on a shy, red-haired boy named Colin who is missing a toe, the constraint seems to facilitate the creative process.
>
> (Tromp & Baer, 2022, p. 1)

Figure 7.1 A writing prompt featuring the boy named Colin

> **Pause to reflect**
> To experience a very broad problem space for yourself, take a blank piece of paper and try to come up with an imaginative drawing. Hard to know where to start, right? Now try the activity in Figure 7.2. You may find it much easier to come up with imaginative and creative drawings when given the constraint of having to start from the squares.

Student perceptions

As the myth above suggests, people may have an intuitive feeling that constraints hamper their creativity, and correspondingly, self-report data suggests that fewer constraints make people *feel* more creative (Sellier & Dahl, 2011). However, a broad field of research has found people's perceptions of their own thinking often fall out of line with reality (Dunning, 2011). In this context, students' subjective judgements may need to be evaluated critically – and supported.

120 *Creativity for Teachers*

How many objects can you draw?

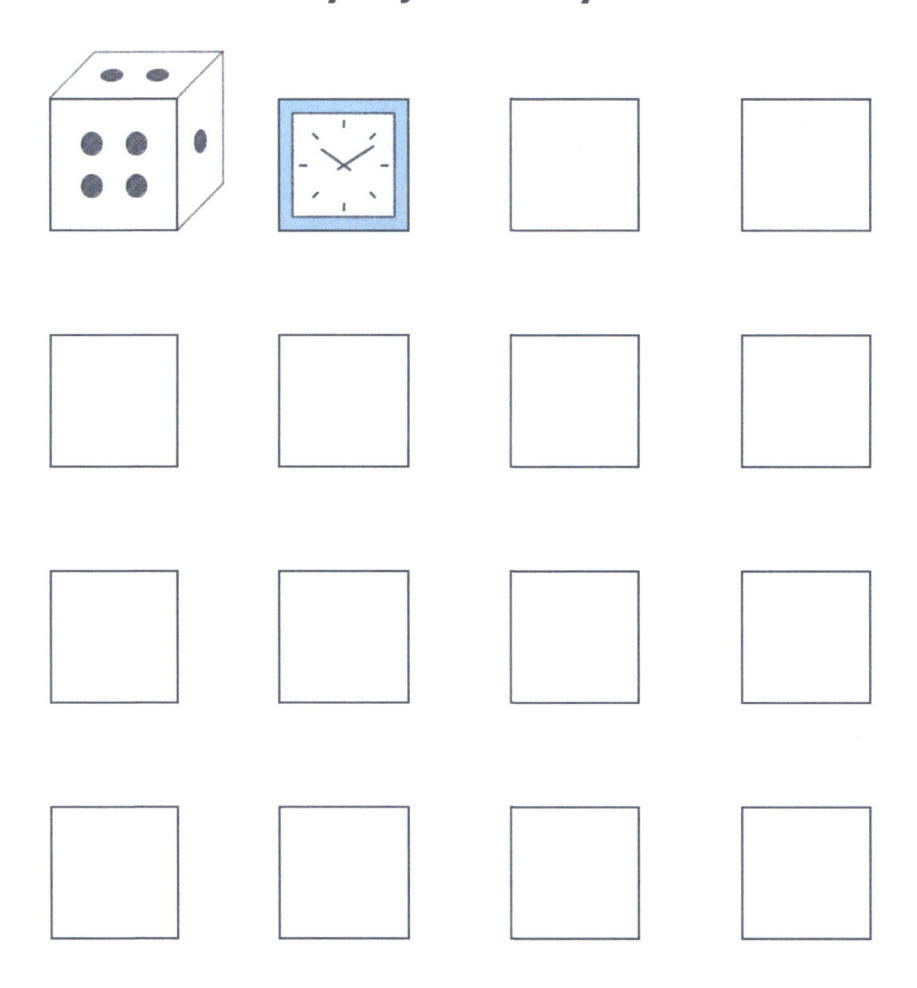

Figure 7.2 Creative drawings task

Parallels can be drawn here with research on desirable difficulties such as retrieval practice and interleaving (see Chapter 6); in both cases, learners' perceptions of what is more effective for learning are out of line with the actual effectiveness of strategies (e.g. Bjork & Bjork, 2023; Janssen et al., 2023). Although the two relate to different processes, in both cases, students are not good at judging what works best, tending to pick an option that intuitively feels easier.

McDaniel et al. (2021) have shown that teaching students about effective learning strategies such as retrieval practice, alongside providing specific opportunities for students to both commit to using these strategies and reflect on their effectiveness, increases the likelihood of them choosing these more effective strategies in the future. Similar discussion over the benefits of constraints in creativity, alongside feedback on how these constraints have led to more creative outputs, could provide a potential way to overcome the mismatch between students' perceptions and reality.

Overall, teachers need to be aware that adding constraints may make tasks feel more challenging, and work to inform students that such challenges can lead to better outcomes.

Mixed benefits of constraints

So far, we have seen that, contrary to intuition, complete freedom can be counterproductive when doing creative tasks. However, the relationship between constraints and creativity is not straightforward. Sometimes, constraints get in the way of producing creative outputs.

When the constraints are too extreme – for example, when there are too many rules or insufficient resources (including time) are given to the problem – then students may fail to make any headway with a task or come up with a very pedestrian response.

> **Pause to reflect**
> Can you think of a creative task you have tackled where the instructions or requirements were just too complicated?

This means that educators need to consider the type and balance of constraints that they deploy. Rather than asking whether constraints are good or bad for creativity, we should instead start to consider which constraints are most productive, how many to use, and under what circumstances. In this respect, constraints are similar to other forms of support and challenge that skilled teachers deploy in the classroom.

According to Tromp and Baer (2022), constraints can have two complementary functions:

- An exclusionary function that specifies something to be avoided
- A focusing function that specifies something to be used

An example of an exclusionary constraint could be an art teacher who doesn't allow colour to be used for a particular project, whereas a focusing constraint would be to say that the outcome must be a pencil drawing. Tromp and Baer suggest that exclusionary constraints without a complementary focusing constraint may not narrow down the problem space sufficiently to improve creativity.

Knowledge as a constraint

As discussed throughout this book, knowledge is an essential prerequisite for creative thinking. One way to conceptualise the value of knowledge is to consider how it imposes constraints on the thinker. Someone with a lot of knowledge is constrained in the sense that they can quickly see which ideas won't work, and are forced to dismiss these, and to keep searching for better options.

We saw an example of this in Chapter 2 – in the 'In depth: Cross-curricular days' case study, learners came up with unrealistic ideas for tackling environmental problems. They didn't have enough knowledge and expertise to constrain their thinking, resulting in worse outcomes on the task.

Tromp and Baer (2022) use the example of setting the problem of cooling a room. One solution might be to use a refrigerator; refrigerators produce cool air, so plugging in a refrigerator and keeping the door open should cool the room. However, if one knows how a refrigerator works then this possible 'solution' will be immediately rejected as the knowledgeable problem-solver realises this will just result in the room heating up. This is an example of knowledge providing an exclusionary constraint. However, knowing what doesn't work is insufficient to solve this problem; knowledge of evaporative cooling provides a focusing constraint to help our problem-solver narrow the problem space further.

However, just as other constraints can be overwhelming, there is the potential for knowledge to provide too many constraints. Knowledge can entrench us in certain ways of thinking, unable to see alternative possibilities. This is illustrated nicely by the candle test created by psychologist Karl Duncker (1935) and discussed in Daniel Pink's book *Drive* (2011). Participants are given a box containing tacks, a box of matches and a candle and tasked with fixing the candle to the wall in such a way that when the candle is lit, the wax will not drip onto the floor.

> **Pause to reflect**
> Take a moment to think about how you might solve the problem described above. Perhaps you might ask students in your class to try it.

The solution to this problem is to tip the tacks out of the box, tack the box to the wall and use it as a shelf to support the candle. Most people fail to see that the box can be used in this way, seeing the box's function as simply to hold the tacks. It is a phenomenon known as 'functional fixedness' – our prior knowledge forms such a strong association that it's hard to think of alternatives. Interestingly, if the tacks are provided as a pile next to the box, participants are far more likely to come up with the correct solution.

Parallels can be drawn here with the concepts of routine expertise and adaptive expertise discussed in Chapter 6. Routine expertise is highly efficient for specific tasks within a relatively narrow domain. However, this routine expertise falls down when people are faced with novel problems that can't be solved by applying a tried and tested method; the knowledge provides too many constraints and the problem cannot be solved. An adaptive expert has flexible knowledge based on understanding; their knowledge provides some constraints but in a less rigid way, meaning that the knowledge doesn't become too constraining.

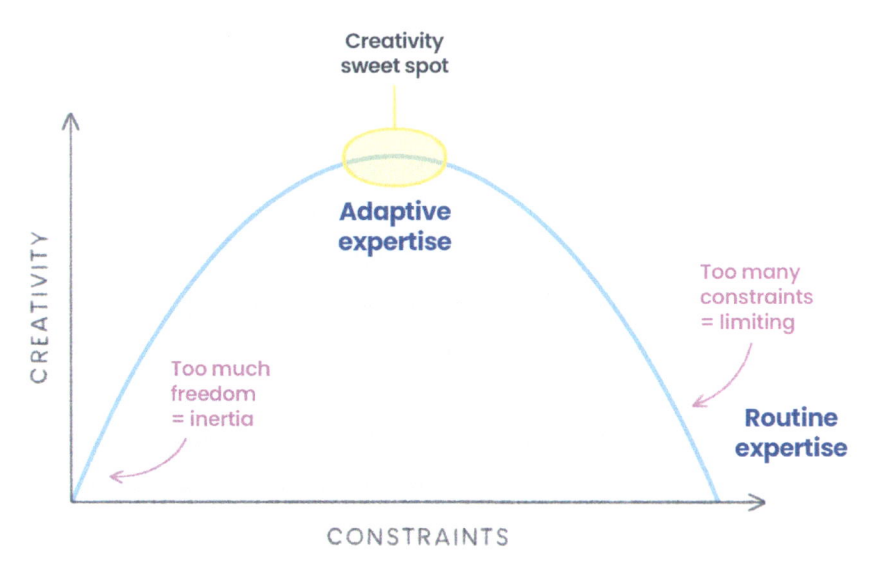

Figure 7.3 The relationship between constraints and creativity

Applications to Practice

As discussed above, a constraint is not harmful to creativity, and often may be beneficial – even if your students don't recognise this! There are some nuances to the issue, though. Focusing constraints are more likely to lead to increased creativity than exclusionary constraints, although we must be careful that these focusing constraints don't narrow the problem space so much that creativity becomes limited. Knowledge, meanwhile, provides a useful constraint in most cases, but is more helpful when it is well understood, and when students are guided to use their knowledge in flexible ways. These notions can help us to provide the right level of constraints to classroom tasks.

Choice within fixed parameters

Completely free choice can be debilitating for students, but providing some choice within some fixed parameters can help students to get started. This can be as simple as providing three or four possible tasks that students could attempt at the end of a topic and allowing them to choose the one that appeals to them most. When discussing topics which have several different applications, students could be asked to find specific examples which have some personal resonance for them; for example, when studying coastal systems in Geography, students could be encouraged to put together a case study from a part of the world they have visited.

In depth: Philosophical essays

In Philosophy, the topic of meta-ethics is usually explored through three primary approaches: naturalism, intuitionism and emotivism. The essay title 'Good is best explained by emotivism – discuss' has an imposed constraint as only one of these approaches should be considered. The best students focus on emotivism and use other meta-ethical theories selectively as comparisons, whereas weaker students just write everything they know about meta-ethics.

Imposing a constraint on the essay results in more sophisticated arguments, as, while the foundational knowledge remains constant, its application can vary significantly in different scenarios.

Research tasks

With the increase in access to electronic devices in the classroom, it has become common to set students independent research tasks. Examples might include:

- Choose an element from the periodic table and research its uses in the real world.
- Research the different ways in which coastlines can be protected and discuss the pros and cons of these different methods.

Without any constraints beyond 'use the internet to research', such tasks are often not very effective for developing students' creative thinking. At one extreme, students simply type the question (often verbatim!) into their device and copy the responses without thought. At the other end of the spectrum, some students may waste time searching through inappropriate sources of information which are either unreliable, inaccurate or simply pitched at the wrong level.

Instead, teachers could provide a focusing constraint in the form of a curated list of sources of information which provide a solid base from which further research could be explored, and give prompts indicating the specific things they expect students to find. Timescales and word counts could also provide constraints that usefully keep students on task and avoid time-wasting.

Rubrics

Well-designed rubrics can provide a clear focusing constraint without suppressing creativity; in the best cases, rubrics can provide guidance allowing students to complete a task more efficiently.

However, there is a danger that when provided with such rubrics students become more concerned about being evaluated against the criteria rather than seeing their supportive function. This is often the case when rubrics are linked to external examination marking and grading systems, and, in these instances, rubrics can hamper creativity. Rather than providing something which could be construed as a marking grid, a rubric could instead be reframed as a list of concepts or sub-topics to consider in a response along with some prompt questions. This could be given as a PowerPoint template for students to complete.

Pause to reflect
Have you any examples of rubrics from your teaching that result in students feeling too controlled by the evaluation and thus inhibiting creativity? Could these rubrics be reframed so that they continue to provide guidance but without the negative effects?

Using worked examples

Using worked examples is a well-researched effective teaching strategy (Sweller, 2006). Worked examples are complete solutions to problems which learners study in order to build their knowledge of how to solve similar problems in the future; studying worked examples is thought to be more efficient than having a student solve the equivalent problems themselves.

Live-modelling of these worked examples by a teacher can help highlight the processes involved in finding the solution. A further modification is completion problems where, following a fully worked example, learners are given incomplete solutions which they have to finish independently. However, care needs to be taken when using worked examples as they are of less benefit to high-expertise learners. When asking students to undertake creative tasks, providing models and examples could result in cognitive fixation where students cannot see alternative approaches. Tromp and Baer (2022) suggest that the most effective examples will be focusing rather than exclusionary and 'they should be either: (a) highly specific and truly original, falling outside the area of fixation; or (b) abstract, referring to categories of possibilities' (p. 5).

This could be a particular problem where students think there is only one right answer or just one approach that could be taken. Here, it may be that the students themselves impose too many constraints on their work as they are only able to follow a specific method demonstrated by their teacher and may not understand the reasoning behind each step. Teachers may therefore want to 'think aloud', modelling how they themselves would experiment, play with options, or try out new approaches. This can pave the way for experimentation and help move students away from fixating on specific examples.

In depth: Poetry

In English, creativity can come from pushing the usual accepted rules of a format as well as working within them. Limericks are usually a humorous form of rhyming poetry, often using predictable rhyming patterns. In a series of creative writing lessons, one group of students were first introduced to the format through some simple examples of the genre and then given examples which had a more serious message or broke the rules in some way, after which students were tasked with creating their own limericks. The idea was for them to generate a lot of different versions in a relatively short time; for the more nervous students, or those who thought they weren't good at poetry, the framework gave a clear starting point, and all students had something they were prepared to share with the class by the end of the session.

Many other poetic forms also provide constraints. Sonnets, for example, have a particular length and rhyme scheme. Beginner poets might find it easier to have these constraints, and later, as they become more experienced and confident, push the boundaries, exploring what happens when they break the standard conventions.

Student engagement with constraints

We also need to be mindful of students' perception that the more freedom they are given, the more creative their responses will be, as noted earlier in this chapter. Discussing how experts use constraints to improve creativity may help overcome these misconceptions. One example that could be given is how poets often choose to follow a particular set of rules such as sonnets, haikus or limericks.

In addition, we can support students to see how increasing levels of knowledge can provide constraints which, in turn, help to narrow the problem space and prevent students from wasting time trying approaches that are doomed to failure. For example, consider the knowledge required to solve the problem in Figure 7.4.

A knowledgeable student will immediately know to discount Pythagoras' theorem or 'SOHCAHTOA' as they recognise they are faced with a

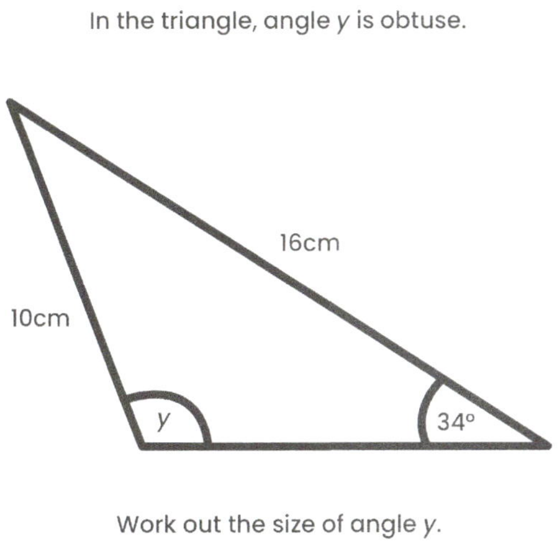
In the triangle, angle *y* is obtuse.
16cm
10cm
y
34°
Work out the size of angle *y*.

Figure 7.4 Triangle problem

non-right-angled triangle; this is an exclusionary constraint. A focusing constraint will then lead them to choosing to use the sine rule. However, if they simply use the sine rule formula in a routine fashion, they will come up with an answer which is less than 90°. This is because there is an alternative triangle with the same side lengths where the angles are all acute.

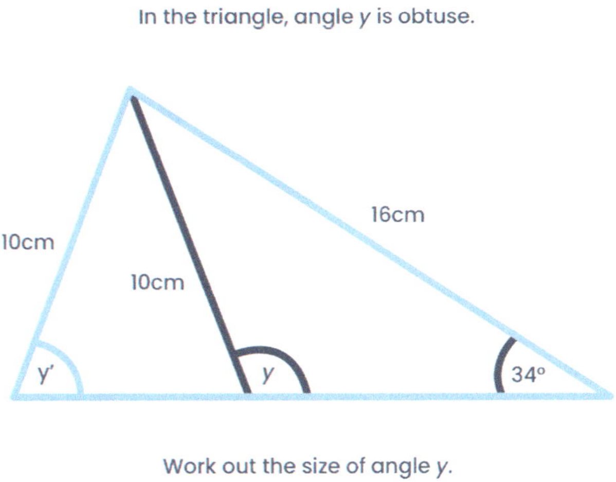
In the triangle, angle *y* is obtuse.
16cm
10cm
10cm
y'
y
34°
Work out the size of angle *y*.

Figure 7.5 Triangle problem version 2

The inverse sine function on a calculator will always return the positive value closest to zero, so rather than giving the angle y, angle y' will be returned. A student with more adaptive expertise would spot that they were asked to find an obtuse angle and adapt their approach accordingly.

Less knowledgeable students will struggle to know where to start with this problem and may spend time unproductively attempting to use Pythagoras' theorem before losing motivation and giving up. For these more novice students, teacher-imposed constraints would help overcome this barrier. With further practice, alongside explicit teaching of metacognitive prompts such as 'Do I have a right-angled triangle?', these constraints can be removed. We will talk more about the links between creativity and metacognition and creativity and motivation in Chapters 9 and 10 respectively.

> **Pause to reflect**
> What examples can you think of in your subject/phase where students take the wrong approach to a problem or task which would never be considered by someone with more expertise?

Avoiding too many constraints

As discussed above, there is a creativity sweet spot. Too many constraints are likely to limit students' creativity, and perhaps leave them feeling frustrated. Too few, and they might not know where to start. It's therefore important that teachers get the level right – and this depends on the students.

For example, providing students with a strict paragraph structure that must be followed in their writing may well lead to students producing very generic work, and therefore less creative outcomes. The use of scaffolding is a common and effective strategy to help with student writing, but as the students get more competent, this scaffolding can be removed. This means taking away a constraint, to ensure we aren't reducing the potential for more creative responses.

A common example of this is the use of the mnemonic PEEL (point, evidence, evaluation, link) to structure students' paragraph writing in various subjects. This is a particular risk when strategies become too focused on requirements for high-stakes examinations; these strategies may increase achievement in the short term but mean students struggle at the next stage of their education, for example when moving from school to higher education. Supports may also lead to short-term success, but act as a barrier to acquiring deeper understanding. A further example is the use of formula triangles in science, discussed in Chapter 6.

As discussed earlier, students with routine expertise may struggle to tackle non-routine problems. For example, a chemistry student who has always followed a linear step-by-step approach to calculating an energy change from an experimentally measured temperature change may be unable to reverse this process to predict a temperature change from a data book value of the energy change. A student with adaptive expertise on the other hand has a deeper understanding of the relationships between energy and temperature changes and is able to complete the unusual problem with ease.

In Chapter 6, we discussed various strategies that teachers could employ to develop adaptive expertise in their students. Scaffolds and worked examples are helpful for novice learners but teachers should have a clear plan for how these scaffolds can be removed so that students don't become too dependent on them. There is a creativity 'sweet spot' but this will change as students gain experience, and hence we might need to force them out of old habits by giving them problems in different formats and finding ways to move beyond superficial understanding of a problem to deeper learning.

Pause to reflect
What examples can you come up with in your subject or phase where students have been fixed in one way of thinking and have been unable to apply this knowledge to a less routine task? Have you tried to tackle this in your practice?

Conclusion

In this chapter, we have seen that counter to many people's intuitions, putting constraints on tasks need not be a barrier to creativity. It can actually increase creativity, or improve the originality of what students come up with.

These constraints can be self-imposed, for example an artist who limits their colour palette to blues and greys, or imposed by external factors, for example a creative writing class where the teacher decides on the specific prompt for that day's writing. Knowledge can itself impose constraints without us realising - more knowledgeable students will know which tools and strategies to apply in which situations, thus narrowing the problem space.

However, imposing too many constraints can limit creativity. This leads to the idea referenced in the title, and which you no doubt recognise - a Goldilocks rule of constraints means aiming for just the right amount of constraints - not too few but not too many.

A complicating factor is that where this creativity sweet spot occurs depends on the knowledge levels of our students. More novice students will probably benefit from more teacher-imposed constraints, but as student expertise increases, these constraints should be removed. Without this, we risk leaving students with only routine expertise, unable to take what they know and apply it to novel situations. One way to avoid this is to introduce a level of uncertainty into lessons, something we will tackle in the next chapter.

Discussion Questions

1) What is the difference between an exclusionary constraint and a focusing constraint? How might these constraints be used in your classroom?
2) Where do you currently use worked examples in your practice? Have you ever used completion examples? Where have you found these worked or completion examples to be effective? Have you seen instances where they are unhelpful for students with higher levels of expertise?

3) What is the relationship between knowledge and constraints? In what ways does knowledge help to 'narrow the problem space'?
4) What is the potential problem with providing students with scaffolds such as formula triangles and strict paragraph structures?

Professional Learning Tasks

Task 1

At the start, we shared the example of writing a story about a shy, red-haired boy named Colin who is missing a toe. Try this task yourself – perhaps you can swap your responses with another teacher for feedback. As an additional constraint, you could try a limited word count – for example, a drabble, which is a story of exactly 100 words in length.

Task 2

Look at an upcoming lesson or scheme. Where might there be opportunities for you to provide students with some choice within fixed parameters? Jot down some ideas, and then have a go at redesigning the lesson.

Task 3

Look at a recent task you have set one of your classes. What knowledge do they have that will impose constraints on that task and help to 'narrow the problem space'? How can you be sure they have the requisite knowledge and won't head off on the wrong path?

Task 4

Consider an upcoming scheme of work. What scaffolds are used to support students over the short-term? What's the plan for gradually removing these scaffolds? Are you aware of students preferring to stick to tried and tested strategies? It may be worth speaking to teachers who work with other year groups for this task.

8 Structured Uncertainty

The COVID-19 pandemic was a time of great global uncertainty. Whilst it is difficult to imagine anyone wishing to go through that experience again, there is no doubt that the uncertainty led to a great deal of creativity and innovation, from the pubs and restaurants who switched to take-away services, to the scientists who invented vaccines in record-breaking time. Not to mention all the teachers who suddenly had to find ways to teach remotely. If you taught through that period, you will no doubt have come up with a variety of creative solutions to the problem of not being in the same room as your students, and it may well be that some of these methods stayed with you when you returned to your physical classroom.

Beghetto (2021) has argued that creativity fundamentally depends on uncertainty, yet many teachers are used to planning everything carefully, and introducing more uncertainty to schools may feel like a scary prospect.

Whilst we acknowledge that the high-stakes accountability systems that many educators find themselves in can make it seem difficult to support students to engage with creative thinking, it is far from impossible. This chapter will use Beghetto's concept of 'structured uncertainty' (Beghetto, 2019), to show how by incorporating some areas of uncertainty into our lessons we can develop creativity without the need for a mass overhaul of the education system (or indeed the return of a global pandemic!).

The Myth

It is rare to find anyone who disagrees with the concept that to thrive in today's society, people will need to be creative thinkers, ready to adapt to the uncertainties that they will no doubt encounter. But in practice, do they *really* like creativity, and its inherent uncertainties? Their actual views may be more complex.

In an experimental study, Mueller et al. (2011) showed that despite espousing creativity as an important goal, participants held an implicit bias against creative ideas. The researchers concluded that despite prior research showing uncertainty is the spur for the search for and generation of creative ideas, their findings suggested that 'uncertainty also makes people less able to recognize creativity, perhaps when they need it most' (p. 16).

This plays out in educational contexts, too. In a study looking at teachers' attitudes towards creativity, Gralewski (2019) found that traits such as independence, impulsiveness, rule-breaking, and striving for spectacular solutions were very strongly associated with creativity for male students, but rarely or never for female students! Creative girls were seen as conscientious and systematic. This suggests that teachers don't always react positively to actions that they associate with creativity, and some see it as being characteristic of only some students. It follows that some people approve of creativity only when it fits their other attitudes and prejudices.

Schools are often characterised by a great deal of certainty, with rules, timetables, routines and a curriculum. Introducing uncertainty into this structured environment for the purpose of supporting creativity may seem like a high-risk strategy to some practitioners. Indeed, it is common for teachers to express the idea that they would support creativity if only they could find the time to do so (Bereczki & Kárpáti, 2018). It is a recognisable and much wider concern – teachers feeling that they are overloaded and/or too busy covering core content. So it is easy to conclude that creativity cannot be taught.

> **Pause to reflect**
> Do you think that creativity is valued in your own school or centre? Have you observed the kind of attitudes towards uncertainty mentioned above? What about the gender biases – is creativity associated only with certain groups of students in your experience? And what (if anything) do schools do to celebrate and encourage genuinely new and useful thinking? How would they react, for example, if a student came up with an original suggestion for changing a school rule for the better?

Exploring the Research

Following the rules

In Chapter 3, we introduced Lego as an analogy for the building blocks that must be in place before creativity can flourish. Provide a child (or adult) with only a few Lego bricks and they are unlikely to produce much of merit; the more Lego bricks available, the more varied and creative the outputs can be. However, many children (or adults) 'playing' with Lego nowadays follow a strict set of instructions to build a specific structure. Many of these structures are quite spectacular and the creativity of the designers is often a delight to see, for example, repurposing Lego frogs to become cherry blossom on a bonsai tree. However, as much as we are 'creating' something when following instructions, the lack of originality means we are not really being creative in our endeavours.

> **Pause to reflect**
> Can you think of any examples from your own experience where you follow instructions to produce a product? To what extent do you feel you are being creative during such tasks? Are you someone who likes to go off-piste, or do you stick rigidly to the instructions? Does this depend on the task or area of your life?

Some commentators have argued that with ubiquitous access to technology, the role of traditional schooling is reduced as students can simply teach themselves (see e.g. Mitra, 2013). You may well have taken this approach yourself when attempting a DIY project at home – the internet is full of step-by-step instructions for any number of home improvement tasks. Similarly, nowadays, most of us rely on satellite navigation systems or Google maps for route planning, even in places we know well. Why bother to learn routes or how to read a map when technology can do this all for us?

This phenomenon has been investigated in a comparison between London black cab drivers (long a source of fascination to cognitive science researchers) and Uber drivers (Noulas et al., 2018). In order to be licensed, all London black cab drivers are required to pass 'The Knowledge', a rigorous test that requires them to memorise the entire urban map of London. Neuroscience researchers have shown that this leads to changes in the brain structure, with London cab drivers having expanded hippocampi, the area of the brain linked to spatial long-term memory (Maguire et al., 2000). Uber drivers, on the other hand, use satellite navigation systems. The researchers showed that, on average, London cabbies were able to navigate faster to destinations than Uber drivers. It appeared as though their extensive and well-structured knowledge allowed the cab drivers to adapt more quickly to changes in traffic conditions, leading to more efficiency than following instructions from a device. This flexible use of expert knowledge may sound familiar – the cab drivers were demonstrating adaptive expertise (see Chapter 6).

> **Pause to reflect**
> Can you think of any examples from your own experience where you have suffered the consequences of over-reliance on technology? Do you feel it's important to increase your own knowledge in this area or is it a price you are prepared to pay?

Chaos and creativity

If creativity can be inhibited by following instructions, then are there any benefits for avoiding instructions? This has been investigated by researchers using paper aeroplanes (Stefl & Rohm, 2017). In this study, participants were tasked with creating a paper aeroplane, with or without Google. The researchers found that solutions using instructions found via Google were better on average, and there were fewer abject failures.

However, the very best outcomes were created without using Google: 'curiosity led a couple of students in the non-Google group to redefine what we consider to be a "proper" paper airplane' (p. 4).

Figure 8.1 Paper aeroplanes created in the study. Image provided by Matt Stefl and reproduced with permission.

Structured Uncertainty 139

That isn't to say that the discipline required to follow the instructions carefully isn't an important skill; it may well in fact be a prerequisite for creative thinking. Being persistent and disciplined are two of the five creative learning habits introduced in Chapter 4. Following instructions may also be an effective way to build a firm knowledge base in a particular domain. However, if students only ever follow instructions or default too quickly to guidance from a Google search, this may limit their potential as creative thinkers.

There is plenty of research to support the idea that disordered environments increase creativity. In a study that did involve Lego, Kim and Zhong (2017) found that participants who were provided with a muddled assortment of Lego bricks produced much more creative outputs than participants who were provided with the same Lego bricks sorted by colour and shape.

Figure 8.2 Organised versus disordered Lego bricks

The researchers found similar results when participants completed sentence construction tasks from categorised and uncategorised lists of words; the participants provided with the uncategorised lists produced more creative sentences. Those of us who have messy desks might be pleased to know that Kathleen Vohs and colleagues (Vohs et al., 2013) found that disorderly environments stimulated creativity – although on the flip-side, their study found that participants with tidier environments were more generous and made healthier choices!

A question for educators is to consider how we introduce uncertainty into schools without them descending into chaos. One of the problems is that with uncertainty comes the risk of failure, something which students (and their teachers) are often keen to avoid at all costs.

Taking beautiful risks

Beghetto (2018) suggests we should encourage students to take 'beautiful risks':

- Bad risks are ones where the potential downsides outweigh the benefits – you wouldn't want to try a new forehand when playing the championship final at Wimbledon.
- Good risks are ones where the potential benefits outweigh the downsides – choosing to work on a new forehand with a coach as part of your preparation for an upcoming tournament.
- Beautiful risks are ones that not only have the potential to benefit an individual but also the potential to make a positive and lasting contribution to the learning and lives of others.

There are clearly times within school where we don't especially wish our students to be creative; safety procedures for using machine tools in a design and technology workshop must be followed exactly, and using an alternative approach here would constitute a bad risk.

However, risks can be beneficial in the right context. As Amy Edmonson puts it, such risks lead to *intelligent failure* (Edmonson, 2023) – the result of thoughtful forays into novel territory. They might not work out, but they are worth the risk, and may lead to creative outcomes with further time and more iterations. Classrooms need to be psychologically safe spaces to encourage students to take both good and beautiful risks and see (intelligent) failure as a positive thing.

> **Pause to reflect**
> Where might you want students to take risks in your lessons and where is it important that they stick to the tried and tested methods? Where might the beautiful risks be found? What would constitute a bad risk?

Applications to Practice

Introducing uncertainty into schools

Beghetto (2021) asserts that when we encounter uncertainty we enter into a state of genuine doubt which requires creative reasoning to resolve. If we wish to develop our students' creativity, we need to find ways in which to bring this uncertainty into our classrooms.

This does not mean removing all structure and allowing complete freedom – creative ideas need to be not only new but also useful, i.e. ideas need to balance originality and task constraints. In a class, if a student comes up with an original idea which is not relevant to the discussion, then that idea cannot be considered creative; equally, if a student is following a well-known method for solving a mathematical problem, then that is also not creative, even though it meets the task constraints by arriving at the correct solution.

In a TED talk, Beghetto (2017b) uses the example of a class being given a simple maths subtraction problem: what is 26 minus 17? One student decides to write a poem about 'how you can get gain through loss; how through subtraction you can add beauty'. Certainly an original response to the problem but not a creative one as it doesn't meet task constraints. Another student follows the teacher-outlined method using column subtraction, coming to the correct answer of 9. This meets task constraints but again is not a creative response as there is no originality.

A third student reaches the answer 9 using a different method from the one modelled by the teacher. It is all too easy to dismiss this response – Beghetto calls this 'killing ideas softly' – and insist that the student follows the prescribed method. By exploring the student's reasoning it is possible to determine whether this truly is a creative response or simply arises from confusion and they have reached the correct answer through incorrect reasoning. Or it might be that the student's method has limited utility beyond this specific example; opening up a discussion to explore why the teacher's method is more effective could be a great way to get deeper understanding from all students.

> ### In depth: Speaking in foreign languages
>
> Speaking is a key component of learning any modern foreign language, and as such oral skills are usually assessed alongside reading, writing and listening skills. This is a frightening prospect for many students, so it is common practice for teachers to provide questions for any oral assessment in advance. However, this can lead to students writing out pre-prepared answers which they then learn by heart. The assessment then becomes a test of memory rather than an assessment of how well the students can converse in a foreign language.
>
> To counteract this, one modern foreign language department decided to stop giving students the questions for end of year assessments in advance, thus introducing some uncertainty into the exercise. To provide some reassurance, the students were still given the topics that could be discussed and lists of relevant key vocabulary to learn. Realising that this more unstructured process would be challenging for many students, teachers built up students' skills throughout the year through regular class discussion where all students were encouraged to participate in the target language.
>
> Over the year, it was found that student confidence increased, and their oral responses in the end of year assessments showed much more creativity. Surprisingly, many students actually found the process less stressful as they were less concerned about learning a pre-prepared script off by heart and knew that they didn't have to be word perfect in the conversation.

Classroom talk

Whilst we may think that much of what happens in schools is highly certain, we never know how students might respond to our lessons, particularly during class discussions. Even if you've taught a topic for several years using the same resources, students still have the capacity to surprise with their unusual responses. As we discussed in Chapter 2, we need to think carefully about our questioning techniques, and how we run classroom discussions is the key to ensuring that we don't unintentionally quash some of these 'creative micro moments', which can, in extreme cases, lead to creative mortification on the part of students.

Lesson unplanning

Beghetto does not advocate the complete removal of structured activities where students are expected to work through routine tasks. As discussed in the previous chapter on constraints (see Chapter 7), it is a misconception to think that creativity thrives best under conditions of complete freedom. However, being too directive, and never allowing students to grapple with uncertainty, may do students a disservice. It would be preferable to equip them with strategies for dealing with uncertainty. Beghetto's solution is a flexible approach that he calls 'lesson unplanning'.

Beghetto suggests that most learning activities can be thought of as having four elements: problem, process, product and criteria.

In the maths example above, the problem would be 'what is 26 minus 17?', the process is column subtraction, the product is the correct answer 9, and the criteria are whether students use column subtraction in reaching their answer. Lesson unplanning involves removing one of these elements to create some uncertainty. In the same example, it could be that the criteria are less rigid by allowing students to use other effective methods to reach the correct solution.

Beghetto emphasises the importance of students having sufficient knowledge of the topic in hand before embarking on lesson unplanning. If students are struggling with basic ideas of subtraction using single digit numbers, then they are unlikely to be able to come up with an efficient method for subtraction using double digit numbers without explicit instruction, and certainly not one that might be generalised to much larger numbers.

In the following sections, we give examples of how lesson unplanning might be applied across different subjects.

Lesson unplanning: Problem

Ask students to make up their own, similar questions on a topic for their peers to answer. This works well for short questions that always follow a similar format, for example common mathematical procedures or simple calculations within the sciences. By making up their own questions, students have to think more deeply about the problem structure and work through common misconceptions. Challenge your students to make up really challenging problems; in our experience they often come up with questions that are more difficult than those in the textbook, and this can lead to really interesting discussions on *why* these questions are more challenging.

Lesson unplanning: Process

Students often have a misconception that there is complete freedom within the arts and humanities – there is no right answer – whereas within science and Maths there is only ever one correct solution. Experts in any of these fields would of course disagree. There are interpretations within arts and humanities that are based on sound evidence and logical reasoning and interpretations that aren't; scientific researchers know very well that evidence can be interpreted in different ways to support different conclusions. All the same, lesson unplanning from a 'process' perspective will look different in these different disciplines.

For Maths and science subjects, unplanning the process might be about setting students the challenge to come up with as many different ways of solving a problem as they can (or even just one alternative approach to that suggested in the textbook or by the teacher). The different methods should all come up with the same answer and the advantages and disadvantages of each can be debated. By playing with possibilities in this way, students may inadvertently start down a path which ends up not leading to the correct solution, which should help them to understand more clearly why problems are approached in a particular way, rather than simply following a standard procedure by rote.

For the arts and humanities, 'process' unplanning may be less about giving space for students to come up with their own interpretations and more about discussing the evidence base on which those interpretations are founded. Another possibility is presenting students with an unsubstantiated interpretation and asking students to explain why this interpretation is unlikely to be correct.

As ever, care must be taken as to when such activities are introduced; too early in the learning sequence and students are likely to become extremely confused and misconceptions more firmly embedded.

Lesson unplanning: Product

There is a strong temptation within education for the product of a sequence of learning to look exactly as it would in the high-stakes assessments for which students are being prepared; this is particularly true within upper primary and secondary schools. For example, after teaching students about genetics in Biology, students complete an assessment consisting of a series of past exam questions, which is then marked by the teacher according to the exam board published mark schemes. Whilst it would be unprofessional to never expose students to the style of assessment they will be facing in these high-stakes assessments, this does not mean that formative assessment designed to build knowledge and understanding during the learning process should follow the same pattern. In fact, research suggests that narrowing the curriculum in this way can be detrimental to learning.

Daisy Christodoulou covers the distinction between formative and summative assessment brilliantly in her book *Making Good Progress?* (2017). In the book, Christodoulou develops an analogy between education and marathon training; you wouldn't train for a marathon by running lots and lots of marathons, so in the same way, you shouldn't prepare students for examinations by having them complete lots of examination practice in every lesson. The analogy is an excellent way to help students (and their parents) to understand the purposes of different forms of assessment within school.

'Product' unplanning can therefore be as simple as not asking students to complete exam-style questions until much later in their schooling. Within the humanities, rather than completing an essay, students could be given a choice to create a video presentation on the same topic or to record a debate between two of their peers looking at both sides of the argument. What about writing an essay in science or Maths? Or asking students to produce a video tutorial explaining how to complete a problem rather than just submitting the solutions? In all subjects, the creation of a one-page graphical summary of a topic can serve as a great way to ascertain whether students have grasped key concepts.

An important caveat here is to ensure that the main focus of students' attention is on the content to be learned. If a student's focus is on learning how to use presentation or video software rather than the content of what they are presenting, then such product unplanning is unlikely to lead to improved understanding. Also, as we discussed in the previous chapter, giving students too much choice over the way they present their work can be paralysing; it is far better to limit the options to two or three that the teacher knows will be suitable within the given timeframe. When given completely free rein, students often default to some of the least creative outputs, producing a piece of pedestrian written work or a superficial PowerPoint presentation.

Lesson unplanning: Criteria

Linked to the above, if as teachers we can become more comfortable with the product of a sequence of learning not looking like that required on high-stakes national assessments, we should be able to become more comfortable with not using the mark schemes from those assessments as criteria for judging all student work. One simple change is not to use marks and grades but just formative comments on work completed early on in a course, even if the questions are taken from past exam papers. Other suggestions include teacher and students together coming up with shared criteria as to what 'good' will look like; this could apply to routines within the classroom as well as academic work.

As ever, it is important to note that teachers ultimately have a professional responsibility to establish learning criteria, as without this, students will not know what is expected of them and will rapidly become confused and demotivated. As Beghetto (2019) says, 'creative expression in the classroom is not about unconstrained originality but rather is more about resolving uncertainty in an otherwise structured and supportive learning environment' (p. 37).

> ### In depth: Practical Chemistry
>
> Two approaches to practical work are usually undertaken within the sciences. The most common is that students follow a predetermined set of steps and then answer questions on data analysis and evaluation. An alternative approach is that students carry out longer inquiry projects where they plan their own experiments to investigate a particular scientific phenomenon. The former usually takes place over a single lesson whereas the latter could stretch over several weeks. However, there are ways of including more open investigative work in science in short bursts.
>
> For example, a common practical in Chemistry is to investigate the effect of concentration on reaction rate, which can be taught as an extended, three-week investigation or as a teacher-led practical taking place in a single lesson. An alternative to both is to set a clock challenge. The iodine clock reaction involves mixing two colourless solutions and measuring the time required for the blue colour to suddenly appear; in a clock challenge, students are given the two colourless solutions and tasked with creating a 'clock' which will change colour after exactly one minute. Students quickly work out that changing the concentration of the stock solutions changes the time taken and many work out the quantitative relationship that halving the concentration doubles the time.
>
> This practical takes no longer than the more common 'follow the teacher's step-by-step method' and students are still exposed to the key chemical theory – increasing concentration increases reaction rate. However, this approach allows students to grapple with uncertainty and realise there is more than one solution to the problem posed.

Anticipating and proactively planning for setbacks

Students may not always respond to uncertainty in productive ways. When students hit problems they cannot immediately solve, this can lead to demotivation and students simply giving up, or deciding they are just bad at your subject.

The concept of a 'premortem' is widely used in the business world (Klein, 2008). This is where before embarking on a project, the assumption is made that the project has failed and team members have to come up with suggestions as to why the failure occurred. This then prompts the team to pre-emptively avoid these failures.

We can also support students with similar thinking on a smaller scale by asking them to predict what might go wrong when carrying out a task and suggest solutions to these predicaments in advance. If they have carried out similar tasks in the past, this also acts as a useful retrieval practice exercise. For example, before carrying out a practical in a science laboratory, students could be asked to write down what mistakes they might make handling equipment and what they could do to limit these errors. Within Maths it could be as simple as asking students to recall common errors when tackling a particular type of problem, e.g. not lining up the decimal point when adding decimals.

> **Pause to reflect**
> What common mistakes do students often make when completing work in your classes? How might you support students to anticipate and thus avoid these mistakes?

In depth: Drypoint in Art and Design

A technique that can be taught as part of Art and Design is drypoint, a printmaking process where an image is made by scratching into a plastic sheet to create grooves and burrs. Although many love the freedom the unfamiliar medium provides, some worry about the outcome and the lack of control they have over the process.

In order to overcome these fears, one teacher specifically asked students to come up with a list of things they thought might go wrong in the process.

- The process was unfamiliar.
- They knew it would take time and that if they made a mistake it would take a long time to re-do.
- The lack of control - scratching into a plastic plate is unfamiliar and isn't the same as drawing with a pencil.
- Marks that are cut into the plastic are more permanent so can't be rubbed out in the way that a pencil drawing can be.
- Fear, embarrassment and disappointment if it doesn't work.

The teacher and students then talked about strategies for overcoming these concerns. For example:

- Ways of trying to burnish out marks
- Feeling the plastic to check for a degree of roughness that would suggest it would hold ink
- How they could gain an understanding/familiarity about what would work (this could include 'ask the teacher who knows the process to check and assess')
- How the process was different from drawing. They talked about the outcome being different from a drawing and how the different marks they made due to the slight lack of familiarity/control were a quality associated with the process rather than a mistake to edit out.

As a result, students embarked on the project with much more confidence, and when faced with challenges, had strategies to fall back on to overcome these challenges rather than becoming demotivated and giving up.

Conclusion

To quote Ron Beghetto, 'there really is no creativity without uncertainty' (Beghetto, 2021, paragraph 1). After all, creativity involves something new – it can't ever be entirely predictable. This chapter has looked at some of the productive ways that uncertainty can be used in education, and shown that even uncertainty and randomness can be structured and planned for.

As we looked at in Chapter 2, many people feel that the structure imposed by formal schooling destroys young people's natural curiosity and creativity, pushing them into a narrow sense of achievement based solely on academic merit. With the high-stakes accountability examinations present in many educational systems, it can seem as though there is a tension between teaching for creativity and achievement in these examinations.

However, even within the restrictions of school systems, we have shown in this chapter that it is possible to infuse the creative benefits of uncertainty into our lessons, and to encourage our students to take 'beautiful risks' with their learning. The young people in our care will be faced with plenty of uncertainty in their future lives, which is one of the reasons that we feel that it's important to support creative thinking, and to consider ways to support its transfer beyond the classroom. If we never expose them to any uncertainty whilst at school, then we are surely failing in our duty to prepare them for the world beyond school.

Discussion Questions

1) In what ways can we create something without actually being creative?
2) What are 'beautiful risks', anyway? Can you share some examples from your own practice?

3) Bearing in mind the idea of lesson unplanning and the broader concept of uncertainty, what do you see as the links between lesson planning and creativity? Are there contradictions for us to wrestle with?
4) To what extent do you agree that there is a balance to be had between efficiency and creativity, or between certainty and uncertainty?

Professional Learning Tasks

Task 1

Choose a particular student in your school and follow them for a day (you could choose to do this as a theoretical exercise, or actually follow them to their lessons). To what extent is their time highly structured? How much uncertainty do they face in a typical day?

Task 2

Get together with a group of colleagues or students and try the paper aeroplane-making activity, with half the group allowed to access instructions via Google and the other half free-styling. Do your results match with those of the researchers? When the authors tried this with a group of sixth form students, it was fascinating to note that the instruction-following group took much longer to produce one paper aeroplane whereas the 'free-stylers' produced their first plane much more quickly and therefore had more chances to adapt and refine their initial designs.

Task 3

Look at a lesson plan for an upcoming lesson. Where might there be opportunities for 'lesson unplanning'? You may wish to break the lesson down into the four components suggested by Beghetto: problem, process, product and criteria. Could one of these components be removed to introduce some structured uncertainty into the lesson? Ron Beghetto (2024) has recently released an AI bot to help with lesson unplanning - what additional ideas for lesson unplanning can you come up with when using an AI assistant?

Task 4

Think about a task or activity that your students undertake that takes place over a few lessons, for example a longer piece of writing. What do you think students' fears or concerns are about tackling this project? How might you set up a discussion to help students to articulate and come up with strategies for overcoming these fears?

9 Metacognition and Strategic Creativity

We associate creativity with flashes of insight. Probably the most famous example is the 'Eureka!' story, which tells how Archimedes discovered the principle of buoyancy and water displacement. King Hiero II of Syracuse tasked Archimedes to determine whether a crown was made of pure gold or had been mixed with lesser metal. This had to be done without damaging the crown, meaning that while it could be weighed, it couldn't be melted down to measure its volume – and its irregular shape made this apparently impossible to calculate.

Archimedes, a mathematician, engineer and inventor, pondered over the problem for a long time. Then, one day, while taking a bath (so the story goes), he noticed the water level rising, and realised that displacement of water could be used to measure the volume of *any* irregular object, and therefore to detect the presence of less dense metals such as silver in the crown. He is said to have run through the streets of Syracuse naked, shouting 'Eureka!' (meaning, 'I have found it!').

There are many other anecdotes of famous creative insights and breakthroughs that seemed to arrive via a flash of insight. The chemist Kekulé is said to have dreamt of a snake seizing its own tail, forming a ring, leading him to develop the concept of the benzene ring, though other accounts suggest that he came up with the idea while daydreaming and gazing out of the window of a horse-drawn bus in London. Elias Howe came up with the design of the sewing machine – with its needle with a

DOI: 10.4324/9781032719221-9

point at the tip – after dreaming of being attacked with spears that had holes in their blades. And Paul McCartney is said to have composed the melody for *Yesterday* in his sleep.

More broadly, many thinkers, including scientists such as Albert Einstein, Marie Curie and Niels Bohr, have attributed some of their ideas to periods of reflection, contemplation and daydreaming, while the popular idea of creativity as being about having a 'brainwave' or flash of insight has taken hold in popular culture.

The Myth

With so many examples mentioned above, you might be surprised to learn that the idea of creativity as a sudden flash of inspiration is often considered to be a myth by researchers (e.g. Benedek et al., 2021). At the very least, it is a simplistic idea. However, as we will see in this chapter, there is an element of truth to the value of contemplation, distraction, and time away from a task. What's more, students can use these strategically as part of their metacognitive control of their creative process. More on that later!

This idea that creativity is a flash of inspiration builds directly on a myth that we looked at earlier in this book – the notion that creativity is so mysterious that it can never really be understood or defined (see Chapter 1). It was literally seen as a mysterious divine gift during the time of Archimedes, when societies such as the Ancient Greeks and Romans believed in god-like beings called muses, who would favour certain artists and thinkers. Nobody knew where creative ideas came from. However, as we have seen, creativity *can* be studied systematically, and we can work to understand its processes.

The main problem with seeing creativity as based on 'Eureka!' moments is that it suggests that thinkers just need to wait for inspiration to strike. It may lead to the assumption that creativity just *happens*, and there is not much that a teacher or educator can do about it. Importantly, it neglects what leads up to a moment of insight; in all of the examples mentioned above, the thinker in question already had vast expertise in their field, and (at least in the case of the scientists) had already been thinking about the problem for a period of time. The insight didn't just happen – a lot of groundwork had been put in place.

Seeing creativity as involving flashes of inspiration therefore puts the emphasis falsely on random chance, and the idea that some people are just lucky. It also implies that people such as Archimedes have an innate creative genius, a view that overshadows the years of work that they put in. In general, the idea unhelpfully ignores context, including the key role of prior knowledge in creativity.

Exploring the Research

A mysterious process?

As we have seen throughout this book, creativity is not actually an inaccessible mystery; it is an active area of scientific inquiry like many others. This inquiry depends on a widely agreed understanding of what the concept means, rooted in cognitive psychology. We explained earlier in this book (see Chapter 1) that creativity certainly can be and has been defined by scientists. To recap, the standard definition of creativity features three key components:

- Making something new
- A product/output that is useful or effective
- A social context in which this novelty and usefulness are judged

Most educators and students are probably unaware that there is such widespread agreement among the research community on what creativity is (and what it isn't). This objective agreement on the nature of the concept dates back to at least the 1950s, with roots further back still (see Runco & Jaeger, 2012).

It is valuable to demystify creativity to educators, students and the general public. In the classroom, students may be getting the message that creativity cannot be understood or scrutinised, with the implication being that they shouldn't think about it or try to develop strategies and solutions. By analogy, this would be like telling a class that physics processes or sports skills are just 'mysteries' that cannot be unpicked or theorised – hardly a helpful way to frame things!

A way to tackle this creativity myth would be to present creativity as something which can be understood and explored. Granted, there are complexities and areas of disagreement, but in this it is just like any other aspect of human behaviour or psychology.

> **Pause to reflect**
> Could you demystify creativity for your students, and tackle the idea that it's impossible to define? How would you start?

It may also be helpful for educators to conceptualise creative thinking in terms of its strong overlaps with problem solving (see Chapter 2). Like other forms of problem solving, certain strategies can be usefully brought to bear in tackling creative tasks, and these can be communicated to students. The role of traits like perseverance and experimentation can also be helpfully highlighted (Durham Commission, 2019; see also Chapter 5). Together, such an approach helps to move away from the myth that creative thinking is divine and mysterious, and towards seeing it as a psychological process which can be usefully studied, understood, and even controlled.

When we start to see creativity as a cognitive process like any other, these difficulties seem less like a mystery and more like a scientific problem. True, we don't know everything about creativity, just like we don't know everything about long-term memory. But we have learned quite a lot, and further research will help to refine this understanding.

Flashes of insight

So far, we have considered and rejected the idea of creativity as a mysterious process. But what about the 'flash of inspiration' idea, and the stories of Archimedes, Kekulé and others? Is there any truth in this concept, and if not, where does it come from?

As noted already, popular views often focus on the moment of insight and ignore the context. When the creative process is looked at over a longer timescale, the idea that a delay may be followed by a moment of sudden insight is highly prominent in the creativity literature, and it starts to make more sense when seen as a part of a greater whole.

Indeed, one of the oldest scientific models of creativity set out a series of processes which included a delay. In his book *The Art of Thought*, English psychologist Graham Wallas proposed a four-stage model that emphasised the importance of the timescale of creativity, including the different thinking that happens at different points of the process (Wallas, 1926). The four stages are:

- Preparation
- Incubation
- Illumination
- Verification

According to this model, a key part of creativity is the *preparation* stage. This is where prior learning – and in particular working on the problem (by a suitably skilled expert) – plays a role. It's easy to link this to the work done by scientists or other problem solvers prior to their breakthroughs.

Next comes *incubation*. This crucial stage is time away from the problem. The analogy is to an egg that is not ready to hatch. The creator has to be patient; at least to an extent, creativity can't be rushed.

Illumination is the moment of insight, after which *verification* processes can be used to make sure that the solution actually works and makes sense (again, drawing on the expertise of the creator to do so, but also on the responses of the community to whom the solution/creative work is relevant).

Preparation
The creator tackles a problem and enhances their relevant prior knowledge.

Incubation
The creator spends time away from the problem, during which ideas continue to develop.

Illumination
The creator comes up with a breakthrough idea which appears to solve the problem or provide a way forward; the "Aha!" moment.

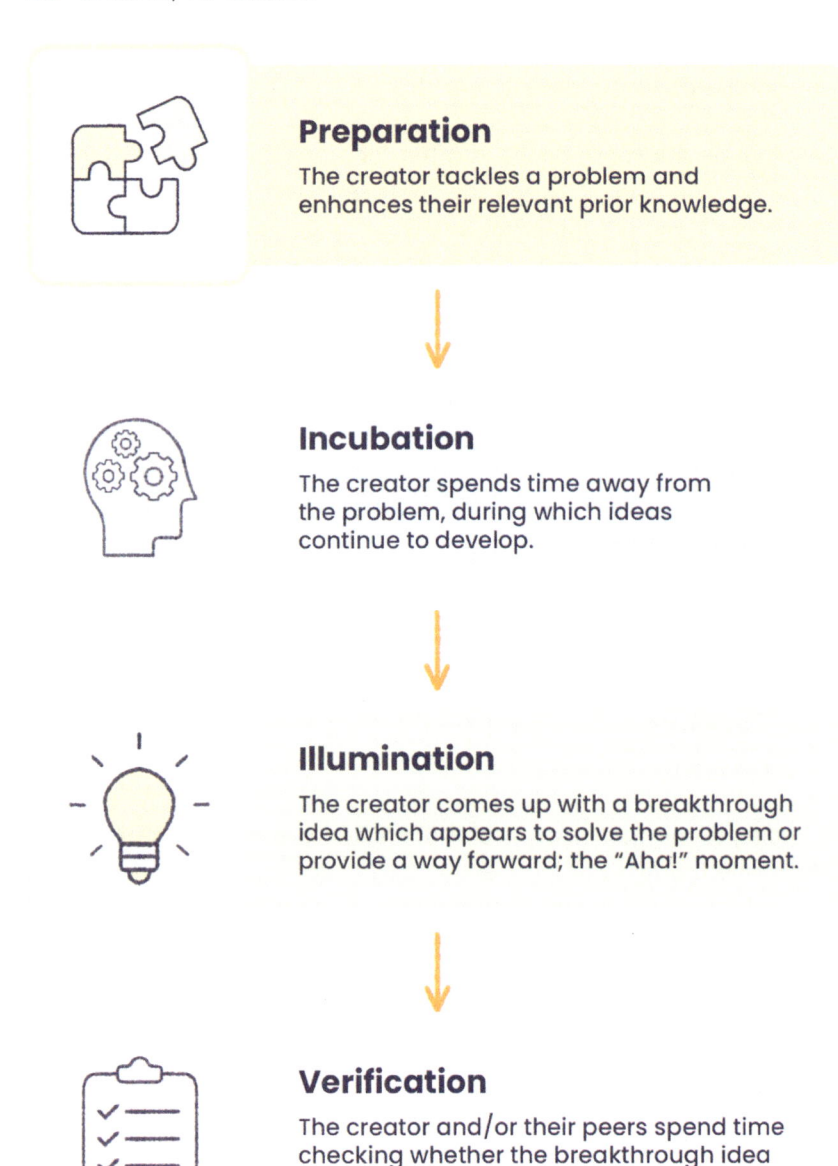

Verification
The creator and/or their peers spend time checking whether the breakthrough idea is workable.

Figure 9.1 The Wallas four-stage model of creativity

Role of incubation

Incubation is an intriguing idea, and it's easy to see the links with education – any creative problem could be designed to include some time away from the task itself. But does incubation actually work?

Although the views of Wallas were simplistic and not grounded on empirical evidence, the idea of incubation caught on, and has been widely studied since. In a review of the evidence, Sio and Ormerod (2009) found that the majority of studies had found a significant benefit of a period of incubation on problem solving, including creative problems and simpler puzzles.

A longer incubation time led to stronger effects, especially with creative problems rather than simpler tasks such as word puzzles. Sio and Ormerod (2009) suggested that this was because of the multi-solution nature of creative problems. A longer time period and more opportunities to think about a problem from different angles and in different contexts led to overall benefits. This was not the case with more straightforward problems.

Control of incubation

An interesting feature of incubation is that it has the potential to be strategically controlled by the creator or student. We can plan to take some time away from a problem, choose to schedule creative sessions over several days, or take the decision to 'sleep on it'. All of these are metacognitive decisions; they reflect the fact that creativity doesn't just happen. It can be planned for.

The idea of strategically controlling one's own creativity further pushes back against the idea that creative thinking depends on luck, rather than judgement and preparation. In line with the famous Louis Pasteur quote, 'Chance favours the prepared mind' (Gibbons, 2013), students and other creators can take steps to learn about how creativity works, and establish a mental toolkit of strategies to manage their own creativity. If they do so, a creative breakthrough is more likely to occur.

While we have championed the key role of foundational knowledge in creativity throughout this book, researchers have established that such metacognitive tools – knowing what you know and how to apply it – can be a better strategy than just practising basic knowledge (Wegerif, 2004).

For the remainder of this chapter, we will explore some of the ways that students can be guided to control and plan for their own creativity. We begin by exploring how incubation can be planned for in the classroom, and then address how some of the other key principles discussed in previous chapters (e.g. connections; constraints; uncertainty) can be seen as metacognitive strategies. In doing so, we begin to outline what a metacognitive toolkit for creativity might look like.

Planning for incubation

In classrooms, a lot of what we do connects to the preparation stage of Wallas' model, but we can also facilitate incubation by building in a delay.

How long should delays be – seconds? minutes? hours? It's not immediately obvious from the research! Ritter and Dijksterhuis (2014) note that incubation could last for various periods of time, from minutes, to overnight, to many days or weeks away from a problem.

Some researchers have used very short delays (a minute or less), but these were tried with simpler problems (Sio & Ormerod, 2009). For creative tasks, a short break could involve taking around 5-15 minutes away from a task, and there is evidence that such breaks can have benefits (Baird et al., 2012). This is good news, as this length of break could be built into a typical school lesson. Meanwhile, other research has focused on the benefits of longer breaks – a day or more.

A general principle is that any break can help, but a longer one is likely to have stronger benefits (Sio & Ormerod, 2009). This may seem familiar – just as with brainstorming (see Chapter 11), a longer period of time can lead to more or better ideas.

> **Pause to reflect**
> What kind of other tasks might your students do if they were to take a short break away from a task – a quarter of an hour or under? At what point in a lesson might this occur?

Productive delays

In terms of what students *do* during a delay, this depends a lot on why incubation helps. In brief, key theoretical explanations have focused on conscious versus unconscious processes:

- Perhaps the thinker is thinking consciously about the problem during the delay, and gradually solving it.
- Alternatively, perhaps any processing is going on without the student's conscious awareness.

Without getting into too many technical details, the evidence seems to favour the idea that at least some 'cognitive work' can happen unconsciously. For example, Baird et al. (2012), in their study of breaks during creative work, found that learners who did a simple task during their break subsequently did better than those who did no task at all. It was better to be occupied. This supports the idea that unconscious work on the problem is taking place; if the efforts were conscious, it would be better to engage in rest with no distractions.

(If this all sounds rather unscientific, be assured that unconscious processing is a mainstream and uncontroversial aspect of cognitive science. All the term means is that some mental processing is happening without our focused attention or awareness – while distracted, for example, or while asleep. For example, researchers agree that 'implicit' memory processes happen without our attention. During time away from a task, as we recall some memories and forget others, the strength of mental connections can change (Anderson et al., 1994). This could affect recall and thinking when we return to a creative task.)

Sleep and associations

As suggested above, there is a lot to be said for a longer period of incubation, even though it will be much harder for the teacher to determine what a student will be doing during that time (the hope will be that for at least some of the time, they will be engaged in reflective mind-wandering!). Longer breaks often include at least one night's sleep, and this can be significant for the creative process.

Our minds appear to be more malleable and open to unusual solutions during or immediately after sleep (again, think how many of the earlier anecdotes involved sleeping/dreaming). Researchers Rasch and Born (2013) found that engaging in sleep, or even a nap, led to a 'hyperassociative' phase, where people were more open to making new connections, particularly after waking up. This suggests that a period of incubation should ideally include at least one night, perhaps more.

A further implication is that students might try engaging with creative tasks at different times of day. They will be in different states of mind, and may find that creative solutions come more easily to mind, especially for more involved creative tasks, such as designing a project, or composing a piece of writing or music.

Of course, another thing that can change over time is a student's mood. The anecdotes about insights often hint that creators might work well in a more relaxed state of mind, but evidence on this is mixed, and attempts to manipulate mood experimentally have not been shown to boost the effects of incubation (e.g. Campbell, 2021). Still, even if it's not worth aiming to change a learner's mood in class, it will naturally vary over longer timescales. It's also well understood that mood has effects on cognition and problem solving (e.g. Shen et al., 2019), even if this is hard to control.

Applications to Practice

Metacognition is a highly practical and applied area of cognitive science. After all, it is all about the strategies that learners use. You may already see some obvious applications, based on what has been said so far. In the next section, we will try to make this more specific and concrete.

Applying incubation

So far in this chapter, we have explained the evidence that incubation – a delay of some kind after first tackling a problem – can be effective, and what's more, students don't need to be resting during this time – they can do another task. Indeed, it appears that a delay where your students are occupied will be more beneficial than a simple rest period. This is a win-win; students can be productively occupied in other work, and incubation will still proceed!

The immediate application of incubation, then, is simply to plan for a gap between students first tackling a creative task or project, and their later work on it. In general, planning a delay comes at little cost to the teacher, and nor does it demand more class time – it is just a matter of scheduling the work over two or more shorter sessions rather than one long one. For example, a creative or problem-solving task that is typically tackled during a two-hour afternoon lesson could instead be started in one hour of day 1, followed by a further hour on the morning of day 2.

Examples of building in incubation in this way might include:

- Taking time away from storyboarding
- Doing an initial plan of an essay then taking a break
- Developing a business plan over several weekly sessions

If possible, give some consideration to the task(s) that happen in between the two sessions. Based on the research discussed earlier in this chapter, it may be that a particularly demanding task counteracts some of the benefits, with the best outcomes – the sweet spot – happening at a medium level of demand. This is in line with the anecdotal evidence, mentioned earlier in this chapter, that creative insights often emerge when people are relaxed but occupied, for example on a walk or bus ride. On balance, then, a delay that is planned mid-lesson should probably involve an occupying but enjoyable task, such as reading, or tackling simple puzzles.

In addition, where possible, you should plan for a gap of a day or more – leaving a task overnight, for example, or returning to it the following week. This would both build in a delay that includes a night's sleep, and vary the time of day at which the work was done. Bear in mind that the students should have prepared for and fully grappled with the creative task. Incubation is not going to occur if they didn't properly get started – or if it was so easy, they finished it in the first session!

Forgetting

Have you ever found that you struggle to recall a name, fact or piece of terminology when asked, only for it to spring to mind a few hours later?

This phenomenon is similar to the moment of insight after incubation, and both link to the workings of long-term memory. When we retrieve words or ideas from memory, different options are in competition with each other, with the retrieved item 'winning' this cognitive competition (Anderson et al., 1994), whether it's correct or not.

It will then be harder to recall or think of related items, especially when they are closely related or competing in memory (Little et al., 2011). This means that there is a benefit to taking enough time to forget unhelpful solutions; simply allowing a few hours to pass before students return to a problem might help them to come up with different ideas. Forgetting does not appear to be the main cause of the incubation benefit (Gilhooly et al., 2013), but the two can work in parallel.

There is a great opportunity to teach students to apply this as a strategy, as it helps to get them thinking about controlling their own thought processes. A good example to start them off is how writing tasks often benefit from returning with 'fresh eyes'. The benefit of forgetting here is that they have to read the text more like an outsider would – and are more likely to notice their mistakes.

From there, you could discuss how other forms of mistakes and automatic assumptions could be overcome with a delay. Accordingly, creative work can benefit from building in a delay and a rethink in the process. This may be particularly useful for classroom tasks where there is a conventional conclusion that students often jump to.

Activating prior learning

The idea of thinking about our own learning and forgetting brings us on to another fundamental idea in metacognition – a learner knowing what they know. Rather than taking knowledge for granted, it helps to shine a spotlight on it, and to invite students to think about the state of their own knowledge and what they might need to address. For example, they might need to reflect on:

- What they know (and can use)
- What needs to be refreshed
- Where they might need to add to their existing knowledge

Much has been said in this book about the role of knowledge in creativity, and of course we tend to think of prior knowledge as something that happens *before* problem solving. However, something that could usefully be done midway through a task, during that incubation period, is to check for gaps and to brush up on factual knowledge.

This again is a good strategy for students to learn as they manage their own creativity. It helps to tackle the myth that creativity is random (see above) or that it's a transferable skill. They may also benefit from reviewing and looking back at their initial ideas and assumptions. Such activities could include:

- Re-reading task instructions
- Looking at model answers
- Doing extended reading around a task
- Retrieving from memory – and then checking – prior knowledge

All of these tasks serve to consolidate your students' expertise, and many also involve exposure to successful models of creative work. And even if the additional reading/learning doesn't directly help them with their creative problem, it won't hurt to have learned a bit more about it!

A toolkit of strategies

The role of forgetting and managing our own knowledge point the way to a couple of further strategies that students can deliberately employ.

Earlier, we talked about how metacognition involves developing in students a toolkit of strategies, and this can be cumulative across their studies. Metacognition is, in general, developmental, and strategies will take time to embed. All the same, students can build up a toolkit of strategies for their creative work, just like they can be taught a set of study habits and revision skills.

Many of the relevant strategies link back to things which were mentioned earlier in this book, and we won't repeat them here. They concern a student managing constraints, connections, cues, and many more factors that help to spark creative ideas. For example, when focusing on connections, students can be taught about deliberately mixing things up and looking for surprising connections. Once they understand this, it becomes a strategy that they can apply for themselves.

Further ideas from this book that can form the basis of strategies include:

- Trying to think of associations/make links between two items or ideas
- Using random prompts or cues
- Asking 'What if …?' questions
- Putting things in unexpected orders
- Brainstorming (see Chapter 11)
- Preparation strategies: brushing up on foundational knowledge
- Applying constraints of various kinds
- Varying your practice

And so on …! You might want to look at these ideas one at a time, perhaps once a month, with your class. One or more of the above ideas could become a regular strategy in your classroom, either done at the start of a task, or something that students learn to do in a self-regulated way when they are feeling stuck. That way, it becomes part of their metacognition, and their capacity to manage their own creative process (read more about creativity and connections in Chapter 5).

Using specific names for techniques could follow. Move slowly; just as with developing a repertoire of study skills, you don't want to overload students by giving them too many things to try at one time. It could also be done on a whole-school basis, emphasising that creativity is not just about the arts subjects (see Chapter 4).

Metacognitive awareness

So far, this section has looked at several strategies that students could use to guide their own creative process. To an extent, this depends on having at least a basic understanding of creativity.

As with other areas of metacognition and self-regulated learning, then, we have to consider the extent to which students have an awareness of how learning works, and to support them to gradually take ownership of the process for themselves (see EEF, 2018; Firth, 2024). After all, you can't use creative tools if you don't know they exist, what they are for, or how they are best used.

We have seen that teachers can build these strategies (such as delays) into their lessons. But there is another side to learning to be metacognitive – students also need to recognise when to apply these strategies. They won't always be appropriate!

For this reason, developing metacognition about creativity involves raising their awareness of what creativity is (and what it is not). Hopefully, you will recognise that this has been a key feature throughout the book. For example, we have explored:

- The standard definition of creativity
- Myths about creativity vs. scientific approaches
- Ideas about the scope of creativity (Big-C and little-c, etc.)
- Creativity across the curriculum
- The connection between creativity and problem solving

Of course, this is too much to cover all at once. However, the point remains that understanding creativity is part of understanding themselves, and understanding learning. If they are going to apply a toolkit of metacognitive strategies to creative tasks, students need to gradually come to know what creativity is. They need to realise that some popular assumptions about it are myths. This is an area where a student's intuition will often lead them astray.

This leads to a metacognitive strategy in its own right – one where we debunk myths and develop in our students an awareness of what creativity is, and how it applies to their learning. At first, coming to understand creativity will probably require a lot of scaffolding and examples from the teacher. Over time, though, they may come up with their own thoughts and ideas about it – creatively!

> ### In depth: Student learning communities
>
> The co-authors of this book have explored the potential benefits of teaching school students about creativity using a student learning community (Badger & Firth, 2023). The student learning community consisted of a group of volunteer Year 12 students who met three times per term to cover topics such as motivation, critical thinking and creativity. Pre-reading fed into sessions where students discussed how ideas could be applied to their own studies and extracurricular pursuits, and reflected on where they had changed their approaches.
>
> These initial sessions also set up a space where students felt free to openly share their ideas, engaging in metacognitive talk about learning. Students were introduced to many of the ideas discussed in this book, for example that creativity applies across all subjects, not just the traditionally 'creative' subjects, the difference between 'little-c' and 'Big-C' creativity, and practical strategies.
>
> Towards the end of the academic year, the student group was tasked with putting together activities for their peers as well as a presentation for staff – novel and authentic tasks. They were given free rein over what they presented to these different groups, and tended to devise their own examples and activities rather than using ones that had been used during the session.
>
> This project showed students' capacity to engage in metacognitive talk about creativity, and to use the strategies to support their own creative thinking.

Conclusion

In this chapter, we have looked in more depth at the popular idea that creativity is mysterious and impossible to define, and that it comes via a flash of insight. We have seen that when looked at over a longer timescale, these insights tend to come as part of a long process of preparation. They are neither random nor impossible to understand, and they often occur following a period of what psychologists call incubation.

What's more, incubation gives rise to a set of strategies that can be applied by the teacher, and which students can use in their own self-regulated study, too.

This idea may appear to conflict with what has been said about creativity as a transferable skill. And certainly, learners will not succeed in creative tasks without the foundational knowledge and routines of the relevant discipline.

However, a strategic, metacognitive approach to learning is about helping students to use their knowledge. It recognises that while knowledge and routines are necessary, they are not always sufficient.

Can these strategies help students to transfer their creative skills from one domain to another? Although transfer is always challenging (see Chapter 6), a key way in which it can be supported is via metacognitive awareness (Bransford et al., 2000). If a learner is to transfer a skill or process from one context to another, it really helps if a learner knows what they know, and they have a clear understanding of how and when that knowledge will be relevant. As we have seen, it is also helpful if they learn specific strategies, have these modelled in class, and practise using them.

As a specific example, the role of constraints is relevant to a range of very different tasks – for example, to both creative writing and designing science projects. The strategy can be transferred between these two very different domains, and help with the same processes (creative problem solving and ideation) in both. But this will only work if the student has the foundational knowledge and skills to succeed in both tasks *and* knows about the creative strategy.

Overall, then, metacognition – a strategic approach to learning whereby learners think about their own learning and make decisions – is highly applicable to creativity. With guidance, students can come to learn about creativity myths and why they are wrong, and about specific strategies and how to use them. Over time, a metacognitive approach to creativity will lay the foundations for them to engage in successful creative work well beyond the classroom.

Discussion Questions

1) Thinking about books or movies that you have enjoyed, how is creativity portrayed across these media? Think of images of scientists, inventors, composers, etc. Do they feature a flash of inspiration?

2) Had you come across the idea of incubation before reading this book? If so, what did you think about it, and did you recognise a possible link to teaching?

3) Can you think of an example in your teaching where the preparation, incubation, illumination, verification model would apply? What would verification involve?

4) How do you feel about students having a mental toolkit of strategies to manage their own creativity. Are your own students close to this? Is it a work in progress?

Professional Learning Tasks

Task 1

The chapter discussed the use of incubation and delays. From your practice, make a list of activities or projects that could be usefully split across more than one day.

Task 2

Reflect on how the ideas in this chapter combine with some of the other things you have read about in the book, for example building blocks (Chapter 3), varied practice (Chapter 6), constraints (Chapter 7). Could any of these things be strategies? And if so, how would you prioritise talking about them to a class? Make a list, in order of priority, of which strategies you might want to practise with a class.

Task 3

Metacognition applies to educators, too. Where do you think your own learning ranks on issues of creativity and cognitive science? Grab a notebook, and try to judge your current level on a scale from 1 to 100 on two key things:

- Your professional learning of cognitive science
- Your professional learning of creativity

Of course, sometimes people misjudge their own expertise (a metacognitive error) and expertise also changes. See Firth (2024) for a fuller exploration of metacognition across classroom situations.

10 Creativity and Motivation

When you were younger, were you asked what you wanted to be when you grew up? How did you answer? And did your response then bear any relation to your current occupation?

It's a commonly asked question, and not just at younger ages. There is a version in secondary schools, too; students are often interviewed or asked to take quizzes about their interests and aspirations, and the responses are used to help guide them towards a future career.

All of this does make some sense, of course; in both school and the workplace, a person is more likely to thrive if they enjoy what they do. And everyone loves to find out what drives a person – what makes them tick.

However, the link between what we enjoy and what we are good at is not as straightforward as it might first appear. In this chapter we will explore this idea of a learner's intrinsic passions, and consider what this means for their engagement in creative activities.

The Myth

Intuitively, it might seem that we should aim to help young people to find their passions. There is an assumption that if they are passionate about something then they should be automatically motivated to follow such passions.

The questions about careers (at any age) imply that learners have an intrinsic motivation to become 'something', and that adults should try to tap into this, uncover it, and then support and encourage students to realise these aspirations.

This approach implies that everyone has an identity and a set of preferences deep within, and, perhaps, that we should strive to 'find ourselves' (this corresponds closely with the idea that children have innate creativity – see Chapter 2). However, psychologists have found both identity and motivation to be more malleable and open to change than we might at first assume.

In short, the reality is a bit more complicated. This means that the idea that only some people have interests and passions that make them suited to creative careers can be considered a myth. And more broadly, whether a student is motivated to do your subject or any other has a lot to do with how the learning is set up.

Exploring the Research

The value of creative motivation

Before returning to the myth and the relevant evidence, it's worth briefly exploring why motivation is so important to creative thinking.

Motivation is one of those cases where we all know it when we see it. We can all think of people who seem incredibly driven and successful. And we can probably think of the opposite case, too – talented people who tell us they're going to make it as a musician or novelist (or, indeed, as a scientist), but fail to put in enough time or work to succeed.

Motivation is notoriously hard to define, but we can look at it in terms of how curious and passionate someone is to engage in tasks, in education or elsewhere. Behaviourally, we can look at how quick they are to get started, how long they persist, and how intensely they work.

Motivation is also a key facet of self-regulated learning. Students have multiple goals, and having the motivation to work towards academic goals, as well as the skills to do so, will impact strongly on whether they master a topic (Boekaerts & Corno, 2005).

Any of the ideas and strategies described throughout this book so far depend to some extent on motivation:

- A more motivated and curious learner will garner more knowledge, and thus have more of the building blocks of creativity. They are more likely to develop expertise.
- Being playful with this knowledge and looking for new and interesting connections depends on motivation.
- A motivated learner may see constraints as an interesting challenge, and persist rather than giving up.
- The metacognition described in the previous chapter (see Chapter 9) depends on learners selecting and applying strategies through their own volition.

There is important evidence from practice, too. In an extensive study of the workplace, Amabile (1996) found that there was a close connection between motivation and creativity – motivated workers came up with better ideas. Amabile developed these findings into a model which considers creativity as stemming from the interaction between three things (Amabile, 1983, 1996):

- Expertise in a domain
- Creative thinking skills
- Motivation

The updated 1996 model also recognises that the social environment surrounds and influences all of these factors, as shown in Figure 10.1.

Amabile's model fits well with the ideas discussed so far in this book. Expertise, built on domain-specific knowledge, is a key factor for having creative ideas. However, it's not sufficient; students also need to use this well, via thinking skills and strategies. Motivation completes the picture.

So, where do our motivations come from? It's not as simple as we might at first assume, and broadly, research suggests that we don't just 'have' motivations and passions. They often arise from circumstances.

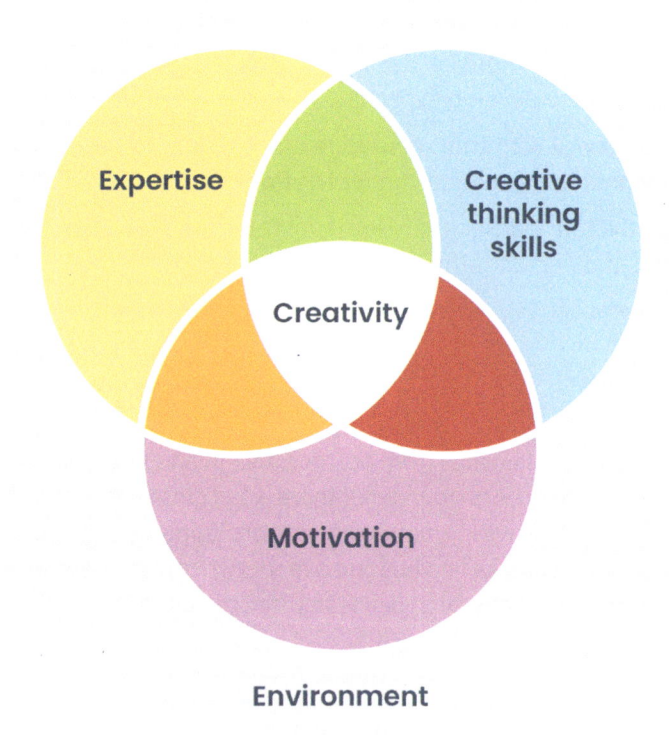

Figure 10.1 Amabile's componential model of creativity

Not always fixed

Let's briefly consider some of the surprising research that suggests that people's motivations are not as fixed as we might assume – even when they themselves believe this to be the case.

In one classic social psychology study by Darley and Batson (1973), men who were training to be a minister were given a personality test about their religious beliefs, and then told that they had to go to another building to give a short talk. Some were told to speak about the parable of the Good Samaritan (a famous Christian story about kindness), while others were told to think on their feet (message condition). Also, some were told, 'you're late, but if you hurry, you should make it', while others were not (hurry condition).

The participants then encountered a person lying on the street. The researchers' true purpose was to find out if the trainees would help or not.

Results from the Darley and Batson study showed that personal beliefs did *not* predict helping behaviour, while message had a weak effect. It was the circumstances (being in a hurry or not) that had the strongest effect on helping. This speaks against the idea of a fixed set of traits, and also implies that we often don't know ourselves very well!

In an even more famous study from the early days of social psychology, researcher Solomon Asch showed that people were willing to deny the evidence of their own eyes. Participants would say that one line was longer than another, even though it clearly was not, simply because a group of (fake) fellow participants all gave the wrong answer. Three-quarters of participants conformed to the group at least once, giving an obviously wrong answer (Asch, 1955). This shows that, at least on occasion, temporary circumstances can motivate behaviour and choices.

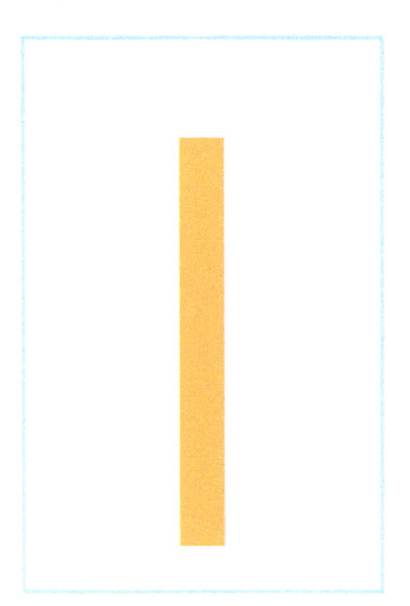

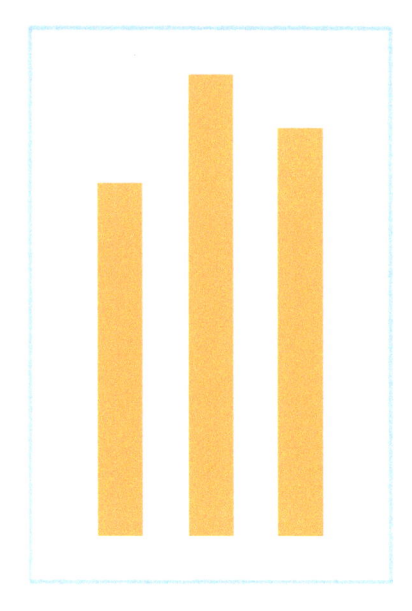

Figure 10.2 Asch's lines

In schools, too, students may think that a particular subject or career is their passion, and fail to account for the role of circumstances, including peer pressure. The studies above may be a little dated, but they speak against the idea that we can just ask people what they want or what they will do, and treat the answer as valid.

Identity foreclosure

Overall, then, motivation is very important to creativity, but we might have some doubts about the accuracy of students' responses to being asked what they want to do when they grow up.

In his book *Think Again*, Adam Grant explicitly warns against asking the question at all. He explains that it has the potential to trap people into 'identity foreclosure – when we settle prematurely on a sense of self without enough due diligence, and close our minds to alternative selves' (Grant, 2021, p. 230). In other words, students may be prone to labelling themselves, and once labelled, this will influence future behaviour.

Many (though not all) people are biased towards appearing consistent in their behaviour (Cialdini et al., 1995), and having said, for example, that they want to be a scientist or an artist, they will strive to play this role. They may, in effect, be self-stereotyping.

Growth theory of interest

The idea that people can have inaccurate beliefs about themselves as a learner may sound familiar to educators. It's not too far away, in principle, from the idea of growth and fixed mindset (e.g. see Dweck, 2006).

For all its detractors, the idea of a growth mindset – whereby students don't see their strengths and weaknesses as fixed, but instead recognise that they can improve these through practice – can highlight the value of learners being open to change. It emphasises that they should avoid labelling themselves (especially if those labels are negative).

In a very similar way, labelling our own interests and passions can impact later motivation to change. Some researchers call this a fixed theory of interest, in contrast to a growth theory of interest. The latter describes people who believe that interests can be developed through experience.

In an experimental study, O'Keefe et al. (2018) looked at how these theories of interest affected a person's motivation to engage with a challenging task. They found that those who had a growth theory of interest were more likely to stick with tasks when things became more complex and challenging. The researchers concluded that 'students endorsing a growth theory may have more realistic beliefs about the pursuit of interests' (p. 1663).

This again casts some doubt on the accuracy of people's beliefs about their own interests. If they choose what they believe to be their passion, but then give up when encountering difficulties and frustrations, then maybe these things weren't really their passions after all.

You might recall that *perseverance* is one of the five creative learning habits introduced earlier in the book (see Chapter 5). Persevering through difficulties is important to produce valuable creative work. The ideas above suggest that having a growth theory of interest would help people to navigate past difficulties and to deal with setbacks and uncertainty (proactively planning for setbacks, as discussed in Chapter 8, might be another way to support this).

Where do motivations come from?

Having cast some doubt on the idea that students' choices or actions are much of a guide to their true self, it's worth asking – where *do* our passions and motivations come from?

There certainly are psychologists who have argued that there *is* such a thing as a true self, and that people can uncover it under the right circumstances. Humanist researcher Carl Rogers (1961), for example, believed that if we are shown unconditional positivity by our parents and educators, we can all discover our true self.

Others have been more sceptical that such a thing as our true self even exists. A group of researchers who have studied identity suggest that it has a powerful effect on our actions, but also that it is quite malleable, and open to change across different social circumstances (Tajfel & Turner, 1979; Turner et al., 1987). They also suggest that people look to categorise themselves as part of one or more prominent social groups – often showing prejudice towards rival groups. Overall, again, human identity and motivations are often more malleable than we might assume.

A compromise position was established by researchers Ryan and Deci (2000, 2017) in their influential *self-determination theory* (SDT). This theory suggests that humans do have certain intrinsic motivators, which the researchers present as basic needs. However, we are also very strongly influenced by circumstances, and in particular by our peer group and our prior learning.

As well as a clearer explanation of the link between intrinsic motivation and extrinsic rewards (see below), the theory sets out three factors in particular, each of which is viewed by the researchers as a fundamental human need:

- Competence
- Relatedness
- Autonomy

We will now look at each of these needs in turn, because each is an important factor in motivation, and each therefore affects creativity.

SDT need 1: Competence

The first need set out by Ryan and Deci is *competence*, meaning having the knowledge and skills to successfully complete a task. The key idea here is that people will be motivated by what they are good at. That is to say, prior learning, and especially their current levels of knowledge and skills, will directly impact on their motivation.

In many ways, this directly contradicts the popular assumption, touched on above, that people need to be motivated towards something *first*, and then later will become skilled. It flips this on its head, suggesting that competence comes first. We tend to enjoy what we are good at, rather than vice versa.

There is a lot of evidence to support that contention. Adding to Ryan and Deci's work, an extensive review of longitudinal studies by Vu et al. (2024) concluded that while each factor (motivation and achievement) affects the other, 'the influence of previous academic achievement wielded twice as strong influence on subsequent motivation compared to the reverse direction' (p. 152).

On balance this is good news for educators, as it is much easier to support students to be successful in their endeavours than it is to try to motivate them more directly. Indeed, focusing our efforts on the motivational side of this relationship by choosing topics and activities linked to our students' passions may in fact backfire.

Overall, the role of competence, as it applies to creativity, means that learners will be more motivated and therefore more creative when they have domain-specific knowledge and knowledge of creative strategies, including the metacognitive knowledge discussed in the previous chapter.

> **Pause to reflect**
> Have you observed students becoming more interested and motivated about a topic once they learn more about it - i.e. when their competence increases?

SDT need 2: Relatedness

A second key need described by SDT is relatedness. In brief, this means that people have an innate need for social interaction, and as a result, we find activities more motivating if we share them with like-minded peers. Far from being an individual trait, motivation depends on our social environment.

This does *not* mean that everything needs to be done in a group in order to be motivating. Things still connect to the social context when we do them alone. Relatedness is feeling a sense of belonging, and also of the social relevance of the task. Does it matter, and specifically, does it matter to people like them? Is it connected to their social identity?

Again, this is good news for educators, because the social environment of our classrooms and schools is something we can influence. In the classroom, 'relatedness is deeply associated with a student feeling that the teacher genuinely likes, respects, and values [them]' (Niemiec & Ryan, 2009, p. 139).

> **Pause to reflect**
> In what ways might you support your students' psychological need for relatedness?

SDT need 3: Autonomy

The third key need described by SDT is autonomy. This means making your own decisions, rather than being told what to do.

Autonomy is often conflated with having absolute freedom, but as discussed in Chapter 7, entirely open choices can be paralysing; creativity often flourishes within some constraints. Instead, we should consider how and when some choice can be incorporated into our lessons, for example adding in some 'structured uncertainty' (see Chapter 8).

As discussed in Chapter 8, creativity involves taking risks; by valuing all students' responses we can build a supportive learning environment that helps students to embrace the uncertainty associated with creativity.

> **Pause to reflect**
> In what ways might you support your students' psychological need for autonomy?

What does the research say about making classes fun and exciting?

One way in which teachers often try to motivate disengaged students is to add an element of fun and competition into activities. Every teacher wants students to enjoy their lessons. However, the research gives cause for caution about this strategy for promoting creativity (Beghetto & Kaufman, 2014).

First, as motivation for a task or topic is mostly developed rather than being inherent in a person, we can't assume that this 'fun' will lead to any lasting enjoyment. Based on the different needs that students have, what one person finds fun may not be enjoyable to another. It may seem to a Maths teacher that an arithmetic game would be loads of fun – but then, the teacher is competent at the task. Things are a lot less motivating if we struggle to make progress.

While games are sometimes really useful in education, the competitive nature of gamified activities encourages social comparisons between students. If students all share a common identity and have an established rapport, they will typically enjoy playing together. However, if there are divisions, games and contests could emphasise these. And many games emphasise competence – if you are the student who always seems to be coming last, such competitions may become demotivating.

Overall, such approaches emphasise the extrinsic features of a task such as rewards and quick completion, rather than requiring students to think deeply. This is not to say that all extrinsic motivators are a problem, but these can be employed in a way that fits better with self-determination theory. This is considered in the next section.

Intrinsic and extrinsic motivation

Motivation is often characterised as coming in just two forms – intrinsic and extrinsic:

- Intrinsic motivation means drives that come from within the person, and derives from the inherent satisfaction from doing the activity itself.
- Extrinsic motivation means drives based on external pressures such as rewards, and is linked to the performance of an activity to attain a separable outcome.

From what we have said so far, you might suspect that lumping motivation into just two types is a bit simplistic. And indeed, SDT tries to move us beyond this simple dichotomy. Instead, it places motivation on a continuum from intrinsic to extrinsic, and shows how it can change over time (Ryan & Deci, 2000).

In particular, something that starts off as being motivated purely by external pressures and rewards can *become* intrinsically motivated. For example, reading may be a chore when you're a child, and later, as a teen or adult, a hobby that you do purely for enjoyment.

As you might imagine, motivations don't change instantly. There are several stages to this process:

- At first, behaviour is driven by the demands or rewards, for example a student who completes a task solely to avoid a detention.
- Over time, the student may seek to maintain self-esteem by complying with expectations and avoiding punishments. They may want to be seen as a 'good student' by teachers.
- Later, the student may see meeting such goals as personally important and in line with their identity. For example, they may pride themselves on meeting deadlines. They may even set external rewards for themselves, consciously managing their own motivation.

There are no end of extrinsic motivators in education – deadlines, rewards, punishments, praise, and the goal of external examinations – and it is easy to assume that such factors would decrease creativity. However, the stages above show that things are more complex. Extrinsic motivation can play a valuable role in educational settings; it can act in synergy with intrinsic motivation (Amabile, 1993), and what starts as external can become more bound up with an individual's choice and identity. Overall, though, things are not going to be truly *intrinsically* motivating unless they meet one or more of the needs discussed in the previous section.

> **Pause to reflect**
> Can you identify an example from your own life where an external motivator had a beneficial effect on motivation and creativity? What about for your students?

In depth: Extended projects

The Extended Project Qualification (EPQ) can be taken alongside A-levels. It is an externally assessed qualification that demonstrates the importance of both extrinsic and intrinsic motivational factors in the production of a creative piece. Students are required to produce a 5,000-word essay or an artefact with an accompanying report and have completely free choice on the topic they choose. Comparable extended projects form part of many other qualification systems internationally.

The free choice aspect of the EPQ provides students with a high level of autonomy, although there are still some constraints as the topic must not be covered in their A-level courses and must be suitable for a sixth form student. The qualification involves taught elements to support students to develop their research skills, which builds their levels of competence. Each student is assigned a supervisor who meets with them regularly for one to one discussions to give feedback on the student's progress, building relatedness.

Alongside the essay or artefact, students are also required to produce a project log where they reflect on their progress, including any challenges they have faced or changes they have made, and record the recommendations from their supervisor. The project log imposes intermediate deadlines on the larger task of completing the full essay or artefact, which prevents procrastination. In addition, the fact that any changes made to the project along the way are celebrated helps students to remain open-minded. The assessment credits both the final essay or artefact and the project log so students can see the value in both the final creative output and the process. In some schools, a showcase event is set up for students to gather feedback on their projects from peers, teachers and parents.

This example illustrates how providing clear structures, along with a consideration of autonomy, competence and relatedness, can help teachers to better motivate students to successfully complete open-ended, creative tasks, even those linked to high-stakes assessments.

Applications to Practice

As discussed earlier, there is an intricate link between motivation and creativity. Our students will be more creative, and more successfully creative, if they are motivated. However, motivation will also follow success and the feeling of competence that accompanies it – a virtuous circle. The following strategies therefore focus on ways to boost and manage motivation in their creative work.

Timing (procrastination, creativity and motivation)

A lack of motivation is often associated with procrastination, which in turn is usually seen as linked to poorer student outcomes. And certainly, it can be frustrating when our students are slow to get started. However, there is some evidence that procrastination is not always detrimental to performance. At times, perhaps we should tolerate it a little more!

In two experiments and a field study, Shin and Grant (2021) found a curvilinear relationship between procrastination and creativity; moderate procrastination led to more creative outputs in all three cases. However, a caveat was that moderate procrastination was more likely to help in cases of high intrinsic motivation. Similar results were found in a study of Chinese factory workers (Adeel et al., 2023).

Surprisingly, this suggests that students can start a task too soon. In *Originals*, Grant (2016) coined the term 'pre-crastination' for the act of starting and finishing a task too quickly. One possible reason why pre-crastination leads to worse outcomes is that it could reflect rushing, or a lack of careful thought. A degree of procrastination, on the other hand, leaves time for novel insights to appear.

This may sound familiar; in Chapter 9 we discussed the idea of incubation. In short, there can be benefits to time away from a task; insights can arise after such a delay. Combine this with motivation, and you can start to see that students may be able to manage delays on tasks, seeing them less as a problem and more as a strategy that can be put to work.

They shouldn't be pushed to get started before they have had time to mull it over. At the same time, as the Shin and Grant study shows, there comes a point where (on average) a delay becomes too long.

The effects might also depend on what students do *during* the delay. Kooren et al. (2024) defined two types of procrastination: active and passive. Passive procrastination is characterised by the inability to act, whereas active procrastination is marked by a preference and deliberate decision to work under pressure. Passive procrastination was more strongly associated with poor academic performance. Active procrastination actually had a small *positive* correlation with academic performance.

Overall, educators should be aware that, especially for creative tasks, delays don't always indicate a lack of motivation. As long as the student has at least some basic level of motivation to do the task, a delay can have a useful purpose.

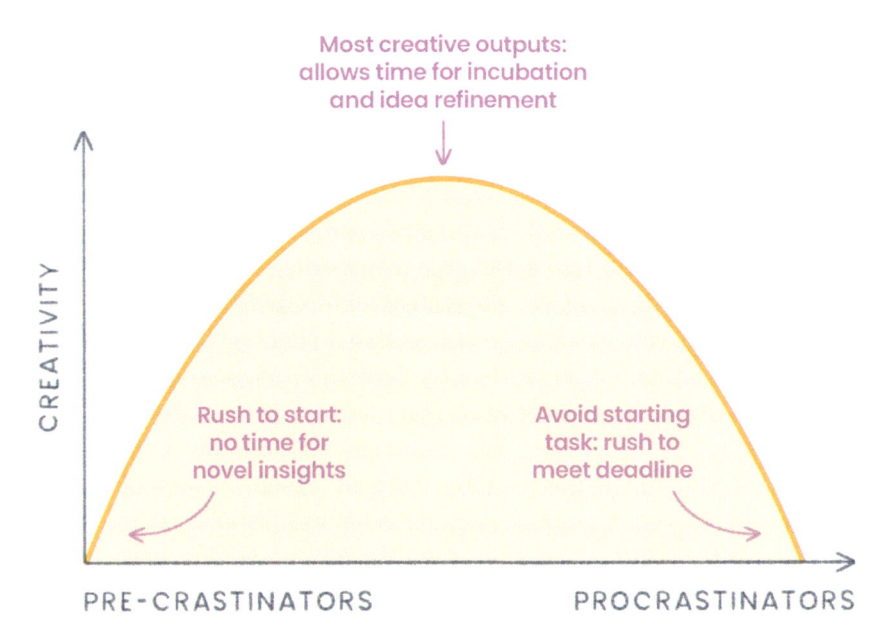

Figure 10.3 The timing of delays can affect creativity

> **Pause to reflect**
> Do you see yourself more as a pre-crastinator (starting things too soon) or a procrastinator? If you are more of a pre-crastinator, how might you incorporate some (active) procrastination into your life to increase your creativity?

Rewards and deadlines

Although they get a bad rap, extrinsic motivators such as deadlines and rewards are not always harmful, as we have seen, and can serve a useful purpose. Many students are poor predictors of how long tasks will take (Buehler et al., 1994), so externally imposed deadlines may help them to manage their productivity and output.

However, the concept of pre-crastination (see previous section) suggests we should think carefully about deadlines, and avoid rushing students into tackling creative tasks without sufficient thought.

Some simple classroom strategies to make better use of deadlines and praise include:

- Increasing wait time after questions. Wait time is a valuable formative strategy, prompting students to think more deeply about questions (Wiliam, 2011; see also Chapter 2), and this certainly applies to creative questions. We've all had students who blurt out the first thing that comes into their head, but would be better off waiting for their ideas to percolate for longer.
- Correspondingly, we might want to reduce or delay feedback, giving students time to think things through. Given time to reflect, their ideas might surprise us!
- Group work involving creative tasks can be dominated by the first idea that someone comes up with, or by louder students. Accordingly, it can be best to set an individual task first, insisting that everyone comes up with their own ideas (see also Chapter 11 for a discussion of group brainstorming).

- Providing students with clear criteria for evaluating their ideas and work. This can support meaningful analysis and discussion of creative work, rather than encouraging completion and speed.
- Set tasks at the end of a lesson, so that a problem can then be returned to at the start of the next lesson when students have had a chance to mull over possible solutions outside of class (allowing for incubation).
- Encourage planning and redrafting. Intermediate deadlines can be set for a plan and a first draft, ideally with time in between for feedback.
- For all of the above ideas, praising students when they rethink or modify their idea (provided theirs is a good idea), rather than for working quickly or getting the 'right' answer.

Strategies linked to competence, relatedness and autonomy

Given the centrality of competence, relatedness and autonomy to motivation, it's worth thinking about simple tweaks to practice we can make to harness these a bit more.

Competence is, as noted earlier, about what students know and can do. Clearly, a major way to boost this is to focus more on developing the knowledge and basic procedures of your subject, working towards learners who show adaptive expertise (see Chapter 6).

However, sometimes students are poor judges of how good they are. They may believe that they lack competence in tasks such as writing or public speaking - or, indeed, creativity - but the evidence may suggest otherwise. This presents an important role for feedback and self-assessment in order to provide a more accurate picture of their strengths.

Relatedness means connecting to students' social identity, but be wary about this - it's easy to make flawed assumptions about what matters to students (stereotyped books about football given to boys, for example). Also, remember that our passions are more developed than discovered, as noted earlier in this chapter. Our emphasis should be more on building a sense of common purpose in the classroom.

Activities that can help to develop a sense of relatedness in the classroom include collaboratively setting targets, and discussing how to craft and improve work within a supportive classroom community. It's also possible to link feedback to relatedness, generating a sense of a common purpose (Lucas & Spencer, 2017). Whilst simplistic rewards are often best avoided, we should feel free to give genuine praise to a student when they make progress.

Regarding autonomy, consider – how motivating do *you* find it to be told what to read, what movies to watch, or what to eat for your lunch? People love a choice! And while free choice isn't always practical (or actually helpful – see above and Chapter 7), we can seek to work in simpler choices. Having a choice between reading book A and reading book B, for example, or between a selection of extension tasks.

Constraints and motivation

It may appear that the discussion above on the importance of autonomy directly contradicts the argument we put forward in Chapter 7 – that adding constraints can improve creativity. In the context of constraints and creativity, autonomy and competence can appear diametrically opposed. Constraints can increase competence and thus support motivation, as in the more novice student attempting the triangle problem discussed in Chapter 7 or the student facing a blank piece of paper who has no idea where to start with their creative writing. On the other hand, constraints reduce student autonomy and thus might be expected to decrease motivation.

A further complication is that the same constraints will be perceived differently by different students; constraints that provide support and guidance for one student may be felt to be overly controlling and restrictive by another. Metacognition has a role to play in supporting student autonomy; in some cases this can help them narrow the problem space for themselves by asking themselves questions about a problem, or seeking more information. For open-ended tasks such as creative writing, we can teach students the benefits that constraints can bring, allow them to experiment with different constraints and support them to impose their own constraints. In this way, we should build students' sense of control and autonomy, and thus motivation.

Conclusion

At the start of the chapter, we raised the idea that people are often told to find their passion. This implies that motivation, including the motivation to engage in creative fields and activities, is something you find within yourself. However, as the research discussed in this chapter has indicated, it can be better to look at a student's passions as something that they need to develop. Rather like dispositions (see Chapter 5), there will certainly be differences between learners in motivation – sometimes large ones! But we can also work to support motivation, and find opportunities to develop it.

The implication is that we should be rather wary of inviting students to introspect, or to find their passions. We also can't just hope for the best, or assume that learners will enjoy certain types of activities. An emphasis on superficially 'fun' lessons misses this important distinction.

SDT explains that three basic psychological needs – competence, autonomy and relatedness – should be supported in order to move people from externally regulated motivation towards more internally regulated motivation.

For a more grounded and lasting motivation to engage in creative tasks, we should try to engage with and harness the SDT needs. This means boosting students' competence, giving them choices, and finding authentic ways to harness their social needs. As mentioned earlier, this doesn't mean every task should be done in pairs or groups (far from it), but it does mean that people are more motivated by activities that seem to have some relevance to their broader lives and interests.

The next chapter provides a focus on a particular kind of task that is very well suited to achieving these needs – larger-scale creative projects.

Discussion Questions

1) What were your own experiences of being asked about your passions or interests as a child or student? Did these things change later in your life?

2) How did you respond to the idea that motivation can arise from success, rather than the other way around?

3) Can you think of examples of people being motivated due to relatedness – that is, more motivated by activities which they have in common with peers?

4) Can you think of any examples of how autonomy would apply in your own classroom/practice? Are there limits to how much freedom of choice you can give? And how does this link to constraints?

5) How does Grant's concept of pre-crastination fit with your own experience? Is it something you've recognised in your own life? Could you apply it in the classroom?

Professional Learning Tasks

Task 1

Take a piece of paper and divide it into three columns, labelled 'competence', 'relatedness' and 'autonomy'. Now review one lesson that you regularly teach. Write down any ways that these three motivational needs are currently met in the lesson. Next, jot down ideas for things that you could add or tweak to increase each one. Finally, note down changes that would be helpful but that you don't intend to make – and your reasons for discounting them.

Task 2

Take some time to speak to students and/or parents about rewards and deadlines. How clear an idea do you have of how these impact on them? This could be a good opportunity for an action research project.

Task 3

The idea of pre-crastination suggests that sometimes doing work straight away does not lead to the best outcomes. Have a look at a scheme of work, including any homework tasks and projects that you set. How might you adapt your schedule to incorporate some productive delays?

11 Creative Projects

Who is the most creative person of all time? Take a moment to think about it. Perhaps an artist such as Picasso springs to mind, or a musician such as Miles Davis. Or perhaps, following the arguments made about the relevance of creativity to science/social science as well as to the arts, you considered the likes of Albert Einstein or Marie Curie.

The question is something of a trick, however. By asking you to think of a 'person', it encourages you to follow the social convention that creativity is located in the individual.

However, a lot of creativity happens in group situations, and everything we think of and do is influenced by the people around us. In this chapter, we will consider the role of peers in creativity, and apply this idea to classroom situations where students develop projects and other extended pieces of work in groups, and across subject disciplines.

The Myth

Is creativity an unusual thing done by unusual people, and best done alone? As discussed earlier in this book, creativity is not just about big ideas, and nor is it completely mysterious, out of reach or inaccessible to scrutiny (see Chapters 1 and 9). Instead, it can be seen as an everyday cognitive process or set of processes, built upon relatively mundane and everyday fundamentals such as knowledge, attention, memory and problem solving.

This leads on to a further myth: the notion that creativity is only about creative geniuses – people who work away in solitude, have an inborn talent, and can't easily be understood by ordinary mortals.

Clearly, from what has been said in this book so far, these people only represent a small fraction of creative thinking across society – and are not a particularly useful model for the teacher. What's more, it presents an image that might be rather unappealing to students. They may already intuitively feel that creative people are a bit eccentric, and might not want themselves to be put in that bracket, even when they recognise the value of the creative work or ideas.

In the classroom, it would be best to avoid perpetuating the stereotype of the lone creative genius, particularly when this is interchangeable with the idea that creativity is the province of strange people and/or loners (Plucker et al., 2004). This notion is a flawed stereotype, as well as supporting the myth that creativity is only accessible to a select few.

The myth of the creative loner therefore makes creativity seem much less appealing or attainable to the school student. It implies that engaging with other people's ideas and thinking is not really part of creativity, and might even be harmful to it. But in fact, creativity can benefit from interactions, at least if these are set up in the right way.

This is why the question at the start of the chapter is misleading. While it's tempting to try to identify great individual creators (who was the *real* genius behind the Beatles, for example?), ideas frequently develop through a process of interaction, rather than in solitude (Sawyer, 2007). Even those who prefer to work alone are carrying with them their awareness of what other thinkers have done before.

Exploring the Research

(Re)considering the lone genius

Why is the idea of the lone creator a myth? First, as discussed already in this book – creativity is based on knowledge. You can't have new ideas without using the 'building blocks' of what you already know and understand (see Chapter 3). In this sense, every inventor or composer, however unique, was developing ideas that they themselves had learned from others. Learning to think creatively is a developmental process (Kaufman and Beghetto, 2009), and schools play a valuable role in supporting this (Karwowski, 2022).

Secondly, the standard definition of creativity states that it depends on a social context (see Chapter 1), including the needs and responses of others. Things are not inherently creative; their level of creativity depends, for example, on current scientific problems, the response of audiences, and social needs. All of this suggests that our students can be creative in valuable and meaningful ways. They need to learn about other people's ideas, discussing and working on their thinking, and building on ideas that have gone before.

Does this mean that it will be better for our students' creative thinking if they work in groups? Here lies a complication. Consider the following two studies:

- Researchers Sawyer and DeZutter (2009) studied the work of improvisational theatre groups, finding that collaborative creativity emerged, with ideas building on those presented by peers.
- However, in studies of brainstorming (see box below), groups do not, on average, produce more ideas than individuals do if they brainstorm alone.

These apparently contradictory findings mirror the confusion that teachers sometimes feel about group work in general, and it is worth exploring the processes involved.

Background to brainstorming

First, some background. Brainstorming in its widely recognised form was proposed by Osborn (1957). The key process was that people would take a period of time to produce as many ideas as they could without attempting to evaluate or judge those ideas. They would simply note down anything that came to mind; distinguishing between good and bad ideas would come later. Osborn also thought that people would come up with twice as many ideas if they worked in a group.

Researchers have since found that brainstorming is a helpful way of coming up with new ideas. However, the notion that it works better in a group has been disputed. Paulus and Dzindolet (1993) found that while groups do come up with more ideas, this is simply because they contain more individuals. If the same individuals were each to work alone, and their ideas to be pooled afterwards, the total number of ideas would in fact be more than the number produced in the group – even if duplicate ideas were discounted.

While surprising in some respects, this does make some sense in terms of what we know about cognition. It is better to do many tasks without social distractions – consider, for example, writing or exam revision. When in a group, it is harder to focus and to retain ideas in working memory, harder to retrieve information from memory, and so forth.

Getting collaboration right

The points above suggest that we should be wary about making group work the default when planning projects in education. However, Paulus and colleagues (e.g. Paulus & Brown, 2007) have argued that groups can still be useful for creativity – if they are set up in the right way (in this, it is not unlike other group work activities in the classroom).

The ideas that other people share can spark connections that we otherwise wouldn't have thought of (rather like drawing random prompts – see Chapter 4). Peers also know things that we don't, leading to ideas that we might not come up with by ourselves. Having to discuss ideas and compromise with peers can also act as a form of constraint – another factor that can boost creativity (see Chapter 7).

One finding from the Paulus and Dzindolet (1993) study was that a group can become more productive if they are set a particular standard. When a group in the study were told how many ideas a comparable number of individuals came up with, they were able to match this.

This finding suggests that it's important for brainstorming groups to have a clear and relatively ambitious target. It also suggests that some of the underperformance of groups in brainstorming is due to group members noticing and being influenced by low productivity in others – something that doesn't happen when they are alone.

Overall, we can see that groups *can* be helpful. However, as in other educational tasks, it's risky to assume that the energy and chatter that comes with group work is actually productive. It's worth giving some thought to how we can set up group tasks such as brainstorming carefully and in an evidence-based way when planning projects.

Pause to reflect
Can you think of parallels between brainstorming and other group work that happens in education? Are there group tasks that your own students do which resemble brainstorming in some way?

In depth: Brainstorming

Brainstorming could be highly relevant to an art project that has multiple parts – students may need to brainstorm several times, not just at the start of the project.

Similarly, a student who is developing a business idea or project, for example in Business Studies or as part of a young enterprise group, may find it helpful to brainstorm several times about different things – the initial product/business, the marketing, the business name, and so forth.

An interesting finding from research on young children by Milgram et al. (1987) was that the best ideas tended to come *later* in a brainstorming session. This has been supported in other studies with older participants. Early on, people think of very common, generic ideas – the sort that anyone could come up with. More original, high-quality ideas arrive at least 10 or 15 minutes into a brainstorming session.

Deuja and colleagues (2014) explored using category prompts when brainstorming, the idea being that prompts should help people to think of a broader range of ideas rather than fixating on a particular issue. For example, if brainstorming on the problem, 'List all the ways your school could be improved', categorisation would involve first thinking about types of issues, such as curriculum, facilities, etc.

Sure enough, Deuja et al. (2014) found that a group produced more ideas when they thought of categories first, and then brainstormed on these one at a time. However, groups did worse when randomly picked categories were provided for them by an experimenter.

Together, these points suggest that it might be best for students to brainstorm on categories that they or group members come up with, one at a time. It also makes sense to give them enough time to reach the more original ideas. This means that, for some projects, students might need to brainstorm several times on different days, with a generous allocation of time to do so where possible.

> **Pause to reflect**
> Are there any situations in your practice where brainstorming could be helpful in your teaching? Would you ask students to do it in groups or alone – or a combination of the two? How much time would you allow? What would be the advantages in asking students not to share their ideas with classmates too soon?

Types of project

Having considered the role of group processes, and the potential of brainstorming for idea generation, it's worth taking a moment to consider what counts as a 'project'.

As explored earlier in this book (see Chapter 5), creativity can apply to all subject areas. It can apply to both brief and extended tasks. What's more, it is at play from early childhood right through to professional practice. This makes the scope of creative projects potentially vast.

For the rest of this chapter, we will be guided by two main ideas in terms of how we define creative projects:

- The output of the task should be new and useful, in line with the standard definition of creativity.
- The task should involve a degree of complexity, thereby distinguishing it from brief, everyday classroom tasks such as answering a question.

Overall, then, we will view a creative project as a task incorporating two or more elements, taking place over two or more days, and with a creative output. Naming a classroom pet is a creative task, but it is not a project. The daily feeding/cleaning of the pet might be a project, but it is (usually) not creative. Designing a new enclosure for the pet *is* a creative project.

Some such projects will be carried out in groups, some individually, and others may involve elements of both – brainstorming and planning in a group, for example, followed by individual execution.

Bear in mind that there are many social interactions that could feature within an extended project. These include:

- Collaboration with a peer
- Collaboration with a group
- Working in a team
- Working with a mentor or supervisor
- Working within a community or movement

When you stop to think about it, a great deal of creativity within an extended project involves one or more of the above social elements. When a doctoral student studies for a PhD, they have a mentor to guide them, and who can support their skills development while also allowing exploration and experimentation. Experienced researchers, too, work as part of teams. Famous artists and authors are not working in a void either – they are part of an artistic community, often responding to the trends and interests of the time. This is how artistic movements such as Cubism arise.

Therefore, we are not assuming that all creative projects are done in a group or pair, or suggesting that they should be. But social interactions of various kinds are present during nearly all projects.

> **Pause to reflect**
> Look at the examples of social aspects of the creative process, above. To what extent do these play a role in your own context? Could a student's creative work be supported by a peer, or by mentoring?

Productive focus

Many teachers will be familiar with a sense that students' project work is not always as focused as it could be. Even when the outcomes are as good as we would like, project work does seem to proceed a little inefficiently at times, with a risk of off-topic chat, and perhaps a fair amount of procrastination, too. So, how do we ensure that students are focused towards the goal? And how can we ensure that it's a worthwhile goal in the first place?

Regarding the first of these points, this touches back on the idea that group brainstorming can be less efficient. Social processes can be useful (or even essential) to creativity, as discussed above. But groups also have their downsides, bearing in mind that a student's working memory is easily overloaded and their attention easily distracted. Deuja et al. (2014) note that when brainstorming, ideas that don't come from the student themselves may be distracting, or simply seem less relevant and motivating.

Overall, teachers might want to avoid group contexts being the default for project work. Instead, discussions can be built in mindfully, and with specific characteristics:

- A specific purpose
- Clear targets, communicated to the students
- A set amount of time allocated

Otherwise, work can often be better done individually, even when there is a notional group to which it contributes, or when it builds on group ideas.

Having said all this, efficiency isn't everything, and there are potential benefits to down time. Recall the discussion in Chapter 9 on the benefits of incubation – time away from a task. Some researchers (e.g. Baird et al., 2012) have found that a period of *low but not zero* demand promotes mind-wandering (see 'In depth', below), and can lead to more creative ideas subsequently.

In terms of how worthwhile the goal of the project is, it's worth recalling that in Chapter 1, we shared some of the common views of teachers about what creativity meant to them, and cautioned against creative tasks and projects that have the veneer of creativity without actually meeting the definition of producing something new and useful. At times, bringing such 'creative elements' into tasks will just be a distraction. For example, if a student decides to create a rap to explain a geological process, is their attention focused on the right rhyming scheme or on the geographical concepts? As this example shows, often these superficial elements that aim at creativity are falling into the trap of conflating creative thinking with arts output (see Chapter 5).

A related risk arises when students have to present or display their project work. The emphasis should be on meaningful work within the subject area, but if students are anxious about presenting back to their peers, their attention may become focused more on creating pretty PowerPoint slides than on the subject matter – or on taking shortcuts such as copying and pasting.

All of this is a reminder that projects and other extended tasks are not 'just creative'. As educators, we need to have a clear purpose, and to think through the process that will take place. As we have seen so far in this chapter, we can carefully consider:

- The use of idea generation techniques such as brainstorming, and the time required
- When group work will be appropriate
- The notion of productive struggle, and the idea that pure discovery is rarely the best strategy
- Strategies that can be used across projects

In depth: Mind-wandering and flow

We are probably all familiar with the sense of being lost in thought. Perhaps a colleague or peer catches us staring into space, and brings our attention back to the task at hand.

Researchers use the term *mind-wandering* for a state where a learner's attention lapses, and they are focused on internal ideas rather than on the external environment or a specific task.

This can, of course, be rather annoying for the teacher, and students who are mind-wandering are often told to pay attention. However, there are benefits to mind-wandering which could play out during creative tasks. Baird et al. (2012) found that setting a simple task that allowed for mind-wandering led to better outcomes than doing nothing at all or doing a complex task.

It perhaps makes sense, in terms of what has been said so far in this book about creative problems, that having the mental space for your mind to wander freely could have some benefits. Therefore, some latitude could be shown to students who are mind-wandering, especially if this happens early in a creative task, for example:

- When planning an essay
- When thinking through the next stage of a science project
- When reflecting on something they have just read
- In a break, midway through an artistic composition

A different but also relevant process is known as *flow*. A flow state is when someone is fully absorbed in a task. The similarity to mind-wandering is that they may appear lost in thought, unaware of their surroundings. However, the difference is that a flow state happens as they are actively working on the task.

You may observe flow states among students who are busy with a creative task, or during activities such as reading. Flow is motivating, and is more likely to occur when a task has a balance between its demands and the learner's ability (Engeser et al., 2021). In other words, it may happen when a task is just hard enough but no more. All the same, there is no guarantee of it happening.

People who have been in a flow state often report that time had rushed by much quicker than they expected it to. They have paid very little attention to what is going on around them. It typically occurs alone, but a creative group can also get a sense of flow.

Flow is also associated with increased performance and focus on creative tasks (Csikszentmihalyi, 1997). It's therefore best not to interrupt students more than necessary when they are in a flow state. We can also make it more likely to occur by setting projects that are challenging, but which students are equipped to tackle in terms of their skills and prior knowledge, and by creating a calm classroom atmosphere.

Discovery learning

Another feature of projects is that they tend to include some unstructured work by students. They differ from typical class formats in that students are often working at their own pace, and on different things. They are self-regulating their learning, and may be, at least to an extent, left to work things out for themselves.

Just like the earlier discussion of group work, this raises educational issues and debates that extend beyond creative tasks.

In brief, some educators (e.g. Bruner, 1966) have advocated for learners to autonomously discover knowledge, rather than being told things directly. Pedagogy based on this approach is known as *discovery learning*. In its purest form, it might imply that students learn things like grammatical rules and scientific principles by themselves, via exploration, experimentation and exposure to examples, rather than being told anything by the teacher.

Others have firmly pushed back against this idea, arguing that telling students things directly is much more effective and efficient. Minimally guided enquiry learning has been shown to be ineffective for long-term learning unless students have a sufficiently high knowledge base (Kirschner et al., 2006). The teacher is, after all, the expert. Pedagogy based on this view is called *direct instruction*.

There are certain compromise positions, and these may be relevant when it comes to planning creative projects in your teaching practice. For example, Mayer (2004), in arguing that 'pure' discovery learning has failed too many times to be viable, suggested that we instead use *guided discovery*. In this approach, the teacher sets up moments of discovery, acting like a tour guide who knows how to lead their group towards what *feel* like 'discoveries'.

This recruits the benefit of surprise and curiosity, helping students to feel engaged and to make the outcomes memorable. It also encourages active learning (e.g. problem solving), but ensures oversight and guidance by an expert (the teacher), so that students are focusing their efforts on productive and relevant problems, and not struggling for too long without help. In short, it's a kind of scaffolding of the process (and in fact, Bruner also advocated for both scaffolding and the benefits of prior knowledge).

Another compromise view to consider is that the degree of active exploration and self-direction can gradually increase in line with a student's expertise (e.g. EEF, 2018). In this, you might see a link to the ideas around structured uncertainty, discussed earlier in this book (see Chapter 8). The degree of uncertainty can rise (and teacher control reduce) in line with the students' level of competence. Beginners won't know what questions to ask, or how to go about exploring a topic autonomously, but more capable students can focus their attention on the right things, and make connections with their existing knowledge. They may also have a set of strategies to help when they get stuck.

Note that competence and expertise are not the same thing as age – even children can be experts, while older students/adults can be novices (see Chapter 6). This latter idea therefore requires judgement on the part of the teacher in terms of what complexity a group is ready for.

Strategies and transfer

In previous chapters (e.g. see Chapter 6) we have discussed the difficulty of transferring skills from one domain to another. As with other skills (or cognitive processes), engaging in creative thinking depends on having a foundation of relevant knowledge. However, creative strategies can transfer from one domain to another – a process that is aided by metacognitive awareness (see Chapter 9).

To take one example that has already been discussed, learners might become aware of brainstorming as an idea generation technique that could be used at various stages of a creative project. Having used it in one context, they could choose to use it in others; all the better if they know its strengths and limitations. They may come to learn how and when to support their brainstorming with categories, for example, when it works better in a group and when it does not, or how long they need to spend on it.

Bear in mind, though, that students find it hard to transfer what they have learned – as with the general and his army problem (see Chapter 6), they may simply fail to realise that a previously studied principle is relevant. One role of the teacher, then, is to draw learners' attention to new applications of previously used strategies. This is an example of metacognitive control in learning – knowing when and how to use strategies, rather than expecting this process to take care of itself. It is also very much in line with Mayer's idea of guided discovery. Students may have the right knowledge, but may still need to be prompted to use it.

Time management is another strategy with obvious applications from one project to the next, and many others could apply, depending on the subject area.

In depth: Extended writing

Researchers who study the teaching of extended writing have established a set of evidence-based practices that can make this more effective. These include explicit teaching of writing and its sub-skills, an authentic purpose to the task, and a real audience (Graham & Harris, 2016).

As part of this, one of the co-authors has studied the use of fan fiction as a form of writing. Fan fiction means writing that is based around an existing fictional work or world – such as *Star Wars* or *Lord of the Rings* – but is unauthorised, and written by fans of those franchises (Jenkins, 2012).

Fan fiction often sits outside of mainstream education, which is a pity – it is highly motivating to learners for many of the reasons discussed in Chapter 10. Fan fiction usually has an audience (among fellow fans), while writing stories to entertain this audience is an authentic task – very different from an arbitrary creative writing task set simply to satisfy course requirements or the exam board.

Fan fiction also provides an instructive example of how creativity, as widely defined, doesn't have to involve a great new idea; more everyday instances are valuable in their own right, such as responding to existing fiction and developing it in new and fun ways. The motivation to engage in this type of writing can be easily explained in terms of SDT theory of motivation, discussed in the previous chapter – it harnesses autonomy and relatedness (see Chapter 10).

> **Pause to reflect**
> Drawing on the idea of fan fiction, can you think of areas where students' own interests could be brought into the school/classroom a little more? Should we be celebrating this kind of creativity?

Authentic projects

Many projects that learners do in education are confined to the classroom. They have often been designed to mimic some real-world process; debates, essay writing, creating podcasts, making posters, collating portfolios – all of these are things that happen in the real world. This is sensible enough in terms of practising application and transfer. Often, though, the educational versions of these activities feel a little artificial.

Naturally, the difficulty level of tasks may need to be reduced for students of any age, but this isn't the only thing that can make school projects feel artificial. Even projects that are a lot of fun often feature some of the following:

- They are designed by the teacher, without student input.
- There is a lack of authentic interactions with anyone outside the classroom.
- In terms of creativity, the outcome may be new to the student, but it is rarely *useful*, beyond meeting the requirements of the task itself.
- There is no lasting outcome.
- There is no tangible impact on the student's life beyond the task.

Contrast this with projects that a student may encounter in their everyday life – redesigning their bedroom, for example, or planning a trip. In such cases, the real-world impact is obvious, and the benefits could be quite lasting. There are opportunities to communicate outside of the learning environment, too.

Creativity researcher Ron Beghetto has argued for the benefits of 'legacy projects'. These projects aim 'to make positive and lasting differences in their lives, schools, communities, and beyond' (Beghetto, 2017a, p. 187). In other words, they are not confined to the classroom, they produce something useful, and their outcome can have a lasting impact.

Examples of what Beghetto would see as legacy projects include:

- A group of bilingual high school students using their language skills and their knowledge of science to design health information leaflets for the local community
- A programme to help the transition from primary to secondary school, researched, set up and managed by older students

These are clearly creative projects as defined earlier, as they are complex and have outcomes that will be both novel and useful. They also involve genuine doubt and uncertainty – educators cannot say in advance what the best outcome will be (Beghetto, 2017a). To succeed, students will need to draw on relevant prior knowledge, and to make connections. Success is not guaranteed, but the possible gains make a risk of failure worthwhile.

There are of course some challenges in setting up some projects, not least the communication with people outside of the educational setting that they tend to involve. All the same, there are benefits to developing projects that involve a genuine creative output, not just a simulated one. Such projects are also more varied, and thereby better for transfer of what is learned to other tasks (see Chapter 6).

> **Pause to reflect**
> Consider your experience of projects, either as a teacher or a student yourself, and Beghetto's notion of legacy projects. Can you see the difference? What kind of 'legacy' projects spring to mind in your context, and can you see any barriers to implementing them?

Applications to Practice

Let's now consider some of the ways that the principles discussed so far can be built into our teaching practice.

Activating everyday tasks

We tend to associate the term 'project' with something very extended, but similar creative principles can be applied to shorter tasks, too. Shorter classroom tasks may fit the definition of 'multi-part' if we are more explicit about the task's stages. Can you say that one of your classroom tasks:

- Involves strategy?
- Would benefit from at least a brief plan?
- Would benefit from an idea generation stage?
- Would benefit from using strategies to activate prior knowledge discussed earlier in this book (e.g. quizzes and reviews, 'what-if?' questions, varied practice)?
- Has more than one stage?
- Has a creative outcome?
- Could benefit from review or redrafting?

If so, it could well benefit from breaking down these stages more clearly.

Take writing a short response to a text in History, for example. This might be seen as just another everyday task. But the response is creative – it has an element of novelty to it, is useful, and depends on recombining prior learning. Such a task could be broken down into stages, with some explicit focus on strategy, brainstorming, and peer review. Via such an approach, students may well get more both from the task itself and in terms of metacognitive understanding of the process.

Brainstorming, short and long

It can be hard to fit a really long brainstorming session into a packed school day. Researchers have found that better ideas come later in a brainstorming session, and that it is more productive to brainstorm on categories one at a time (see 'In depth', above). But how do we fit that in?

Given the amount of time needed to come up with original ideas, it's worth thinking about how this might be divided up across several sessions. One way would be to build more than one brainstorming session into projects in your classroom. Perhaps the students brainstorm on their initial goal for example, then brainstorm categories of solutions, and then brainstorm on the solutions themselves – each in a different lesson.

Another approach to managing the time requirements would be to initiate the brainstorming ahead of a student's free time. It could begin near the end of a lesson/near the end of the school day, for example. This would allow students to go away and think about the problem or task ahead of their next session – a form of incubation (see Chapter 9, 'Applying incubation').

Perhaps brainstorming could also be set as homework, or prior to a lunchtime interval. You could experiment with different options, and seek feedback from your students.

Legacy questions

In setting up legacy projects (see above), Beghetto (2017a) recommends asking the following questions to yourself or peers:

- What is the problem? Take time to look for a need affecting people in the school or the wider community.
- Why does it matter? It will be useful to communicate the importance of the issue or the risks involved when discussing the problem and advocating for solutions.
- What are we going to do about it? This question helps to focus on action, and not treating issues as simply of academic interest. The classroom work becomes all about crafting a workable plan.
- What lasting legacy will our work leave?

Students will often be overambitious; the first question above is a great opportunity to tackle this impulse. It is great for brainstorming, but also allows the teacher to guide students towards something more specific and realistic. They may want to solve all the problems in the world! It's important to keep their ideas focused.

The third question above is also an opportunity for the teacher to intervene. In line with what was said earlier about the benefits of a guided discovery approach, teachers may want to give students some latitude to explore at times – reading about the issue, for example, and carrying out their research – while also intervening to ask powerful, critical questions and keep the focus on the issue at hand.

> ### Pause to reflect
> Internationally, many education systems and curricula involve an extended project of some kind. These may or may not include features that make them more authentic, such as the need to communicate with researchers or businesses external to the school. What are the options in your area or education system? Could these be more widely used? Are they appropriate for your students? And if not, could your school devise its own project?

In depth: A legacy project in Food and Nutrition

Project work in a subject such as Food and Nutrition is widespread, but can suffer from feeling artificial, as discussed above. For example, a student might be asked to create a meal for a fictional family with specific dietary requirements.

In order to have a more authentic project, one school partnered with the school's catering company and set students the challenge of designing healthy snacks that could be sold in the school's canteen. To heighten motivation, the problem was set by a professional chef from the company who also gave some fixed parameters that the snacks needed to fulfil, such as the sugar content and the relative amount of fruit and vegetables compared to other ingredients.

The project was carefully structured with opportunities for students to carry out research, trial a range of recipes, and gain feedback from fellow students in a break-time sale. The students worked in collaborative groups of four, but there were also opportunities for individual reflection, as each student kept an online project log with findings from the research, initial ideas, and notes on any changes they made as a result of feedback.

The final snacks were judged by the school's catering company and the best examples included in the break-time sales for the following year. Despite some students finding the initial freedom of the project overwhelming, the vast majority thoroughly enjoyed the experience, commenting that they liked working as a team and being able to choose their own recipes. It was also noticeable that virtually every group changed their mind at least once over the course of the project and that they were comfortable doing so due to the way the project had been framed.

Many facets of authenticity

While legacy projects can be very appealing, they won't be practical in every situation. Sometimes, for example, the format of a project is constrained by exam board rules, or just by practicalities such as time constraints.

All the same, there are aspects that can make projects *feel* more authentic to the learners. Each project has multiple facets, and in each of these, tasks could be relatively more or less authentic. Such features include:

- The degree of student choice
- Whether there is an extended rather than one-off approach to the project or topic – is it ever talked about again, or followed up on?
- Collaboration with students from other year groups or schools, which might include mentoring next year's students
- Input from outside speakers
- The involvement of parents
- An authentic audience, such as sharing the work publicly or even aiming to have it published

Overall, these areas represent a kaleidoscope of options for projects. Even if you don't have scope to create a true legacy project, perhaps there are ways that you can increase the authentic feel of the projects you already use. They may well be more motivating as a result.

Conclusion

In this chapter we have considered the idea that creativity is not always just a solo effort, and have explored the role of creative projects – extended tasks which are not always done in pairs or groups, but which generally involve some kind of social input.

More broadly, it is worth tackling the idea that creativity is just for eccentric loners. This, like several other myths in the book so far, presents a view of creativity as only accessible to the few. In fact, just as anyone can have an original idea (even if it's only a mini-c idea), anyone can do a creative project. Processes such as brainstorming can be used by anyone to help come up with new ideas, and there is research into how to make them more effective. Mind-wandering and flow are further examples of cognitive processes that anyone can experience, but which depend in part on how the project work is set up, and the approach taken by the teacher.

Projects can involve group work and an element of discovery, and we have seen that both of these tie into wider educational debates. In both cases, it makes sense to avoid assuming that these are the right approaches in all situations. Just because creativity involves social processes, it doesn't mean that working in a group should be the default, and we can't assume that eager chatter in class is actually productive! Likewise, we should be cautious about leaving students to discover things by themselves, and embrace the use of scaffolding and guided discovery, especially when students are new to a subject or topic.

We can also make projects more impactful and memorable – and more motivating – by making connections outside the classroom. As we have seen, legacy projects can vary the skills used in projects, and have an impact that goes beyond the learning outcomes or assessment of the task itself. Even where this seems impractical, it's worth looking at how some aspects of these principles can be built into projects or other extended tasks.

Discussion Questions

1) Who did you think of in response to the question at the start of the chapter about the most creative person of all time?
2) Can you think of any good examples of collaborative creativity?
3) What are your own experiences of brainstorming? Do you do it in your own practice, or use it in class?
4) How do you feel about legacy projects, or about making projects more authentic in general?
5) When students work together on projects, what can we do to make sure that there is a productive focus, and minimise time-wasting and distractions?

Professional Learning Tasks

Task 1

How well do your students' views of creative projects align with the research? This could be a good opportunity to check their assumptions – and to build their metacognitive awareness. Try giving a group the following questions, based on the ideas from this chapter:

1) Who would come up with more good ideas – three students working in a group, or the same three students each working individually and in silence?
2) When do the best new ideas tend to occur to people – when they first encounter a problem, after 10 minutes or so, or after 20 minutes or more?
3) What could be done to make a brainstorming group come up with more ideas?

It may also be instructive to find out how much students like working with others. The results could surprise you!

Task 2

Focusing on one project in particular, develop an outline proposal for how it could be developed as a 'legacy project', with more of a lasting impact, and connections to outside audiences. Perhaps there could be an element of student design of the project, too (or perhaps guided student input, bearing in mind what has been said about expertise and discovery learning). When your proposal is ready, why not share it with peers or your institution's senior management? Ron Beghetto (2024) has developed an AI tool to support legacy project planning – to what extent does collaboration with AI help to develop your ideas?

12 Assessing Creativity

Assessment in education does not have a good reputation. In England in 2016, there were mass boycotts of the primary school SATs (standardised assessment tests). Protests saw parents waving banners reading 'I learn best when I have fun' and 'Testing is not learning'. Similarly, there have been boycotts of standardised assessments in the US, most notably in 2015 when new assessments linked to the Core Common Standards were introduced across 43 states.

In these and similar cases, tests have been accused of causing stress among young children, and of being more about the government's desire for data to rank and compare schools than about supporting children's learning. Tests and assessment are certainly not associated with creativity in most people's minds.

Having read our discussion of the role of knowledge (e.g. see Chapter 3), you may be able to see a counter-argument based on the cognitive science research. However, in some respects educational assessment deserves its reputation – it's all too easy for it to be done ineffectively, or for the wrong reasons. In this chapter we will look at the ways in which creativity can be assessed, and consider how this might enhance a teacher's understanding of assessment issues more broadly.

DOI: 10.4324/9781032719221-12

The Myth

In their research on the prevalence of creativity myths, Benedek et al. (2021) found 'strong support for the claim that creativity cannot be measured' (p. 4). Indeed, the fourth most endorsed creativity myth in their research was that *'Most people would not be able to distinguish abstract art from children's art'*. You might recall that we discussed earlier in the book how creativity is often seen as an elusive phenomenon, difficult or even impossible to recognise (see Chapter 1). An obvious extension of this idea is that it is seen as impossible to judge or assess. To some people, at least, it's impossible to decide whether creative outputs are good or bad.

The notion that assessing creativity is impossible may be linked to teachers equating creativity with the arts, and with these domains, in turn, being seen as inherently subjective. Perhaps there is also unease that any standards or rubrics provided to assess creative work would end up stifling creativity.

However, it is certainly not the case that we can't try to measure creativity or judge creative outputs – there is a wealth of evidence from creativity research, including more recent work specifically looking at creativity in schools, that creativity can be assessed. We discuss that research next.

Exploring the Research

Washback effects

Assessment can have both positive and negative impacts on teaching and learning – so-called 'washback' effects. Unintended and detrimental effects of assessments – negative washback effects – include teachers focusing their instructional practices solely on the requirements for high-stakes examinations. For example, if a summative assessment consists of only multiple-choice questions, a negative washback effect would be teachers never giving students a chance to produce extended pieces of writing or construct their own arguments. Equally, it has been argued that removing the requirement for assessed practicals in science will be detrimental to the development of students' practical skills as teachers will no longer spend so much time carrying out experimental work in class (Abrahams et al., 2013).

From a creativity perspective, high-stakes examinations that reward factual knowledge recall and routine skills may deter teachers, and students, from developing the adaptive expertise required for true creative thinking.

The negativity associated with assessment doesn't always feature outside of educational establishments, where the need to test competence may seem straightforward and necessary. An example where there is little debate – and perhaps a positive washback effect – is the driving test. In most countries you cannot legally drive without passing a test, but there is little or no protest against these assessments or the stress they cause (more likely, there would be uproar if they were removed). The test may not guarantee that everyone is a good driver, but the purpose of establishing a baseline level of competence seems uncontroversial.

Educational assessment can also have positive washback effects. If something is assessed, then this can increase student motivation, meaning they study more, or it may improve teacher feedback, leading to better learning.

There is therefore a need to maximise the positive washback effects whilst minimising the negative washback of assessment. Let's consider how this plays out in the assessment of creativity specifically.

Assessments used in creativity research

Many assessments used in creativity research have focused on divergent thinking in particular. As we have discussed previously in this book, levels of divergent thinking can be measured by setting tasks such as 'how many uses of a paperclip can you think of' (this was cited by

Ken Robinson in his claims that schools kill creativity – see Chapter 2). While such a task is certainly simplistic, the idea is to compare a person's responses to those of (thousands of) previous participants, to see, for example, how many ideas someone comes up with for uses of an everyday object, and how unusual these are.

This is the approach taken by the *Torrance Tests of Creative Thinking* (Torrance, 1974), which score responses against four criteria overall:

1) Fluency. The total number of interpretable, meaningful, and relevant ideas generated in response to the stimulus.
2) Flexibility. The number of different categories of relevant responses.
3) Originality. The statistical rarity of the responses.
4) Elaboration. The amount of detail in the responses.

It's not hard to see the appeal of these tests. They are easy to do, and if someone were to come up with dozens of rare and elaborated ideas from many categories, it would certainly be impressive! We can see links here with ideas we have discussed earlier in the book such as playfulness and originality, flexible thinking, and more. Of course, the question needn't just be about paperclips – any everyday object could be prompted in the same way.

> **Pause to reflect**
> Have you ever tried the everyday uses task discussed above? What other objects would work well as a prompt?

However, there are some serious limitations of tasks such as the everyday uses test. It doesn't consider the utility of ideas within specific social contexts. Remember, according to the standard definition of creativity, an idea which is highly original but not suited to the task constraints cannot be considered truly creative.

Another issue is the connection with knowledge. Knowledge will play a role in responses. However, some ideas that people come up with on the test might be unworkable in practice. As we looked at in Chapter 7, knowledge can provide constraints and some highly original ideas may be quickly dismissed by experts in the field who understand why such ideas would be impossible to implement.

Baer (2017) has suggested that due to the importance of subject knowledge, general tests of creativity can be superficial. It may be better, then, to measure the creativity of outputs of specific tasks. This is the basis of the Consensual Assessment Technique, CAT, often referred to as the 'gold standard' of creativity assessment (Amabile, 1982). In the CAT, creative outputs are judged by a panel of experts, mirroring the approach taken in the highest levels of domains – artwork is judged by expert art critics, Nobel prizes in Physics and Chemistry are awarded by pre-eminent scientists. The expertise of the judges is an essential part of the CAT and these experts must come to their judgements independently – interrater reliability has been shown to be very high across a number of studies (Baer, 2017).

Self-assessment

Tests aside, how well can people judge their own creativity? Baer (2017) discusses how he asks his students to rate their own creativity on a scale of 1–10. A rating of 10 would put them on the same level as the most creative people of all time – the Big-C creators we have discussed in previous chapters. Creativity ratings of 10 can only be applied posthumously so are impossible to award on a self-assessment. The lowest rating 'goes to the most boring rock one can imagine, one even a geologist couldn't love'. Ratings of 1 are therefore also impossible on a self-assessment!

Baer goes on to say that this exercise shows students that creativity is a continuum; it is not possible to answer the question 'am I a creative person?', but the question can start conversations around the domain specificity of creativity because a single scale breaks down as soon as you specify a creative field.

> **Pause to reflect**
> Try the exercise suggested by Baer yourself. Where would you rate your own creativity on a 1-10 scale? Does your rating depend on the domain you consider? For example, perhaps you are much more creative at some tasks than others.

However, as Baer discusses, self-assessment within creativity research is problematic. Student self-assessments show little correlation with the judgements of experts (Kaufman et al., 2010; see also Chapter 7 for students' perceptions of constraints). In short, we are not good at assessing our own creative skills! One reason could be that many students simply do not possess sufficient knowledge to effectively assess their own creative ideas and outputs. It may also be the case that they do not have a sufficiently refined conception of what creativity is.

Why assess creativity?

Given the difficulties associated with assessing (or self-assessing) creativity, it might be all too easy to conclude that we should abandon attempts to assess creativity in schools. Lucas (2022a) identifies three reasons for why pursuing creative thinking assessments is a valuable endeavour. These *positive* washback effects are:

1) **Improving the status of creative thinking.** Although there may be lofty philosophical reasons for why not everything in schools should be measured or assessed, it remains the case that what is assessed tends to have a higher status – it comes to be seen as an important part of a school's purpose. If we are serious about improving our students' creative thinking skills then we should highlight this by making assessment of those skills a key part of our assessment practices.

2) **Enhancing the quality of teaching and learning.** In order to be able to assess something, teachers need to understand it and to have a sense of what progress in that area looks like. The creativity assessments

discussed earlier in this chapter are summative assessments, but creativity is also amenable to formative assessment – assessment which provides valuable feedback to learners, supporting the creative process.

3) **Promoting a shared understanding of creative thinking.** A common framework is required for any assessment. Creativity and creative thinking are often seen as vague and undefinable; an assessment framework helps to clarify what is meant by these terms, creating a shared understanding for students, teachers and parents, as well as those outside of educational establishments.

Pause to reflect

To what extent do you agree with Lucas' reasons for assessing creativity in schools? Can you think of any other reasons? What about reasons to *not* assess creativity?

In depth: PISA Creative Thinking Assessment

PISA (Programme for International Student Assessment) has run tests for 15-year-olds on reading, science and Maths since 2000. For the first time, in 2022, PISA added a creative thinking assessment. The publication of PISA data provokes debate and discussions within governments, and one of the rationales for introducing such an assessment was to improve the status of creative thinking by making creative thinking a topic for such debates.

The assessment examined students' capacities to generate diverse and original ideas and to evaluate and improve ideas across a range of domains – written expression, visual expression, social problem solving and scientific problem solving. Thus it assesses divergent thinking whilst recognising that creativity cannot be separated from domains. The assessment included several innovative and interactive assessment methods. For example, in some items, students were required to produce a visual artefact rather than a written response and the assessment included only open-ended tasks with no single solution (see OECD, 2022, for more details).

Results from the assessment were published in June 2024 (OECD, 2024). As the data were gathered during the COVID-19 pandemic, results do need to be interpreted with caution as not all participating countries met the PISA sampling standards. However, some general patterns were drawn from the data.

- Academic excellence is not a prerequisite for excellence in creative thinking, but few students below a baseline proficiency in mathematics excelled in creative thinking.
- Students demonstrated relative strengths in creative expression tasks but relative weaknesses in creative problem-solving tasks.
- Girls outperform boys on average and in no country did boys outperform girls in creative thinking.
- Students with higher socio-economic status performed better in creative thinking, although this association is weaker than it is for mathematics, reading and science.
- Only around 50 per cent of students believed their creativity was something they could change; having a growth mindset on creativity positively related to performance.
- Classroom pedagogies make a difference. Students who reported that their teachers valued their creativity scored higher than their peers.

These data support many of the assertions we have made throughout this book – whilst knowledge is necessary for creative thinking, it is not sufficient and teachers *can* make a difference to students' creativity.

Whilst not a perfect assessment – no assessment can be – the PISA assessment has shown that creative thinking can be assessed on an international scale, and can begin to draw out interesting patterns, as well as making comparisons across education systems. The assessment may also help to raise the status of creative thinking. The future role of this kind of data as part of PISA will be interesting to follow.

Modes of assessment

Many of the formal assessments undertaken in schools consist of traditional pen and paper tests, essays written under timed conditions or multiple-choice questions. These tend to favour the assessment of more routine skills, shallow or narrow learning which can be equated with the routine expertise discussed in Chapter 6. Lucas (2022b) argues that creative thinking is a broader disposition and cannot be assessed in the same way as typical academic tasks where syllabuses outline specific knowledge and skills that need to be acquired. Instead, the assessment of creative thinking should take place over time and include longer, deeper investigations; these can take place within any subject discipline or as part of interdisciplinary problem-based learning, or indeed as part of extra-curricular activities. Lucas and Spencer (2017) group possible types of assessment into four different approaches – pupil, teacher, real-world and online. For example, pupil self-reflection tasks, teacher grading based on predetermined criteria, an authentic product such as a podcast, or an online portfolio showcasing student work.

Assessing creativity in schools

Despite the scepticism from many teachers, there is plenty of evidence to suggest that assessment of creativity is possible within schools. Bolden et al. (2020) carried out a scoping review of 51 research articles looking at creativity and assessment. Rather than simply looking at summative assessments of creativity, such as those discussed earlier in this chapter, they were particularly interested in broadening the view of classroom assessment to include formative assessment processes. They drew out two main findings:

- **The importance of creativity assessment criteria**. Providing frameworks and/or clear assessment criteria was found to produce much more accurate assessments of creativity. Such frameworks help to conceptualise creativity into more tangible processes and outcomes. The researchers also found that criteria helped to move teachers away from their tendency to overemphasise academic appropriateness above originality when assessing student work.

- **The value of self-assessment**. As discussed earlier, self-assessment is problematic in creativity research, as students may misjudge their capabilities. However, the review by Bolden and colleagues suggests that when a clear assessment framework and teacher guidance are in place, self-assessment can help to support student creativity, and thus be a helpful formative assessment process.

Creative assessment criteria

Several frameworks and criteria have been suggested for conceptualising and assessing creativity. The PISA Creative Thinking Assessment discussed earlier used a framework which was designed to assess creativity in a standalone test for international comparisons, but this is probably less helpful as a framework for developing and assessing creative thinking within a school.

The creative learning habits introduced in Chapter 5 provide a more promising example; several case studies looking at schools where the habits have been used for assessment are described in Lucas and Spencer's book *Teaching Creative Thinking* (2017). More recently, this framework has been used in a variety of Australian primary schools to assess creative thinking (Lucas, 2022b). The five learning habits and associated sub-habits proved particularly useful as a self-reflection tool and as a way of making creative thinking visible.

Another example is Rethinking Assessment's three-dimensional model of creative thinking. Its three dimensions – being imaginative, inquisitive and persistent – are each further broken into three substrands. The effectiveness of this model has been studied in English schools with students aged between 9 and 14 (Krstic, 2024). The study involving 13 schools and 45 teachers was run over the course of one school term, and three assessment modes were chosen – pupil self-report, teacher assessed product/process assessment and pupil portfolios. Schools strongly endorsed the model of creative thinking in the study and were able to develop and apply the three modes of assessment. Pupil portfolios were liked by teachers; however, the researchers noted that 'teachers found the process of evaluating their pupils' progress against the progression framework challenging ... and the organisation of teacher moderation sessions took considerable amounts of time and planning' (Krstic, 2024, p. 7).

A further example is the Australian Council for Educational Research's (ACER) model of creative thinking (Ramalingam et al., 2020) which consists of three strands and associated aspects:

1) Generation of ideas - number and range of ideas
2) Experimentation - shifting perspectives and manipulating ideas
3) Quality of ideas - fitness for purpose, novelty and elaboration

Applications to Practice

The research into assessing creativity in schools suggests that not only can creativity be assessed but that such assessments can bring positive benefits to learners. However, rather than attempting to produce highly reliable summative assessments with their associated high stakes and unintended consequences of 'teaching to the test', we may be better off focusing on formative assessment practices using a variety of assessment methods. These different assessment methods should be spaced across time and used in combination with one another - no single assessment is likely to produce an accurate picture of a student's creativity.

Formative assessment

Bolden et al. (2020) discuss the relationship between creativity and Black and Wiliam's (2006) five key formative assessment/assessment for learning (AFL) strategies. These are summarised in Figure 12.1.

> **Pause to reflect**
> Which of the assessment for learning strategies that you currently use in your classroom could be adapted to assess creativity?

AFL strategy	Application to creativity
Clarifying and understanding learning intentions and criteria for success.	Providing students with descriptive rubrics, or frameworks such as the creative learning habits, supported by examples of high and low quality work.
Engineering effective classroom discussions, questions and tasks that elicit evidence of learning.	Supported by open-dialogue and psychologically safe classroom environments – see Chapter 2 on classroom discussions.
Providing feedback that moves learning forward.	Feedback should reference specific criteria and strike a balance between not being overly harsh (which could be demotivating) and providing sufficient challenge.
Activating students as instructional resources for each other.	Peer discussion focused on evaluating and improving ideas can be beneficial for the creative process – see Chapter 11 on the power of collaboration in project work.
Activating students as owners of their own learning.	Providing opportunities for self-assessment and reflection as well as helping students to develop creative metacognition – see Chapter 9 for further details.

Figure 12.1 The links between creativity and assessment for learning

Decision filters

Both peer and self-assessment have been shown to improve creativity but only when accompanied by clear criteria. Projects involving creative thinking often entail coming up with multiple initial ideas and then narrowing down these ideas to possible solutions. One way to do this is to use a decision filter where three or four separate criteria are identified as being required for an optimal solution – depending on the knowledge level of the class, these can be provided by a teacher or co-constructed with the students.

An example decision filter for a stall at a school fair is given below.

1) **Flair**: How unique and interesting is the idea?
2) **Audience**: Has a 'buying' audience with their needs/wants been clearly identified? How likely are they to buy the product or service?
3) **Profit**: How likely is it that a profit could be made?
4) **Implementation**: How feasible is the idea? How easily can it be brought to reality?

For each of their ideas, students are asked to give a score out of five against each criterion, either as a self-assessment or peer-assessment process. The total score can be used to decide which idea is worth taking forward, or indeed whether parts of different ideas could be combined. Another option is for students to use a sliding scale against each criterion – for some reason, this feels less judgemental than assigning a numerical score. When used as a peer-assessment tool, decision filters can provide a clear framework for peer feedback to help students improve their ideas.

> **In depth: Self-reflection using creative learning habits**
>
> As shown by Lucas (2022b), the creative learning habits can be used to encourage student self-reflection. In order to help students move away from too narrow a focus on marks and grades in standardised academic subjects, one secondary school used the habits to help students notice where they were developing their creative thinking.
>
> The process started with an assembly. Students were first encouraged to discuss myths associated with creativity in order to dispel common misconceptions before being introduced to the definition of creativity and the creative learning habits. Examples were shared from teachers' personal experiences to show the value of creativity across a range of different areas.
>
> In the following session, students were first asked to list the accomplishments they were proud of, both within their academic lessons and their extra-curricular pursuits, and both within and outside of school. This list was then annotated in different colours to show where and how the creative learning habits had helped them in their pursuits. Starting from concrete experiences, rather than the abstract creative learning habits, helped students to notice where they had already shown these habits and hence to consider in subsequent weeks where these habits might be useful in developing their learning. Rather than being a one-off task, the reflection was returned to after a few weeks and students were encouraged to add further examples. The student reflection provided a useful starting point for discussions with form tutors and could, in the future, be adapted to form part of reporting to parents.

Authentic assessment

As discussed in Chapter 11, we can heighten student engagement in, and learning from, creative projects if we provide them with purposeful, authentic tasks. Such projects lend themselves brilliantly to less traditional forms of assessment. For example, students could be asked to produce a film or a podcast or an exhibition of work or even to set up a small business or charity initiative. The Consensual Assessment Technique (CAT) used by creativity researchers can be adapted for use in schools by asking experts in a particular field to judge this work, for example, using professional scientists to judge the school science fair or journalists to judge a news podcast.

In depth: Assessing authentic projects

Partnering with the local community is one way to find real-life, authentic projects for students to complete. In one such project students were asked to develop a campaign for the local council to encourage residents to use more sustainable travel methods. The project was launched by an expert from the council and the same expert returned to give feedback on the students' final campaigns. This was a very informal feedback session and the school also wanted a way to formally recognise the students' achievements without having to give marks or grades. To this end, they decided to conclude the project with a self-assessment.

The school identified the following key learning outcomes:

- Understanding the problem
- Use of evidence
- Embracing different perspectives

These three outcomes were shared with students towards the start of the project. The school also wished the students to be able to reflect on how they could apply their learning in this project to their future work and their own key learning, making five outcomes in total.

Students were given a Google form to complete which included some prompt questions under each of these five categories. The form was set up so that the students' responses were exported to an editable Google doc which enabled the teacher to add a supporting comment. The whole document was then printed off as a certificate which was awarded to the students by their form tutor as a celebration of their achievements.

Use of technology

The ubiquitous use of various technologies in school gives huge scope for not only producing a wider variety of creative outcomes but also curating and assessing this work. Digital portfolios can be created where students can upload examples of their work which showcase the development of their creative thinking skills. These can be organised in line with specific assessment frameworks, or set up so that students can provide evidence to allow them to be awarded digital badges in different categories. Rethinking Assessment's Learner Profile is an example which is being trialled in several schools (Rethinking Assessment, 2024).

There is also a role for technology in supporting student self-assessment, as highlighted by Bolden et al. (2020). Technology can enable students to experiment with and assess multiple possibilities before committing to a final product – for example, using tablets to experiment with different brush strokes, music composition software or computer aided design in design technology. Artificial intelligence can also be utilised to provide feedback on ideas and promote better self-reflection.

Reporting to parents

Few parents are likely to disagree with a school that prioritises developing students' creative thinking but if the only information shared with them is marks and grades then this becomes the parents' only measure of success. Many students find the uncertainty associated with creativity challenging; if their fears about not 'succeeding' in school are reinforced by messages from home then it will be difficult to shift the culture within a classroom. A reporting structure that moves beyond marks and grades to celebrate other skills can help shift this mindset. Another option is to invite parents into showcase events where they can see examples of student work; having students explain how they changed their mind or developed their ideas in producing the work can help parents (and students) to see the value in the process and not just the final outcome.

In depth: The role of parents

An important part of developing creative thinking is receiving feedback and improving as a result. Involving parents in this process can provide a powerful way to engage them with the school culture that is focused on developing students' creative thinking. In one project, students were tasked with coming up with a new business idea to support a local café. The final outcome of the two-day workshop was a presentation to the café owner. However, rather than inviting parents into school to view the final presentations, parents were invited in at the end of the first day and asked to give feedback on the students' prototype ideas. Parents were given information on the project brief and some suggested questions and many reported afterwards that they enjoyed being part of the process. At the end of the second day, students were then able to report back to their parents on how they had improved their ideas and presentations as a result of the feedback.

Conclusion

In this chapter we have shown that, despite the fears of many teachers, it is possible to assess creativity in both summative and formative ways. There is no such thing as a perfect assessment and assessing creativity is no different. Any assessment can have positive and negative washback effects; as educators we should endeavour to maximise the positive and minimise the negative effects. A major positive washback effect of assessing creativity in schools is that it shows that creativity is valued and celebrated in that institutional setting. However, to avoid some of the negative washback effects, we suggest that it is more productive to focus on formative assessment practices using a range of assessment methods. Rather than summative assessment methods, which tend to judge students with a simple mark or grade, such formative assessment processes can be used to improve teaching and learning of creativity.

Discussion Questions

1) What are the two commonly used tests for assessing creativity used by creativity researchers? What do you think are the advantages and disadvantages of each? To what extent do you feel these tests are applicable to school contexts?
2) What were the main conclusions drawn from the PISA Creative Thinking Assessment? To what extent do you feel the PISA assessment is a valid assessment of creative thinking?
3) What do you understand by the terms formative and summative assessment? Which of these types of assessment is more useful for assessing creativity and why?
4) Come up with some examples of multi-modal assessments that can be used to assess creative thinking. Which do you think are most appropriate for your subject/phase?
5) In what ways might technology be used to develop and assess creative thinking in your setting?

Professional Learning Tasks

Task 1

Carry out Baer's creativity self-assessment task with a group of students or colleagues. Do people's self-assessment results change when they consider creativity in different domains? For the students, how do their self-assessments match up with their teachers' assessments?

Task 2

You can find various examples of divergent thinking tests on the internet – try Googling 'Divergent Thinking Test' and see what you can find. Carry out a test yourself or with a group of colleagues or students. Although divergent thinking is only one aspect of creativity, such tests can provide an interesting starting point for discussion. For example, did people who scored higher use particular strategies?

Task 3

Several models or frameworks for assessing creative thinking have been suggested in this chapter:

- PISA Creative Thinking Assessment (OECD, 2022)
- The Centre for Real-World Learning's Creative Learning Habits (Lucas and Spencer, 2017)
- Rethinking Assessment's three-dimensional model (Krstic, 2024)
- ACER Creative Thinking Skills Framework (Ramalingam et al., 2020)

With a group of colleagues, compare and contrast these different frameworks. Which do you think would be most appropriate for assessing creative thinking in your context?

Task 4

Consider the interactions you have with parents in your school. To what extent do these interactions celebrate successful, measurable outcomes such as performance on standardised tests or assessments? Are there more opportunities for celebrating less measurable qualities such as the skills and dispositions students have shown during the process of a task or activity?

13 Developing Creative Teachers

The inspirational teacher that transforms the lives of a group of troubled students. It's a common theme in Hollywood films – think Robin Williams as John Keating in *Dead Poets Society*, or Jack Black as Dewey Finn in *School of Rock*.

According to Hollywood, these hero-teachers are ones that buck against the tyrannical school regime. They are mavericks and rule-breakers who rip up textbooks and get students to stand on their desks to see a different perspective. This, according to Hollywood, is the way to encourage your students to think creatively! There is no room for discipline or structure or a focus on knowledge building – indeed, as we discussed in Chapter 2, teachers who have such high expectations are usually objects of derision in these movies. With role models like John Keating and Dewey Finn, it is no wonder that a myth has developed that only *some* teachers have the personality to teach creatively.

In this chapter we will look at the cultures that can be created in schools to support every teacher to teach for creativity.

The Myth

In their review study, Bereczki and Kárpáti (2018) found that just like with creative students, creative teachers were viewed as having particular characteristics. In line with the media representations mentioned above, they tended to be seen as being confident and sociable.

The researchers also found that creative STEM teachers were seen as those who taught the subject in a novel and non-traditional way. This perhaps suggests that anyone who is seen as too much of a rule follower or traditionalist won't be seen as creative – a rather simplistic way to see creativity! In other settings, researchers have found that the most effective teachers represented a broad range of personalities and teaching styles – what they had in common was a set of effective classroom practices (Bransford et al., 2006a).

But does a teacher's personality or taking a non-traditional approach to the classroom actually help with fostering creativity? Given that successful creativity rests on skills and knowledge, it is more important to be effective than to seem creative. The Bereczki and Kárpáti study describes conceptions of who might be a creative teacher as 'somewhat narrow', and tending to emphasise teachers' creativity outside of the classroom. Widespread views of what makes a creative teacher appear to be rather simplistic, and perhaps neglect the value of supporting the skills needed for creative thinking in favour of celebrating a particular personality – the teaching maverick.

Pause to reflect
Which teachers in your school do you consider to be 'creative'? Are they the more maverick teachers? Are they teaching the 'creative' subjects such as Art, Music and Drama? To what extent do their teaching practices develop creative thinking in their students?

Exploring the Research

It is widely recognised that it's important for teachers to be creative in their practice (Morais et al., 2015). Teaching involves creating materials, lesson plans, crafting explanations, and responding to unpredictable classroom situations. As Bramwell and colleagues put it, 'it is difficult to imagine successful teaching that does not depend on teachers' creativity' (Bramwell et al., 2011, p. 228).

All the same, there is a difference between being a creative practitioner and teaching in ways that support creativity among students. The Durham

Commission on Creativity (2019) explains that teaching for creativity involves using a particular set of pedagogies that help to develop and cultivate creative thinking among students, and highlights that these pedagogical skills may differ sharply from creative thinking in everyday life.

However, it must be acknowledged that there are several barriers to teaching for creativity in schools. A review article by Bullard and Bahar (2023) identified three challenges to teaching for creativity:

1) **Teacher creative self-efficacy and beliefs.** Teachers who believe some of the myths we have tried to dispel throughout this book, such as that children's creativity is innate and therefore cannot be fostered or that creativity is associated solely with the arts, are less likely to be motivated to teach for creativity. On the other hand, teachers who believe that students can cultivate and strengthen their creativity are more inclined to teach for creativity. Thus a first step in developing creative teachers may be to work towards shifting these beliefs, something we hope this book has already started to do.

2) **Environmental constraints.** The school environment needs to be conducive to this shift in teaching for creativity; in the absence of this supportive environment, even teachers who believe creativity can be developed in young people struggle to do so. A key reason why teachers feel they are unable to teach for creativity is because they are concerned about meeting curriculum objectives; this concern is also felt by students who are often convinced that exam scores are more important than creativity. They are also likely to feel uncomfortable with the organised chaos that stimulates creativity.

3) **New teacher training with old practices.** Even if teachers are persuaded to teach for creativity, they often default back to their traditional methods. Suggested reasons for this were teachers' own school experiences, their teacher training and assessment-driven instruction. This is supported by other research which shows that changing teacher habits is hard and sustained professional development is required to overwrite and upgrade existing habits (Hobbiss et al., 2020).

Bullard and Bahar conclude by suggesting three possible solutions to overcome the barriers they identified:

1) Teaching teachers to consider and/or apply creative theories in their pedagogy
2) Using helpful tools that reinforce creativity, such as creative checklists to self-evaluate teaching methods
3) Shaping school culture around creativity

> **Pause to reflect**
> Looking at the barriers identified by Bullard and Bahar, which ones do you think are the most significant in your school context? How might the solutions they suggest for overcoming these barriers be applied?

The idea of teachers being fearful of the potential chaos and uncertainty that teaching for creativity involves is also addressed in a quirkily titled article, 'In Praise of Clark Kent', by Kaufman and Beghetto (2013). Here they explain that there is a time and place for creativity and it is not something that we should be focusing on all of the time. The article starts with a wonderful description of what a date with Superman might actually look like, which is worth quoting in full.

> Imagine going out on a date with Superman. He comes to your door with flowers, but his super-strength crushes the stems. You climb onto his back and hold on; with his power of flight, he does not need a car. So instead of engaging in pleasant conversation or listening to music, you spend the travelling time dodging bird waste. As you enter the restaurant, Superman tells you, 'That was a bold choice to wear those undergarments.' You realise that he has used his X-ray vision to invade your privacy. He coughs, and his superbreath slams you against a wall. As you struggle to get up, you realise from

the unpleasant look on his face that his super-smelling ability can detect the garlic that you had with lunch. During dinner, he uses his heat vision to turn his steak from medium to well done and almost sets the restaurant on fire. When the bill arrives, his eidetic memory inspires him to argue with the waiter over a price discrepancy. By the end of the night, you decide you will never go out with him again.
(Kaufman and Beghetto, 2013, p. 155)

Their point being that sometimes you need the innovation and excitement of Superman but most of the time the steady, predictable, mild-mannered Clark Kent is preferable.

One of the problems is that although creativity has benefits, it also has costs. In businesses for example, creativity costs time and money, and although it can bring innovative performance, it can also come with poor attention to detail and lower performance quality. CEOs need to decide when to prioritise creativity and when to stick to business as usual; the same is true in our classrooms and for our leaders in schools.

The influence of leadership on creativity

The culture set by school leaders can help to support teachers to overcome the barriers associated with teaching for creativity. We introduced Teresa Amabile's componential theory of creativity (Amabile, 1996) in Chapter 10. This theory suggests that three overlapping factors – domain-relevant skills, creativity-relevant processes and motivation – are required for creativity, but in addition, there needs to be a supportive social environment for this creativity to flourish. These factors are as important for developing creative teachers as for developing creative students.

Considering this theory from a leadership perspective, Amabile (1998) looked at various factors which lead to businesses undermining creativity. In this article, she considers expertise and creative thinking as raw materials but the motivation component as the part that actually determines what we do; these motivating factors are highly influenced by the social environment. Her research suggests that intrinsic motivation is far more important for creativity than extrinsic motivation and that often the root of problems in businesses is that they rely on extrinsic motivational factors. Promising a bonus if a solution to a problem is reached or threatening redundancy if targets are missed are extrinsic motivational factors, whereas people will be most creative when they are motivated primarily by interest, satisfaction and the challenge of the work itself, not external pressures.

As was also explained earlier in the book, self-determination theory (Ryan & Deci, 2000) offers a nuanced approach to extrinsic motivation; it can be looked at on a scale from very controlling (if you don't do this piece of work you'll be sacked) to more autonomous (I believe in the value of this work and want to do a good job for my boss because I respect them). The culture of a workplace is therefore highly influential in supporting the internalisation of motivating factors, and hence increasing creativity. And from a leadership perspective it may be easier to influence a culture than increase an individual's expertise or creative thinking skills.

Amabile suggests six categories where managers can enhance creativity:

1) **Challenge**: Managers can ensure that people are matched to the right assignments so they are faced with a challenge that stretches their abilities, but not too much.

2) **Freedom**: Whilst there may be specific goals a business needs to achieve, managers can give people autonomy over the means by which they obtain these goals. One way in which managers can unintentionally mismanage freedom is by changing these overarching goals too frequently.

3) **Resources**: Deciding how much time and money to give to a team or project is a judgement call that can either support or kill creativity. Time pressures under some circumstances can heighten creativity but fake deadlines or impossibly tight ones can create distrust and undermine intrinsic motivation.

4) **Work-group features**: Mutually supportive groups with a diversity of perspectives and backgrounds have been shown to produce more creative ideas; often managers kill creativity by assembling homogeneous teams.

5) **Supervisory encouragement**: Rather than offering specific extrinsic rewards, managers can foster creativity by recognising creative work and by meeting new ideas with open minds. They encourage responsible risk-taking but recognise that not every risk will pan out and treat failures as useful learning opportunities.

6) **Organisational support**: Leaders can support creativity by mandating information sharing and collaboration and by ensuring that political problems do not fester.

> ### Pause to reflect
> To what extent do you see the categories identified by Amabile as relevant to educational contexts? Are some more important than others? Can you think of any leaders who have undermined creativity, quite possibly unintentionally, by failing to support the intrinsic motivation of the people they lead?

Creely et al. (2021) carried out a case study in a secondary school in Melbourne looking at perspectives of leadership for creative thinking and risk-taking. In their study, they found the school principal had a clear vision for implementing change and teachers wanted to implement that vision. However, there was uncertainty amongst teachers on exactly how to implement the vision and implementation met with an uneven reception from students. One of their conclusions was that not only teachers but also students need to be motivated to change their approaches. Even if teachers are prepared to take risks and embrace uncertainty, if this approach is alien to the students then it will be faced with resistance. In addition, the researchers recommended that leadership for change should be led not only by formal leadership but also on a collegial teacher level. Involving students in this process, for example through a group such as a student learning community might be a way to embed a culture throughout a school that supports teaching for creativity.

> **Pause to reflect**
> Have you tried implementing change in your school or classroom only to be met with resistance from students? How did this impact your willingness to pursue the change? Did you find any strategies successful in overcoming this resistance?

Applications to Practice

Rather than our usual set of strategies for the classroom, the focus in the following sections is more on what school leaders can do to support the colleagues they work with.

Adaptive expertise

Just as with our students, teachers need to develop adaptive expertise in order to be effective creative practitioners. It is not sufficient to simply give teachers a list of pedagogical tools that can be used to develop creative thinking (although it is necessary and our hope is that the preceding chapters of this book have provided exactly that); teachers need to have a firm understanding of the underlying principles so they can choose the correct strategies at the correct time. They need to deal with situations flexibly, using their expertise to tackle the unexpected. They need adaptive expertise.

Developing this among teachers can depend on the support they get, and the overall professional development environment. Schwartz et al. (2005) note that there is an 'optimal adaptability corridor' where experimentation and playfulness are in balance with support to develop efficiency in core skills:

- Too much of the former could lead to an imaginative novice teacher feeling frustrated.
- Too much of the latter could lead to a routine expert, good at basic tasks but poor at handling unexpected situations.

Moving up this optimal adaptability corridor therefore means avoiding either extreme. It's a path that ultimately leads to adaptive expertise, but the route there won't be quick or easy. To quote Bransford et al. (2006b, p. 49): 'adaptive experts are much more likely to change their core competencies and continually expand the breadth and depth of their expertise. This restructuring of core ideas, beliefs and competencies may reduce their efficiency in the short run but make them more flexible in the long run.'

In developing adaptive expertise among teachers, those who support them need to be willing to take risks and allow colleagues to try something different. And when supporting their teaching for creativity specifically, the need to embrace uncertainty becomes even more central, as this must apply to learners' work, too. Ron Beghetto's work on the role of uncertainty (Chapter 8) is applicable to teacher learning:

> Without uncertainty, there is no creative learning. This is because uncertainty establishes the conditions necessary for new thought and action. If students (and teachers) already know what to do and how to do it, then they are rehearsing or reinforcing knowledge and skills.
>
> (Beghetto, 2021, p. 483)

Embracing uncertainty and engaging in metacognitive reflection are essential for developing adaptive expertise. As Creely et al. (2021) suggest, whilst formal leadership for change in this area is necessary, collegial teacher support is likely to be as important. The Education Endowment Foundation identifies 'Arranging practical social support' and 'Providing feedback' as two of 14 mechanisms for effective professional development (EEF, 2021), implying that leaders should consider providing opportunities for collaboration between colleagues. Importantly, the guidance does not recommend specific forms of professional development but rather encourages leaders to consider the mechanisms underpinning teacher professional development. Depending on the set-up of your workplace, social support and feedback could be provided as part of one to one coaching conversations, discussions within subject or phase groups or across subjects or phases, or indeed between schools; building adaptive expertise takes time, and leaders need to ensure that teachers are given sufficient time to consider how pedagogical principles to develop creative thinking can be enacted in their specific phase or subject.

In depth: Teacher Learning Communities

Teacher Learning Communities (TLCs) are one way in which teachers can be supported to develop their practice in teaching for creativity (Wiliam & Leahy, 2014).

In one school, which has been running TLCs over a number of years as part of their in-house professional development programme, the groups tackle different issues, with each one focused on a different school priority. Each TLC consists of a group of volunteer teachers from across a range of subjects and experience who meet after school for an hour every half term to discuss a particular aspect of educational research and how it might apply in the school's context.

An essential part of the process is that, at the end of each meeting, teachers set an action plan for a change, often very small, they wish to make in their practice, with the expectation that they feed back their findings at the start of the next meeting. Peer observations within the group are also strongly encouraged. A powerful aspect of the TLCs is the lack of hierarchy; chairs provide the structure for meetings but are also learning alongside their colleagues, trying out ideas, asking other teachers to observe lessons and provide feedback, and sharing both the successes and challenges of adapting their own teaching. TLC chairs may be in a formal leadership role within the school or may be classroom teachers who are interested in developing their leadership skills.

For the last couple of years, one of the TLCs has focused on creativity. In initial discussions, it became apparent that different teachers had very different conceptions of what creativity meant. Some thought in terms of being more creative as a teacher, for example, coming up with different activities within lessons which would engage students more in learning, others linked creativity to a creative output, whereas others associated creativity with critical thinking and problem solving. In order to dig into this further, the extent to which these different conceptions of creativity depended on the subject and the way in which knowledge in those subjects is built up over time was debated. Although this didn't allow teachers to reach an exact consensus on a definition of creativity, it did enable a shift in focus away from the activities planned by the teacher to the impact these activities had on student learning.

A turning point in discussions was discovering the work of Lucas et al. (2021), which introduced the group to the creative learning habits (see Chapter 5). Having a clear framework for developing creative thinking enabled discussions to become more focused and helped teachers to see practical ways in which changes might be implemented in their classrooms. Sharing this model, alongside initial forays into implementation, with other teachers within the school as part of a staff meeting developed a shared language of what creative thinking meant in the school's context.

Leadership and school culture

School leaders have a key role to play in developing a culture that supports teachers to both teach creatively and teach for creativity. Bullard and Bahar (2023) give the following suggestions to shape a school culture centred on creativity:

1) Revising class schedules to provide more time for the creative process
2) Including creativity and/or related terms in curriculum standards

3) Professional development on assessing students' creative thinking rather than relying solely on standard multiple-choice questions

4) Strategically selecting textbooks and/or calling for textbooks that support creativity

5) Encouraging and acknowledging positive and effective chaos as students engage in creativity

Revising class schedules

It may seem as though the constraints imposed by external systems do not allow for much flexibility in terms of revising class schedules, but there are plenty of examples of schools that have managed to do this – see for example case studies discussed as part of the Creativity Collaboratives, an action research programme set up by Arts Council England in collaboration with the University of Durham (Creativity Exchange, 2024). Revising class schedules doesn't necessarily have to involve a complete rewrite of a school timetable. It is possible to take classes off timetable for a day to engage in project work of the types discussed in Chapter 11; these can be more effective if some spacing across several days or weeks is incorporated into the project timeline. Equally, it is possible to revise class schedules within a subject by repurposing a sequence of lessons to have more of a focus on developing creative thinking.

Adapting curricula and assessment practices

Incorporating creativity as part of curricula standards may seem beyond the remit of individual schools and their leaders, and indeed it is pleasing that many international organisations and national school curricula are increasingly recognising the importance of creative thinking (see Lucas, 2022b). However, whether or not your school is working within a broader system which has creativity as an explicit part of its curriculum, there is a need to support teachers to operationalise what creative thinking and teaching *for* creativity look like in your specific context. Adapting models such as the creative learning habits can help to develop a shared language for creativity across an institution.

Such models can also support the assessment of creative skills, as discussed in Chapter 12, and leaders should also consider to what extent they can remove any barriers to teaching for creativity associated with assessment. Although in many countries external assessment systems do not incorporate aspects of creative thinking, leaders do have control over their own internal assessment processes. Do these internal assessment processes have to follow the same criteria as those external examinations? Can leaders reduce the number of 'data drops' where teachers are expected to report student progress against standardised criteria developed from those external assessments? None of these questions are easy to answer, and we would be doing our young people a disservice if we never exposed them to the criteria required for success in these external assessments, but it is worth considering whether they need to dominate all assessments within a school environment.

> ### In depth: End of year assessments
>
> End of year examinations are a common feature in many secondary school settings. However, even exams sat in the early years of secondary school can end up focusing too much on the demands of an external examination system to the detriment of developing students' wider subject knowledge and understanding. Despite the shift in many schools towards more comment-only marking and formative assessment practices throughout the year, it is often common for secondary school students to sit more formal, graded assessments at the end of each school year. These assessments can have negative washback effects with demands from students and their parents to provide more exam-style practice throughout the year, which can lead to a focus on short-term performance to the detriment of long-term learning. Thus the end of year assessment can drive curriculum and teaching decisions.
>
> In one school, the school leadership therefore dropped the requirement for all departments to set a more formal end of year examination, and several departments came up with alternative assessment systems.

The Chemistry department replaced the exam with an extended investigation, spread out over several weeks. Students undertook some initial exploratory practical work and then planned a more formal practical investigation. The structured write-up assessed not only their practical skills but also the chemical theories studied during the year, such as particle theory and reactions of acids. The new style of assessment proved much more effective at assessing students' understanding of the first year of the Chemistry course, without the negative washback effects of students demanding more formal tests throughout the year.

In Geography, they used to have an assessment at the end of the first year of the course focused on map skills, a skill that was relatively easy to assess in a 45-minute test paper. The unintended consequence of this assessment was that map skills began to dominate the curriculum to the detriment of other geographical concepts. With the removal of the exam, the department was able to focus much more on building the foundations of what makes a good geographer, using ongoing formative assessment to check progress through the curriculum.

In History, they found that short essays completed under timed conditions in the first year inevitably ended up being more about memorising facts and less about skills acquisition and development. The department wanted to communicate to students something that more closely emulated what historians actually do – research, examining primary resources, identifying trends, etc. To that end, they replaced their formal examination with a project that covered several lessons. Students were given access to a curated set of resources and asked to consider the question 'How did rulers in Medieval England and the Islamic Empire maintain power?' The project introduced no new content but encouraged students to consider the theme of maintaining power through three categories: use of violence/coercion, religion and architecture. They have found this approach a far better way to assess the development of students as historians and prepare them for future study, particularly as the factual content of the first year course was not required in subsequent years.

Motivating teachers to embrace uncertainty

Bullard and Bahar's (2023) final point on leaders encouraging and acknowledging positive and effective chaos is possibly the hardest one for leaders to embrace. As indicated by Amabile's work discussed earlier in the chapter, there is a link between creativity, risk-taking and failure; this chimes with research that has found that in order to be creative, people need to have creative confidence but also be willing to take intellectual risks (Beghetto et al., 2021). However, failure within an educational context is often seen in a negative light as it does not align with easily measurable outcomes of success such as scores on standardised tests or with traditional approaches to performance management. So what can leaders do to shift their school's culture towards one more supportive of risk-taking and forgiving of failure?

One avenue to explore is teacher motivation. To what extent are teachers driven by extrinsic motivational factors such as professional development associated with one-off, high-stakes lesson observations or quality assurance predicated on every teacher following a prescribed lesson structure. Such practices may enable a school to quickly reach a certain level of alignment between teachers and student experiences but will almost certainly limit their ability to take risks and embrace failure. And if teachers are unwilling to embrace the uncertainty that is essential for creativity to flourish then it is highly unlikely that students will feel comfortable doing so.

As ever, there is a balance to be struck. Leaders should carefully consider where alignment is required and where it is appropriate to give teachers more freedom; this should be considered at both the whole school and departmental/phase level.

As discussed in Chapter 10, self-determination theory (Ryan & Deci, 2000) provides a helpful framework to move beyond the simplistic intrinsic/extrinsic motivation dichotomy. It emphasises certain basic psychological needs: competence, relatedness and autonomy. These concepts are just as important for supporting teacher motivation as student motivation.

Clear systems and structures around behaviour, for example, support teacher competence – if there is no accepted whole school behaviour protocol then it becomes challenging for teachers to establish a safe and supportive learning environment, decreasing their levels of competence in the classroom. This can rapidly become highly demotivating. Equally, teachers need a clear set of pedagogical practices that support teaching for creativity – a shared language across a school helps build competence in this area. On the other hand, an environment which restricts teacher autonomy and does not allow for adaptation to subject, phase, the specific children in front of them and indeed a teacher's own personality is only ever going to produce teachers with routine rather than adaptive expertise.

Autonomy can be seen as in opposition to relatedness, which refers to the need to feel connected and a sense of belonging; however, within self-determination theory, autonomy is not associated with individualistic behaviours or being independent and detached but rather with the extent to which your behaviour is controlled by others. Ensuring teachers have a sense of agency within their own classrooms is possibly a better way to conceptualise these ideas. Social support from peers and a culture of mutual trust and respect throughout a school will serve to develop more intrinsically motivated staff.

Pause to reflect
Do the leaders in your school support teachers to embrace the uncertainty required to teach for creativity? To what extent does your school culture develop teachers' intrinsic motivation by supporting their needs for competence, relatedness and autonomy? If you are in a leadership role, do you see any tensions between teacher autonomy and accountability measures?

Involving parents

Parents play an important role in developing a school's culture, and sharing the school's vision for developing creativity with parents through newsletters, talks, social media, etc. will be an important part of any school's implementation. In the same way that students can be resistant to change, parents can also undermine teachers' attempts to teach *for* creativity if they fear that such practices might be detrimental to their children's performance in external standardised assessments. As discussed in Chapter 12, whilst it is unlikely that many parents will disagree with the broad conception that part of a school's role is to develop students' ability to think creatively and thrive beyond school, it is important to share with them exactly what this looks like in practice. In Chapter 12 we suggested changes to reporting structures and inviting parents to showcase events. Other ideas could be using parents as a source of expertise in particular fields; they could provide the inspiration for a legacy project or act as an external judge for creative work. Maybe they could even come into school and complete some short projects or activities alongside their children?

Conclusion

In this chapter we have dispelled the myth that only certain teachers have the personality to teach creatively. Teaching for creativity does not have to involve a maverick teacher who fights against the school system. Indeed the opposite is true – for a school to truly develop creative students, the principles and practices associated with teaching for creativity should be part of the whole school culture and embraced by all stakeholders, teachers, students and parents alike. Leaders have a responsibility to set the vision but collegial teacher support is also required to help embrace the uncertainty that is a prerequisite for developing creativity. Equally, it needs to be recognised where teaching for creativity is appropriate and where it is not. There is still a place for traditional, teacher-led instruction within a school that champions creativity – as we have said repeatedly throughout this book, knowledge and skills are intertwined and creativity stems from a sound knowledge base.

Discussion Questions

1) What barriers might be in place to prevent your school developing creative teachers? What could you do to mitigate these?

2) What does 'adaptive expertise' mean in the context of a teacher? How might this differ from 'routine expertise' in teaching? In what ways can teachers be encouraged to develop adaptive expertise?

3) In what ways can self-determination theory be applied to motivating teachers to develop their practice to teach for creativity?

4) How might frameworks for assessing creative thinking (such as those discussed both in this chapter and the previous chapter) be used to develop a shared language or culture within a school for teaching creativity?

Professional Learning Tasks

Task 1

Consider the professional development opportunities available to you in your school and beyond. Carry out an audit of these opportunities against the 14 mechanisms suggested by the EEF Guidance Report on Effective Professional Development (2021). To what extent do these opportunities allow you to develop adaptive expertise in your context? Which mechanisms might you wish to focus on in order to improve your personal practice in teaching for creativity (or that of your teaching staff if you are in a leadership position)?

Task 2

Download the *Noticing Creative Thinking* resource found on the Leading for Creative Thinking website (Leading for Creative Thinking, n.d.). Use the resource to observe some lessons in your school and/or ask some colleagues to observe your own teaching. In what ways are you already developing creative learning habits in your students? Are there any habits that you could be developing further?

Task 3

Undertake an audit of the more formal assessment practices currently undertaken within your school/phase/department. To what extent do these practices align with high-stakes, external examinations or standardised tests? Is there room for changing the success criteria to acknowledge students' improved capacity for creative thinking? Are there opportunities to change how results from these assessments are reported to parents?

14 Looking Back and Looking Forward

Creativity: Important but Misunderstood

There is widespread agreement that creativity is an important process in education. Everyone wants creative students. Everyone wants school leavers to be creative in the workplace. Everyone wants teachers to be creative in their practice.

However, as we have seen, there is much less of a consensus about what creativity actually is. Indeed, there are many misconceptions about it throughout the education system – a situation that could be a problem for teachers and policy makers alike. Some teachers may feel that it is an optional extra that they often don't have time for, while others feel that it will take care of itself.

We hope that by presenting a cognitive science approach to creativity throughout this book, we have provided a clearer and more granular explanation of the fundamentals of creativity. Once the concept is defined, with a breakdown of how it works and what kinds of things support it, it's easier to see why just hoping for the best won't work. Some focus on supporting and providing opportunities for creativity, informed by an understanding of what it looks like across tasks and subjects, will be much more valuable to educators.

In this book, we have worked through various aspects of creativity, trying to cut through the confusion and presenting a more concrete picture of what creativity looks like in education, as well as how to teach for creativity. We hope you now recognise more fully what creativity is, how relevant it is to all students on an everyday basis, and how it can't be separated from learning knowledge across the curriculum.

Reflecting on the Myths

As part of the process of unpacking and exploring creativity, it has been necessary for us to spotlight and debunk the various myths and popular misconceptions that are associated with creativity.

The myths were shared in part because they provided a useful starting point for exploring some of the cognitive science research into creativity. However, there is another reason. We also feel that it's important to push back against misconceptions that might impact teachers and students at a policy level. If decisions are made based on myths about creativity, this is not in the best interests of students.

For example, if it is assumed that students will develop creativity if left alone and given as much freedom as possible, then schools might fail to develop the building blocks of creativity that are so important, and may actually undermine creativity by not providing any structure or constraints. Similarly, the idea that creativity only belongs to some subjects could have a distorting effect on curriculum policy. Arts subjects play a valuable role in their own right – their purpose is not to make students more creative in other fields.

Skills vs. Knowledge, Revisited

One of the myths shared in the book is the idea that creativity is a transferable skill, and again, this is widely shared by policy makers, along with the assumption that teaching generic creative skills will more or less automatically transfer to everyday life or to the workforce. However, we have seen throughout the book that this is simplistic and over-optimistic.

This returns us to the skills vs. knowledge debate discussed towards the start of the book. We have placed a great emphasis on the role of knowledge in creativity. At the same time, we hope we have clarified that while knowledge and other fundamentals of your teaching are the basic building blocks of creativity, that is not the whole story. Learners also need to know what to do with that knowledge. Consider the following ideas we have discussed:

- There are certain 'initial requirements' that apply across domains, including dispositions such as a tendency to be playful with ideas.
- Gaining more expertise does not always help with creative thinking – it only helps with creative transfer to novel tasks if the expertise is adaptive, rather than routine.
- How well learners understand a problem makes a huge difference, and learners also need to make connections and reorder their 'building blocks'.
- The set-up of tasks and social circumstances can make a difference, as can a student's capacity to think about and control their creativity (metacognition).

These subtleties are often absent from policy documents and curricula, which tend to fall on one side of the argument or the other – a strong skills or knowledge focus. We hope that a more detailed, nuanced and evidence-based approach to creativity will lead to more thoughtful discussions about how to support creativity. As discussed in Chapter 1, recent years have seen a huge growth in interest in cognitive science and its insights for the classroom. A key theme that has run throughout all the chapters of the book is that this cognitive science approach can be applied to creativity, too.

After all, the process of creative thinking needn't and shouldn't sit separately from discussions of how educators build knowledge, teach reading, or raise attainment. Creativity connects directly to concepts such as motivation and metacognition, and applies both to everyday tasks and to extended projects at all ages and stages.

Part of the reason for this is that creativity is such an everyday thing and draws on the same cognitive systems that students use to think about and process other tasks. It is subject to the same limitations of working memory as other learning tasks, for example, and draws on the same schemas that make up long-term memory, and on a learner's broader dispositions and attitudes.

The Big Challenge

Even armed with a better understanding of the concept, there are many challenges to supporting creativity in education. Creativity is not impossible to teach – but it does involve introducing some uncertainty into your classes. It may not entail rewriting the entire school curriculum, but it does involve making space for divergent thinking and providing opportunities for students to explore ideas. These are issues that draw on careful judgement and planning on the part of the professional.

As students begin to apply creativity (and, we hope, to better understand creativity), they will benefit from support with strategies to help them apply their curricular knowledge. They will also benefit from practising flexibly, so that their knowledge becomes part of adaptive rather than routine expertise. And they will benefit from the thoughtful use of constraints as a form of scaffolding of their thinking.

As students become more successful at everyday creative tasks, they may find themselves relishing the opportunities to engage in them. Metacognitive awareness of their own creative potential will motivate them to try new things in the future. Certainly, some will show more of a creative disposition than others, and more enjoyment of these aspects of their learning. Still, creative dispositions such as curiosity and playfulness can be encouraged through simple tasks done on a regular basis. As discussed in Chapter 10, motivation is built, not found. Once students realise that they can do something, and that it's not just for other people, the prospect becomes much less threatening – it may even be enticing.

Therefore, despite the challenges both to understanding creativity and to supporting it among learners, there is plenty of reason for optimism about the state of creativity in schools. Consider, for example:

- Creativity applies to all subjects, meaning that everyone is invited.
- Creativity can be encouraged and explored within the existing curriculum – good news for those who don't feel they have enough time to add it to their courses.
- Tasks such as varied practice can help to develop adaptive expertise among students, which will help with problem solving.
- Many tasks that boost creative thinking are quick, easy and fun to do, such as playfulness, brainstorming, spotting connections, and using prompts. Others connect to rather than conflict with good practice, for example by boosting knowledge or making use of scaffolding and formative assessment.

The Big Picture

After so much discussion of school-age students and the classroom, it may feel that we have not focused enough on creativity beyond the classroom – on its vital role in the workplace or in everyday life.

Well, a cognitive science approach can help us to prepare students for life beyond education, too. It would be unrealistic to suppose that many school or college leavers will immediately be ready to engage in Pro-C or Big-C creativity. All the same, we feel that the view of teaching presented in this book will help to prepare students for future experiences. For example, as discussed in Chapter 9, students who know how to learn are better prepared. Learning how to learn can include gaining a metacognitive awareness of what creativity is, and how to harness it, as recommended in this book.

Many commentators feel that creativity is at the very top of the skills that students will need in the future. For example, the World Economic Forum identified creative thinking as the second most important skill required by employers in 2023 (after analytical thinking) and the skill judged to be increasing in importance most rapidly between 2023 and 2027 (WEF, 2023).

While we can't predict what roles our students will end up in, it's reasonable to suppose that their capacity to be creative may lead to more success wherever they end up. Fortunately, in line with Karwowski's (2022) propositions which were discussed in Chapter 2, as well as the points made about knowledge (Chapter 3), academic learning is not a barrier to this – it correlates with creativity, and students who know more are better placed to achieve in creative work.

Still, we have also seen that students need to be able to use knowledge flexibly, and schools don't always provide the best preparation for this. Classrooms are often rather predictable compared to the workplace. Openness to uncertainty and willingness to be creative and to tinker with ideas will pave the way for doing the same in more authentic settings, as will engagement in legacy projects (see Chapter 11). The strategies and dispositions that students apply during creative tasks will become part of a toolkit, all of which will be supported by their metacognitive understanding of creativity and of themselves as creative individuals.

Researchers who have explored creative ideas among many thousands of artists, musicians, writers and scientists have noted many common characteristics among those who are successful. Sternberg (1999) noted that much creative work involves incremental progress within the existing parameters of the field, such as writing a detective story in a new way. Others may in some way redirect their field or spark an entirely new genre – Jane Austen's novels, for example. Still others combine elements from two or more sources to make something new – George Lucas fusing samurai movies and sci-fi when making *Star Wars* is a widely discussed example. Such work doesn't happen without both expertise in the field(s) and a willingness to explore ideas in a context of uncertainty.

Most students we teach will not become the next George Lucas or Jane Austen. However, we would still argue that the building blocks of creativity are put in place early – and that this can often be done better than is currently the case. Infusing creativity into academic tasks helps learners both to consolidate basic content and to get used to using this flexibly and playfully. By facing uncertainty and taking risks in the classroom, where the low-stakes nature of most tasks means failure rarely has long-lasting detrimental consequences, learners will become more comfortable with facing this uncertainty later in life.

Overall, just because creativity can be a small-scale, everyday process in the classroom, it doesn't mean that we can't dream big for our students. We can't predict where our students' career paths will take them, but we can set them up as best we can.

We hope you have enjoyed exploring the ideas in this book, and that you are inspired to apply them (creatively!) to your own classroom. And if so, why not use the discussion questions and tasks to explore them with colleagues, too? This could become your very own legacy project.

References

Abrahams, I., Reiss, M. J., & Sharpe, R. M. (2013). The assessment of practical work in school science. *Studies in Science Education, 49*(2), 209-251.

Adeel, A., Sarminah, S., Jie, L., Kee, D., Daghriri, Y., & Alghafes, R. (2023). When procrastination pays off: Role of knowledge sharing ability, autonomous motivation, and task involvement for employee creativity. *Heliyon, 9*, e19398.

Agarwal, P. K., & Bain, P. M. (2019). *Powerful teaching: Unleash the science of learning*. John Wiley & Sons.

Amabile, T. M. (1982). Social psychology of creativity: A consensual assessment technique. *Journal of Personality and Social Psychology, 43*(5), 997-1013.

Amabile, T. M. (1983). The social psychology of creativity: A componential conceptualization. *Journal of Personality and Social Psychology, 45*(2), 357-376.

Amabile, T. M. (1993). Motivational synergy: Toward new conceptualizations of intrinsic and extrinsic motivation in the workplace. *Human Resource Management Review, 3*(3), 185-201.

Amabile, T. M. (1996). *Creativity in context: Update to "The Social Psychology of Creativity"*. Westview Press.

Amabile, T. M. (1998). How to kill creativity. *Harvard Business Review, 76*(5), 76-87.

Anderson, L. W. (Ed.), Krathwohl, D. R. (Ed.), Airasian, P. W., Cruikshank, K. A., Mayer, R. E., Pintrich, P. R., Raths, J., & Wittrock, M. C. (2001). *A taxonomy for learning, teaching, and assessing: A revision of Bloom's taxonomy of educational objectives (Complete edition)*. Longman.

Anderson, M. C., Bjork, R. A., & Bjork, E. L. (1994). Remembering can cause forgetting: Retrieval dynamics in long-term memory. *Journal of Experimental Psychology: Learning, Memory, and Cognition, 20*(5), 1063-1087.

Anderson, R. C. (1984). Some reflections on the acquisition of knowledge. *Educational Researcher, 13*(9), 5-10.

Asch, S. E. (1955). Opinions and social pressure. *Scientific American, 193*, 31-35.

Badger, C., & Firth, J. (2023). A metacognitive approach to developing creativity. *Impact, 19*. https://my.chartered.college/impact/issue-19-effective-pedagogy-and-applying-research-in-practice/

Baer, J. (2017). Why you are probably more creative (and less creative) than you think. In M. Karwowski & J. C. Kaufman (Eds), *The creative self* (pp. 259-273). Academic Press.

Baer, J., & Kaufman, J. C. (2005). Bridging generality and specificity: The amusement park theoretical (APT) model of creativity. *Roeper Review, 27*(3), 158-163.

Baird, B., Smallwood, J., Mrazek, M. D., Kam, J. W. Y., Franklin, M. S., & Schooler, J. W. (2012). Inspired by distraction: Mind wandering facilitates creative incubation. *Psychological Science, 23*(10), 1117-1122.

Barnett, S. M., & Ceci, S. J. (2002). When and where do we apply what we learn? A taxonomy for far transfer. *Psychological Bulletin, 128*, 612-637.

Barton, C. (2024). SSDD Problems: 10 tips to supercharge them in the classroom. https://eedi.substack.com/p/ssdd-problems-10-tips-to-supercharge

Beghetto, R. A. (2013). *Killing ideas softly? The promise and perils of creativity in the classroom*. IAP Information Age Publishing.

Beghetto, R. A. (2017a). Legacy projects: Helping young people respond productively to the challenges of a changing world. *Roeper Review, 39*(3), 187-190.

Beghetto, R. A. (2017b). Uncertainty in school contexts. https://youtu.be/yE8feb5Vc8Q?si=ozwMuvg9O2RTIrnD

Beghetto, R. A. (2018). Taking beautiful risks in education. *Association for Supervision and Curriculum Development, 76*(4), 18-24.

Beghetto, R. A. (2019). Structured uncertainty: How creativity thrives under constraints and uncertainty. In C. A. Mullen (Eds), *Creativity under duress in education? Creativity theory and action in education*, vol. 3 (pp. 27-40). Springer.

Beghetto, R. A. (2021). There is no creativity without uncertainty: Dubito Ergo Creo. *Journal of Creativity*, *31*, 100005.

Beghetto, R. A. (2024). Creativity and possibility thinking bots. https://www.ronaldbeghetto.com/ptbots

Beghetto, R. A., & Kaufman, J. C. (2014). Classroom contexts for creativity. *High Ability Studies*, *25*(1), 53-69.

Beghetto, R. A., Karwowski, M., & Reiter-Palmon, R. (2021). Intellectual risk taking: A moderating link between creative confidence and creative behavior? *Psychology of Aesthetics, Creativity, and the Arts*, *15*(4), 637-644.

Benedek, M., Karstendiek, M., Ceh, S. M., Grabner, R. H., Krammer, G., Lebuda, I., Silvia, P. J., Cotter, K. N., Li, Y., Hu, W., Martskvishvili, K., & Kaufman, J. C. (2021). Creativity myths: Prevalence and correlates of misconceptions on creativity. *Personality and Individual Differences*, *182*, 11068.

Benedek, M., Beaty, R. E., Schacter, D. L., & Kenett, Y. N. (2023). The role of memory in creative ideation. *Nature Reviews Psychology*, *2*(4), 246-257.

Bereczki, E. O., & Kárpáti, A. (2018). Teachers' beliefs about creativity and its nurture: A systematic review of the recent research literature. *Educational Research Review*, *23*, 25-56.

Bereiter, C., & Scardamalia, M. (1987). *The psychology of written composition*. Erlbaum.

Birnbaum, M. S., Kornell, N., Bjork, E. L., & Bjork, R. A. (2013). Why interleaving enhances inductive learning: The roles of discrimination and retrieval. *Memory & Cognition*, *41*(3), 392-402.

Bjork, R. A. (1994). Memory and metamemory considerations in the training of human beings. In J. Metcalfe & A. Shimamura (Eds), *Metacognition: Knowing about knowing* (pp. 185-205). MIT Press.

Bjork, R. A., & Bjork, E. L. (2023). Introducing desirable difficulties into practice and instruction: Obstacles and opportunities. In C. E. Overson, C. M. Hakala, L. L. Kordonowy, & V. A. Benassi, (Eds), *In their own words* (pp. 19-30). Society for the Teaching of Psychology.

Black, P., & Wiliam, D. (2006). Developing a theory of formative assessment. In J. Gardner (Ed.), *Assessment and learning* (pp. 81-100). Sage.

Boekaerts, M., & Corno, L. (2005). Self-regulation in the classroom: A perspective on assessment and intervention. *Applied Psychology*, *54*(2), 199-231.

Bolden, B., DeLuca, C., Kukkonen, T., Roy, S., & Wearing, J. (2020). Assessment of creativity in K-12 education: A scoping review. *Review of Education, 8*(2), 343-376.

Bramwell, G., Reilly, R. C., Lilly, F. R., Kronish, N., & Chennabathni, R. (2011). Creative teachers. *Roeper Review, 33*(4), 228-238.

Bransford, J. D., Brown, A. L., & Cocking, R. R. (2000). *How people learn: Brain, mind, experience and school*. National Academy Press.

Bransford, J. D., Darling-Hammond, L., & LePage, P. (2006a). Introduction. In J. D. Bransford & L. Darling-Hammond (Eds), *Preparing teachers for a changing world: What teachers should learn and be able to do* (pp. 1-39). Jossey-Bass.

Bransford, J. D., Derry, S., Berliner, D., Hammerness, K., & Beckett, K. L. (2006b). Theories of learning and their role in teaching. In J. D. Bransford & L. Darling-Hammond (Eds), *Preparing teachers for a changing world: What teachers should learn and be able to do* (pp. 40-87). Jossey-Bass.

Bruner, J. S. (1966). *Toward a theory of instruction*. Harvard University Press.

Buehler, R., Griffin, D., & Ross, M. (1994). Exploring the "planning fallacy": Why people underestimate their task completion times. *Journal of Personality and Social Psychology, 67*(3), 366-381.

Bullard, A. J., & Bahar, A. K. (2023). Common barriers in teaching for creativity in K-12 classrooms: A literature review. *Journal of Creativity, 33*, 100045.

Campbell, G. (2021). The influence of mood during incubation on subsequent design ideation. Doctoral thesis, University of Strathclyde.

Caviglioli, O. (2019). *Dual coding with teachers*. John Catt.

Chase, W. G., & Simon, H. A. (1973). Perception in chess. *Cognitive Psychology, 4*(1), 55-81.

Christodoulou, D. (2017). *Making good progress? The future of assessment for learning*. Oxford University Press.

Cialdini, R. B., Trost, M. R., & Newsom, J. T. (1995). Preference for consistency: The development of a valid measure and the discovery of surprising behavioral implications. *Journal of Personality and Social Psychology, 69*(2), 318-328.

Creativity Exchange (2024). *Creativity Collaboratives*. https://www.creativityexchange.org.uk/creativity-collaboratives

Creely, E., Henderson, M., Henriksen, D., & Crawford, R. (2021). Leading change for creativity in schools: Mobilizing creative risk-taking and productive failure. *International Journal of Leadership in Education*, https://www.tandfonline.com/doi/abs/10.1080/13603124.2021.1969040

Csikszentmihalyi, M. (1997). *Creativity: Flow and the psychology of discovery and invention*. HarperCollins.

Darley, J. M., & Batson, C. D. (1973). "From Jerusalem to Jericho": A study of situational and dispositional variables in helping behavior. *Journal of Personality and Social Psychology*, 27(1), 100-108.

de Jong, T., Lazonder, A. W., Chinn, C. A., Fischer, F., Gobert, J., Hmelo-Silver, C. E., ... & Zacharia, Z. C. (2024). Beyond inquiry or direct instruction: Pressing issues for designing impactful science learning opportunities. *Educational Research Review*, 44, https://www.sciencedirect.com/science/article/pii/S1747938X24000320.

Deuja, A., Kohn, N. W., Paulus, P. B., & Korde, R. M. (2014). Taking a broad perspective before brainstorming. *Group Dynamics: Theory, Research, and Practice*, 18(3), 222-236.

Douven, I. (2021). Peirce on abduction. https://plato.stanford.edu/entries/abduction/peirce.html

Dunning, D. (2011). The Dunning–Kruger effect: On being ignorant of one's own ignorance. In M. Zanna & J. Olson (Eds), *Advances in experimental social psychology, vol. 44* (pp. 247-296). Academic Press.

Durham Commission (2019). *Durham Commission on Creativity and Education*. London, Arts Council England.

Dweck, C. S. (2006). *Mindset: How you can fulfil your potential*. Robinson Books.

Edmonson, A. (2023) *Right kind of wrong: Why learning to fail can teach us to thrive*. Cornerstone Press.

EEF (2018). *Metacognition and self-regulated learning: Guidance report*. https://educationendowmentfoundation.org.uk/education-evidence/guidance-reports/metacognition

EEF (2021). *Effective professional development: Guidance report*. https://educationendowmentfoundation.org.uk/education-evidence/guidance-reports/effective-professional-development

Eglington, L. G., & Kang, S. H. K. (2017). Interleaved presentation benefits science category learning. *Journal of Applied Research in Memory and Cognition, 6*(4), 475-485.

Engeser, S., Schiepe-Tiska, A., & Peifer, C. (2021). Historical lines and an overview of current research on flow. In C. Peifer & S. Engeser (Eds), *Advances in flow research*, 2nd edn (pp. 1-29). Springer.

Epstein, D. (2019). *Range: Why generalists triumph in a specialized world.* Riverhead Books.

Ericsson, K. A. (2017). Expertise and individual differences: The search for the structure and acquisition of experts' superior performance. *WIREs Cognitive Science, 8*(1-2), e1382.

Facione, P. A. (2015). *Critical thinking: What it is and why it counts.* Insight Assessment.

Feltovich, P. J., Spiro, R. J., & Coulson, R. L. (1997). Issues of expert flexibility in contexts characterised by complexity and change. In P. J. Feltovich, K. M. Ford, & R. R. Hoffman (Eds), *Expertise in context* (pp. 125-146). American Association for Artificial Intelligence.

Fink, E., Mareva, S., & Gibson, J. L. (2020). Dispositional playfulness in young children: A cross-sectional and longitudinal examination of the psychometric properties of a new child self-reported playfulness scale and associations with social behaviour. *Infant and Child Development, 29*(4), e2181.

Fiorella, L., & Mayer, R. E. (2015). Eight ways to promote generative learning. *Educational Psychology Review, 28*(4), 717-741.

Firth, J. (2024). *Metacognition and study skills: A guide for teachers.* David Fulton Books.

Firth, J., & Riazat, N. (2023). *What teachers need to know about memory.* Sage.

Firth, J., Rivers, I., & Boyle, J. (2021). A systematic review of interleaving as a concept learning strategy. *Review of Education, 9*(2), 642-684.

Fyfe, E. R., & Nathan, M. J. (2019). Making "concreteness fading" more concrete as a theory of instruction for promoting transfer. *Educational Review, 71*(4), 403-422.

Fyfe, E. R., McNeil, N. M., & Borjas, S. (2015). Benefits of "concreteness fading" for children's mathematics understanding. *Learning and Instruction, 35*, 104-120.

Geisinger, K. F. (2016). 21st century skills: What are they and how do we assess them? *Applied Measurement in Education*, *29*(4), 245–249.

Gibbons, G. H. (2013). Serendipity and the prepared mind: An NHLBI Intramural Researcher's breakthrough observations. https://www.nhlbi.nih.gov/directors-messages/serendipity-and-the-prepared-mind

Gick, M. L., & Holyoak, K. J. (1983). Schema induction and analogical transfer. *Cognitive Psychology*, *15*(1), 1–38.

Gilhooly, K. J., Georgiou, G., & Devery, U. (2013). Incubation and creativity: Do something different. *Thinking & Reasoning*, *19*(2), 137–149.

Graham, S., & Harris, K. R. (2016). A path to better writing: Evidence-based practices in the classroom. *The Reading Teacher*, *69*(4), 359–365.

Gralewski, J. (2019). Teachers' beliefs about creative students' characteristics: A qualitative study. *Thinking Skills and Creativity*, *31*, 138–155.

Grant, A. (2016). *Originals: How non-conformists move the world*. Viking

Grant, A. (2021). *Think again: The power of knowing what you don't know*. Penguin Random House.

Gube, M., & Lajoie, S. (2020). Adaptive expertise and creative thinking: A synthetic review and implications for practice. *Thinking Skills and Creativity*, *35*, 100630.

Harford, T. (2016). *Messy: The power of disorder to transform our lives*. Little, Brown.

Harrington, D. M. (2018). On the usefulness of "value" in the definition of creativity: A commentary. *Creativity Research Journal*, *30*(1), 118–121.

Haskell, R. E. (2001). *Transfer of learning*. Academic Press.

Hatano, G., & Inagaki, K. (1986). Two courses of expertise. In H. W. Stevenson, H. Azuma, & K. Hakuta (Eds), *Child development and education in Japan* (pp. 262–272). W. H. Freeman/Times Books/Henry Holt & Co.

Hirsch, E. D. (2008). Plugging the hole in state standards. *American Educator*, *32*(1), 8–12.

Hobbiss, M., Sims, S., & Allen, R. (2020). Habit formation limits growth in teacher effectiveness: A review of converging evidence from neuroscience and social science. *Review of Education*, *9*(1), 3–23.

Holyoak, K. J. (1991). Symbolic connectionism: Toward third-generation theories of expertise. In K. A. Ericsson & J. Smith (Eds), *Toward a general theory of expertise: Prospects and limits* (pp. 301–335). Cambridge University Press.

Howard-Jones, P. A. (2014). Neuroscience and education: Myths and messages. *Nature Reviews Neuroscience, 15*(12), 817-824.

Janssen, E. M., van Gog, T., van de Groep, L., de Lange, A. J., Knopper, R. L., Onan, E., Wiradhany, W., & de Bruin, A. B. H. (2023). The role of mental effort in students' perceptions of the effectiveness of interleaved and blocked study strategies and their willingness to use them. *Educational Psychology Review, 35*(3), Article 85.

Jenkins, H. (2012). *Textual poachers: Television fans and participatory culture*. Routledge.

Karwowski, M. (2022). School does not kill creativity. *European Psychologist, 27*(3), 263-275.

Kaufman, J. C., & Baer, J. (2002). Could Steven Spielberg manage the Yankees? Creative thinking in different domains. *Korean Journal of Thinking & Problem Solving, 12*(2), 5-14.

Kaufman, J. C., & Beghetto, R. A. (2009). Beyond big and little: The Four C model of creativity. *Review of General Psychology, 13*(1), 1-12.

Kaufman, J. C., & Beghetto, R. A. (2013). In praise of Clark Kent: Creative metacognition and the importance of teaching kids when (not) to be creative. *Roeper Review: A Journal on Gifted Education, 35*(3), 155-165.

Kaufman, J. C., Evans, M. L., & Baer, J. (2010). The American idol effect: Are students good judges of their creativity across domains? *Empirical Studies of the Arts, 28*(1), 3-17. https://doi.org/10.2190/EM.28.1.b

Kim, Y. J., & Zhong, C.-B. (2017). Ideas rise from chaos: Information structure and creativity. *Organizational Behavior and Human Decision Processes, 138*, 15-27.

Kirby, J. (2013). What Sir Ken got wrong. https://joe-kirby.com/2013/10/12/what-sir-ken-got-wrong/

Kirschner, P. A., & Hendrick, C. (2020). *How learning happens: Seminal works in educational psychology and what they mean in practice*. Routledge.

Kirschner, P. A., Sweller, J., & Clark, R. E. (2006). Why minimal guidance during instruction does not work: An analysis of the failure of constructivist, discovery, problem-based, experiential, and inquiry-based teaching. *Educational Psychologist, 41*(2), 75-86.

Klein, G. (2008). Performing a project premortem. *Engineering Management Review, IEEE, 36,* 103–104.

Kooren, N. S., Van Nooijen, C., & Paas, F. (2024). The influence of active and passive procrastination on academic performance: A meta-analysis. *Education Sciences, 14,* 323.

Krstic, S. (2024). *Putting creative thinking at the core of the English school curriculum: An exploratory study.* Australian Council for Educational Research UK.

Land, G. (2011). The failure of success. https://youtu.be/ZfKMq-rYtnc?si=I98jE6i2TB3nAFLN

Larcom, S., Rauch, F., & Willems, T. (2017). The benefits of forced experimentation: Striking evidence from the London Underground network. *The Quarterly Journal of Economics, 132*(4), 2019–2055.

Lassig, C. (2021). Creativity talent development: Fostering creativity in schools. In S. R. Smith (Ed.), *Handbook of giftedness and talent development in the Asia-Pacific* (pp. 1045–1069). Springer.

Lave, J., & Wenger, E. (1991). *Situated learning: Legitimate peripheral participation.* Cambridge University Press.

Leading for Creative Thinking (n.d.). *Noticing creative thinking.* https://leadingforcreativethinking.org/index.php/noticing-creative-thinking

Little, J. L., Storm, B. C., & Bjork, E. L. (2011). The costs and benefits of testing text materials. *Memory, 19*(4), 346–359.

Lovell, O. (2020). *Cognitive load theory in action.* John Catt Educational.

Lucas, B. (2022a). *Creative thinking in schools across the world: A snapshot of progress in 2022.* Global Institute of Creative Thinking.

Lucas, B. (2022b). *A field guide to assessing creativity in schools.* Perth: FORM.

Lucas, B., & Spencer, E. (2017). *Teaching creative thinking: Developing learners who generate ideas and can think critically.* Crown House Publishing.

Lucas, B., Spencer, E., & Stoll, L. (2021). *Creative leadership to develop creativity and creative thinking in English schools: A review of the evidence.* Mercers' Company.

Maguire, E. A., Gadian, D. G., Johnsrude, I. S., Good, C. D., Ashburner, J., Frackowiak, R. S. J., & Frith, C. D. (2000). Navigation-related structural change in the hippocampi of cab drivers. *Proceedings of the National Academy of Sciences of the United States of America, 97*(8), 4398–4403.

Mayer, R. E. (2004). Should there be a three-strikes rule against pure discovery learning? *American Psychologist, 59*(1), 14-19.

Mccrea, P. (2023). Variation theory: Using positive & negative examples. https://snacks.pepsmccrea.com/p/variation-theory.

McDaniel, M. A., Einstein, G. O., & Een, E. (2021). Training college students to use learning strategies: A framework and pilot course. *Psychology Learning & Teaching, 20*(3), 364-382.

Mednick, S. A. (1962). The associative basis of the creative process. *Psychological Review, 69*(3), 220-232.

Miao, P., & Heining-Boynton, A. L. (2011). Initiation/response/follow-up, and response to intervention: Combining two models to improve teacher and student performance. *Foreign Language Annals, 44*(1), 65-79.

Milgram, R. M., Moran III, J. D., Sawyers, J. K., & Fu, V. R. (1987). Original thinking in Israeli preschool children. *School Psychology International, 8*(1), 54-58.

Mitra, S. (2013) Build a school in the cloud. https://www.ted.com/talks/sugata_mitra_build_a_school_in_the_cloud

Morais, M. D. F., Jesus, S. N. D., Azevedo, I., Araújo, A. M., & Viseu, J. (2015). Intervention program on adolescent's creativity representations and academic motivation. *Paidéia (Ribeirão Preto), 25*, 289-297.

Mueller, J. S., Melwani, S., & Goncalo, J. A. (2011). The bias against creativity: Why people desire but reject creative ideas. *Psychological Science, 23*(1), 13-17.

Niemiec, C. P., & Ryan, R. M. (2009). Autonomy, competence, and relatedness in the classroom: Applying self-determination theory to educational practice. *Theory and Research in Education, 7*(2), 133-144.

Nijstad, B. A., Stroebe, W., & Lodewijkx, H. F. (2002). Cognitive stimulation and interference in groups: Exposure effects in an idea generation task. *Journal of Experimental Social Psychology, 38*(6), 535-544.

Nijstad, B. A., De Dreu, C. K., Rietzschel, E. F., & Baas, M. (2010). The dual pathway to creativity model: Creative ideation as a function of flexibility and persistence. *European Review of Social Psychology, 21*(1), 34-77.

Noulas, A., Salnikov, V., Hristova, D., Mascolo, C., & Lambiotte, R. (2018). *Developing and deploying a taxi price comparison mobile app in the wild: Insights and challenges*. IEEE.

OECD (2022). Thinking outside the box: The PISA 2022 Creative Thinking Assessment. https://www.oecd.org/en/topics/sub-issues/creative-thinking/pisa-2022-creative-thinking.html

OECD (2024). New PISA results on creative thinking: Can students think outside the box? *PISA in Focus*, 125. OECD Publishing, Paris.

O'Keefe, P. A., Dweck, C. S., & Walton, G. M. (2018). Implicit theories of interest: Finding your passion or developing it? *Psychological Science*, *29*(10), 1653-1664.

Osborn, A. F. (1957). *Applied imagination: Principles and procedures of creative thinking*, rev. edn. Scribner.

Patston, T., Cropley, D., Marrone, R., & Kaufman, J. (2018). Teacher implicit beliefs of creativity: Is there an arts bias? *Teaching and Teacher Education*, *75*, 366-374.

Paulus, P. B., & Brown, V. R. (2007). Toward more creative and innovative group idea generation: A cognitive-social motivational perspective of brainstorming. *Social & Personality Psychology Compass*, *1*, 248-265.

Paulus, P. B., & Dzindolet, M. T. (1993). Social influence processes in group brainstorming. *Journal of Personality & Social Psychology*, *64*(4), 575-586.

Perkins, D. N., & Salomon, G. (1988). Teaching for transfer. *Educational Leadership*, *46*(1), 22-32.

Perkins, D. N., & Salomon, G. (1992). Transfer of learning. *International Encyclopedia of Education*, *2*, 6452-6457.

Pink, D. H. (2011). *Drive*. Canongate Books.

Plucker, J. A., & Beghetto, R. A. (2004). Why creativity is domain general, why it looks domain specific, and why the distinction does not matter. In R. J. Sternberg, E. L. Grigorenko, & J. L. Singer (Eds), *Creativity: From potential to realization* (pp. 153-167). American Psychological Association.

Plucker, J. A., Beghetto, R. A., & Dow, G. T. (2004). Why isn't creativity more important to educational psychologists? Potentials, pitfalls, and future directions in creativity research. *Educational Psychologist*, *39*(2), 83-96.

Proyer, R. T., Tandler, N., & Brauer, K. (2019). Playfulness and creativity: A selective review. In S. R. Luria, J. Baer, & J. C. Kaufman (Eds), *Creativity and humor* (pp. 43-60). Elsevier Academic Press.

Quigley, A. (2023). What is the problem with 'skills' in schools? https://alexquigley.co.uk/what-is-the-problem-with-skills-in-schools/

Ramalingam, D., Anderson, P., Duckworth, D., Scoular, C., & Heard, J. (2020). *Creative thinking: Skill development framework*. Australian Council for Educational Research. https://research.acer.edu.au/ar_misc/40

Rasch, B., & Born, J. (2013). About sleep's role in memory. *Physiological Review, 93*, 681-766.

Rethinking Assessment (2024). Building a learner profile. https://rethinkingassessment.com/learner-profile/

Rhodes, M. (1961). An analysis of creativity. *Phi Delta Kappan, 42*(7), 305-310.

Ritter, S. M., & Dijksterhuis, A. (2014). Creativity – the unconscious foundations of the incubation period. *Frontiers in Human Neuroscience, 8*, 73722.

Robinson, K. (2006). Do schools kill creativity? https://www.ted.com/talks/sir_ken_robinson_do_schools_kill_creativity

Rogers, C. (1961). *On becoming a person: A therapist's view of psychotherapy*. Constable.

Rohrer, D., Dedrick, R. F., & Stershic, S. (2015). Interleaved practice improves mathematics learning. *Journal of Educational Psychology, 107*(3), 900-908.

Rosch, E. (1978). Principles of categorisation. In E. Rosch & B. B. Lloyd (Eds), *Cognition and categorisation* (pp. 27-48). Lawrence Erlbaum.

Rotherham, A. J., & Willingham, D. T. (2010). "21st-century" skills: Not new, but a worthy challenge. *American Educator, 34*, 17-20.

Rowe, M. B. (1986). Wait time: Slowing down may be a way of speeding up! *Journal of Teacher Education, 37*(1), 43-50.

Runco, M. A., & Jaeger, G. J. (2012). The standard definition of creativity. *Creativity Research Journal, 24*(1), 92-96.

Ryan, R. M., & Deci, E. L. (2000). Self-determination theory and the facilitation of intrinsic motivation, social development, and well-being. *American Psychologist, 55*(1), 68-78.

Ryan, R. M., & Deci, E. L. (2017). *Self-determination theory: Basic psychological needs in motivation, development, and wellness*. Guilford Publications.

Said-Metwaly, S., Fernández-Castilla, B., Kyndt, E., Van den Noortgate, W., & Barbot, B. (2021). Does the fourth-grade slump in creativity actually exist? A meta-analysis of the development of divergent thinking in school-age children and adolescents. *Educational Psychology Review, 33*(1), 275-298.

Sawyer, K. (2007). *Group genius: The creative power of collaboration*. Basic Books.

Sawyer, R. K. (2006). The new science of learning. In R. K. Sawyer (Ed.), *The Cambridge handbook of the learning sciences* (pp. 1-18). Cambridge University Press.

Sawyer, R. K., & DeZutter, S. (2009). Distributed creativity: How collective creations emerge from collaboration. *Psychology of Aesthetics, Creativity, and the Arts, 3*(2), 81-92.

Schwartz, D., Bransford, J., & Sears, D. (2005). Efficiency and innovation in transfer. In J. Mestre (Ed.), *Transfer of learning from a modern multidisciplinary perspective* (pp. 1-51). Information Age Publishing.

Sellier, A. L., & Dahl, D. W. (2011). Focus! Creative success is enjoyed through restricted choice. *Journal of Marketing Research, 48*(6), 996-1007.

Shen, W., Zhao, Y., Hommel, B., Yuan, Y., Zhang, Y., Liu, Z., & Gu, H. (2019). The impact of spontaneous and induced mood states on problem solving and memory. *Thinking Skills & Creativity, 32*, 66-74.

Shin, J., & Grant, A. M. (2021). When putting work off pays off: The curvilinear relationship between procrastination and creativity. *Academy of Management Journal, 64*(3), 772-798.

Simonton, D. K. (2012). Teaching creativity: Current findings, trends, and controversies in the psychology of creativity. *Teaching of Psychology, 39*(3), 217-222.

Sio, U. N., & Ormerod, T. C. (2009). Does incubation enhance problem solving? A meta-analytic review. *Psychological Bulletin, 135*(1), 94-120.

Soderstrom, N. C., & Bjork, R. A. (2015). Learning versus performance: An integrative review. *Perspectives on Psychological Science, 10*(2), 176-199.

Spencer, E., Lucas, B., & Claxton, G. (2012). *Progression in creativity: Developing new forms of assessment – Final Research Report*. Newcastle: CCE.

Stefl, M., & Rohm, A. (2017). Is the internet killing your creative potential? Lessons from the art of paper airplane making. *Graziadio Business Review, 20*(1).

Sternberg, R. J. (1999). A propulsion model of types of creative contributions. *Review of General Psychology, 3*(2), 83-100.

Sternberg, R. J., & Lubart, T. I. (1996). Investing in creativity. *American Psychologist, 51*(7), 677-688.

Sternberg, R. J., & Lubart, T. I. (1999). The concept of creativity: Prospects and paradigms. In R. J. Sternberg (Ed.), *Handbook of creativity* (pp. 3-15). Cambridge University Press.

Storm, B. C., Bjork, E. L., & Bjork, R. A. (2008). Accelerated relearning after retrieval-induced forgetting: The benefit of being forgotten. *Journal of Experimental Psychology: Learning, Memory, and Cognition, 34*(1), 230-236.

Sweller, J. (2006). The worked example effect and human cognition. *Learning and Instruction, 16*(2), 165-169.

Sweller, J., & Levine, M. (1982). Effects of goal specificity on means-ends analysis and learning. *Journal of Experimental Psychology: Learning, Memory, and Cognition, 8*(5), 463-474.

Syed, M. (2011). *Bounce: The myth of talent and the power of practice*. Fourth Estate.

Tajfel, H., & Turner, J. C. (1979). An integrative theory of intergroup conflict. In W. G. Austin & S. Worchel (Eds), *The social psychology of intergroup relations* (pp. 33-47). Brooks/Cole.

Torrance, E. P. (1974). *The Torrance tests of creative thinking: Norms-technical manual*. Personal Press.

Tromp, C., & Baer, J. (2022). Creativity from constraints: Theory and applications to education. *Thinking Skills and Creativity, 46*, 101184.

Turner, J. C., Hogg, M. A., Oakes, P. J., Reicher, S. D., & Wetherell, M. S. (1987). *Rediscovering the social group: A self-categorization theory*. Blackwell.

van Broekhoven, K., Cropley, D., & Seegers, P. (2020). Differences in creativity across Art and STEM students: We are more alike than unalike. *Thinking Skills and Creativity, 38*, 100707.

Vohs, K. D., Redden, J. P., & Rahinel, R. (2013). Physical order produces healthy choices, generosity, and conventionality, whereas disorder produces creativity. *Psychological Science, 24*(9), 1860-1867.

Vu, T. V., Scharmer, A. L., van Triest, E., van Atteveldt, N., & Meeter, M. (2024). The reciprocity between various motivation constructs and academic achievement: A systematic review and multilevel meta-analysis of longitudinal studies. *Educational Psychology, 44*(2), 136-170.

Wallas, G. (1926). *The art of thought*. Franklin Watts.

Wammes, J. D., Meade, M. E., & Fernandes, M. A. (2016). The drawing effect: Evidence for reliable and robust memory benefits in free recall. *The Quarterly Journal of Experimental Psychology, 69*(9), 1752-1776.

WEF (2023). The Future of Jobs Report 2023. https://www.weforum.org/publications/the-future-of-jobs-report-2023/

Wegerif, R. (2004). Towards an account of teaching general thinking skills that is compatible with the assumptions of sociocultural theory. *Theory and Research in Education, 2*(2), 143-159.

Whitehead, A. N. (1929). *The aims of education and other essays*. The Free Press.

Wiliam, D. (2011). *Embedded formative assessment*. Solution Tree Press.

Wiliam, D., & Leahy, S. (2014). Sustaining formative assessment with teacher learning communities. *USA: Learning Sciences Dylan Wiliam Center*.

Willingham, D. T. (2007). Critical thinking: Why is it so hard to teach? *American Educator, 31*, 8-19.

Wittrock, M. C. (1974). Learning as a generative process. *Educational Psychologist, 11*(2), 87-95.

Index

Note: Page locators in *italic* refer to figures.

achievement: age and creative 84; creativity and academic 18; motivation and 181
active procrastination 188
adaptive expertise 100-102; boosting variation to develop 107-108; cab drivers demonstrating 137; and curriculum 104-105; deep understanding important for 105-106, *106*; developing teachers' 243-245; and tackling non-routine problems 124, 131
Agarwal, P. K. 49
Amabile, T. M. 175, *176*, 185, 221, 240, 241
Amusement Park Theoretical (APT) model 79-80, *80*
Archimedes 153, 155
Art and Design: drypoint 149; teachers' views on creativity in 74, 75
artificial intelligence (AI) 8, 232
arts: creativity is not just for 72; differences between students in sciences and 83-84; engaging in a non-creative way with 70, 72; lesson unplanning process 144, *145*; overcoming student preconceptions 86; planning for setbacks 149; policy to increase creativity through teaching 71, 78, 95-96, 255; STE(A)M education 78; views on creativity in 14, 51, 71, 74, 75, 85
Asch, S. E. 162, 177, *177*
assessment: end of year 248-249; for learning (AFL) strategies 227, *228*; lesson unplanning and criteria for 146-147; lesson unplanning and product for 145-146; standardised 217, 252
assessment of creativity 217-235; adapting curricula and assessment practices 248; applications to practice 227-233; assessing authentic projects 231; assessment for learning (AFL) strategies 227, *228*; assessments used in creativity research 219-221; authentic assessment 230; conclusion 233;

Index

criteria for creative assessment 225, 226-227; decision filters 228-229; discussion questions 234; exploring research 218-227; formative assessment 227-228, 233; modes of assessment 225; the myth 218; PISA Creative Thinking Assessment 223-224, 226; professional learning tasks 234-235; reasons for 222-223; reporting to parents 232; role of parents 233; in schools 225-226; self-assessment 221-222, 226, 232; self-reflection using creative learning habits 229; use of technology 232; washback effects 218-219
Australian Council for Educational Research (ACER) model of creative thinking 227
authentic assessment 230
authentic projects 208-210; assessing 231; many facets of 213-214
autonomy 182-183, 191, 251

Badger, C. 169
Baer, J. 33, 34, 47, 76, 77, 79, 81, 118, 122, 127, 221
Bahar, A. K. 238, 239, 246, 250
Bain, P. M. 49
Baird, B. 160, 161, 203
Barton, C. 108
Batson, C. D. 176-177
beautiful risks, taking 140-141
Beghetto, R. 6, 15, 19, 20, 21, 24, 25, 44, 81, 84, 134, 140, 141, 143, 147, 150, 152, 183, 196, 209, 212, 216, 232, 239-240, 244, 250
Benedek, M. 2, 4, 13, 53, 117, 154, 218

Bereczki, E. O. 4, 15, 135, 236, 237
Big-C creativity 6, 20, *21*, 84
the big challenge 257-258
the big picture 258-260
Bjork, R. A. 102
Bjork, R. A. and Bjork, E. L. 35, 42, 104, 116, 120
Black, P. 227
Blackberry 81
Blockbuster 81
Bloom's taxonomy 39
Bolden, B. 225, 227, 232
brainstorming 198, 202, 206; background to 197; in groups and alone 196, 197, 199; short and long 211
Bransford, J. D. 33, 40, 45, 60, 98, 101, 105, 170, 237, 244
bridging 113-114
Broekhoven, K. van 76, 83
building blocks 31-49; analogy 35-37, *36*, 58; applications to practice 41-47; cognitive science of knowledge 34-35; conclusion 47-48; creative writing 38; discussion questions 48; drawing as a mnemonic strategy 43; exploring research 34-41; fundamentals of creativity 34; knowing what you know 44-45; making most of memory 41-43; the myth 33-34; professional learning tasks 48-49; seeking novelty and usefulness 45-47; skills vs. knowledge 38-39; thinking skills 40-41; 'what if?' 43-44
Bullard, A. J. 238, 239, 246, 250
business, leadership and creativity in 240-242

cab drivers study 137
candle test 123
categorisation of quotations 28
challenge, the big 257-258
chaos and creativity 137-140, *138*, *139*, 239; teachers' discomfort with 238, 239-240, 250
Chase, W. G. 77, 105
ChatGPT 8
Chemistry: end of year assessment 249; halogen displacement reactions 66; practical 147; reflection on creativity in 70
chess masters 77, 105
children's creative thinking 13, 14-16
choice within fixed parameters 125
Christodoulou, D. 145
class schedules, revising 247
classroom talk 143
cognitive flexibility 54
cognitive science: and creativity 6-7, 52, 256; of knowledge 34-35, 58; view of expertise 99-100
commuters 94
competence 180-181, 190, 250-251
competitions in education 183-184
concreteness fading 109-110, 113
confident humility 83
connections: halogen displacement reactions 66; making 53-54, *55*, 57-58; mind maps to support 63-64; prompts and sparks to make new 65; seeking out 62-63
Consensual Assessment Technique (CAT) 221, 230
constraints and creativity 117-133; applications to practice 124-131; avoiding too many constraints 130-131; choice within fixed parameters 125; conclusion 132;

discussion questions 132-133; exclusionary and focusing functions 122, 124; exploring research 118-124; knowledge as a constraint 122-124, 128; mixed benefits of constraints 121-122; and motivation 191; the myth 117-118; philosophical essays 125; poetry 128; problem space 118-119, *120*; professional learning tasks 133; relationship between *124*; research tasks 125-126; rubrics 126; student engagement with constraints 128-130, *129*; student perceptions 119-121, 128; sweet spot, creativity *124*, 130, 132; using worked examples 127
convergence schemas 99
convergent vs divergent thinking 9-10, *9*
creative learning habits model 87-90, *88*, 226, 246; reflecting on teaching for creativity with 90; self-reflection using 229
'creative mortification', tackling 25-26
creative projects 194-216; activating everyday tasks 210-211; applications to practice 210-214; authentic projects 208-210; authentic projects assessment 231; brainstorming 196, 198, 199, 202, 206; brainstorming, background to 197; brainstorming, short and long 211; conclusion 214-215; contradictory findings on working in groups 196; discovery learning 205-206; discussion questions 215; exploring research 196-210; extended writing 207;

flow 204; Food and Nutrition 213; getting collaboration right 197-198; legacy projects 209-210, 213; legacy questions 212; the lone genius 195, 196; making projects feel more authentic 213-214; mind-wandering 202, 203-204; the myth 194-195; productive focus 201-203; professional learning tasks 216; social elements 201; strategies and transfer 206-207; types of project 200-201
creative writing 38; constraints facilitating 118, 191; fan fiction 207; poetry 128; prompts 65
creativity: the big challenge 257-258; the big picture 258-260; building blocks 236; building blocks analogy 35-37, 36, 58; and cognitive science 6-7; debates and disagreement 1-2; defining 4-6, 5, 53, 155; demystifying 155-156; as distinct from problem solving 9-10; importance of 7-8; as important but misunderstood 254-255; knowledge boosting 58-61, 59; myths and misconceptions 2-3; teachers' views on teaching creatively 3
creativity as a skill 1, 16, 33; linking knowledge to 57-58; a thinking skill 33, 40-41; a transferable skill 95-96, 255
Creativity Collaboratives 247
creativity models: Amabile's model 175, *176*, 240-241; Australian Council for Educational Research's (ACER) model 227; 'four C' model 20-22, *21*, 22-23, *23*; PISA Creative Thinking Assessment 223-224, *226*; Rethinking Assessment's 3D model 226-227; Wallas' four stage stage model 157, *158 see also* creative learning habits model
Creely, E. 242, 244
cross-curricular days 17
Csikszentmihalyi, M. 204

Darley, J. M. 176-177
darts, underwater 105-106
Darwin, C. 50-51
deadlines 189-190, 241
Deci, E. L. 180, 184, 241, 250
decision filters 228-229
definition of creativity, standard 4-6, 5, 53, 155
delays: creativity and timing of 187-188, *188*; to facilitate incubation 160, 164; productive 161-162
Deuja, A. 199, 202
DeZutter, S. 196
digital portfolios 232
direct instruction 205
discovery learning 205-206
divergent thinking 14-15, 18-19, 219-220; vs. convergent thinking 9-10, *9*
domains and creativity 76-77; Amusement Park Theoretical (APT) metaphor 79-80, *80*; creativity as domain-general or domain-specific 76-77; domain-general vs. domain-specific debate 79-81, *80*, 83; examples 77-79
drawing: constraints activity 119, *120*; as a memory strategy 43
dreaming 154

drypoint in Art and Design 149
Duncker, K. 123
Dzindolet, M. T. 197, 198

Ed-c (educational creativity) 22-23, *23*, 84, 85
Edmonson, A. 140
Education Endowment Foundation (EEF) 45, 168, 206, 244, 253
Eglington, L. G. 111
end of year assessments 248-249
English 24, 85; categorisation 28; poetry 85; teachers' views on creativity in 74
Eno, B. 65
Epstein, D. 93
evolution, theory of 50-51
expertise *see* adaptive expertise; routine expertise
Extended Project Qualification (EPQ) 186
extended writing 207
extrinsic and intrinsic motivation 184-185, 241

fan fiction 207
Firth, J. 49, 111, 168, 169, 172
fixed theory of interest 179
flexible knowledge 50-69; applications to practice 61-67; boosting creative thinking 58-61, *59*; Charles Darwin 50-51; classroom-relevant combinations 56; conclusion 67; discussion questions 68; existing knowledge 53; exploring research 53-61; flexible thinking 54-55; halogen displacement reactions 66; links to creativity as a skill 57-58; making connections 53-54, 55, 57-58; music 57; the myth 51-52; note taking 63-64; professional learning tasks 68-69; prompts and sparks 64-65; reminders 61-62; Remote Associates Test (RAT) 55; seeking out connections 62-63
flexible thinking 54-55, 81
flow 204
Food and Nutrition legacy project 213
forgetting 61-62, 164-165
'four C' model of creativity 20-22, *21*; adding Ed-c to 22-23, *23*
'functional fixedness' 123
future, looking to 258-260
Fyfe, E. R. 109, 110

games in education 183-184
geniuses, creative 20, 51, 155; idea of children as 13; the lone genius 195, 196
geographical landforms 113
geography 113, 249
Gick, M. L. 99
goal-free problems 86
Gralewski, J. 135
Grant, A. 81, 82, 83, 178, 187
group work 189, 215; brainstorming 196, 197, 199; contradictory findings on 196; getting collaboration right 197-198; productive focus and 202 *see also* creative projects
growth theory of interest 178-179
guided discovery 205, 207, 212

habits, creative learning *see* creative learning habits model
halogen displacement reactions 66
Harford, T. 117

Haskell, R. E. 96, 97
Hatano, G. 101, 102
Hendrick, C. 49
History 86, 211, 249
Holyoak, K. J. 99, 102
Howe, E. 153-154
humanities 144, 145, 146; teachers' views on creativity in *74*
humility, confident 83

identity foreclosure 178
illumination stage 157, *158*
Inagaki, K. 101, 102
incubation: applying 163-164; control of 159-160; planning for 160-161; role of 159; stage 157, *158*
insight, flashes of 153-154, 154-155, 156-158
instructions: avoiding 137-139; following 136-137, 137-138, 139
intelligent failure 140-141
interleaving 63, 108, 110-112; blocking vs. *111*; geographical landforms 113
intrinsic and extrinsic motivation 184-185, 241

Jaeger, G. J. 4, 5, 72, 155
Jarrett, K. 117
Jenkins, H. 207

Kang, S. H. K. 111
Kárpáti, A. 14, 15, 135, 236, 237
Karwowski, M. 18-19, 27, 40, 196, 259
Kaufman, J. C. 6, 20, 29, 76, 77, 79, 81, 84, 183, 196, 222, 239-240
Kekulé, A. 153
Kim, Y. J. 139
kind learning environments 93
Kirschner, P. A. 49, 205

knowledge: building block of creativity 18, 35-37, *36*, 47-48, 58; cognitive science of 34-35, 58; as a constraint 122-124, 128; creativity tests and 221; foundational 34, 37, 38, 40-41, 56, 160; knowing what you know 44-45; as powerful 37; vs. skills 38-39, 255-257; structure in memory 58-61; Theory of Knowledge (TOK) 87 *see also* flexible knowledge
Kodak 81
Kooren, N. S. 188
Krstic, S. 226-227, 235

Land, G. 13
landforms, geographical 113
languages: speaking in foreign 142; teachers' views on creativity in *74*; using creative learning habits in 90
Larcom, S. 94
Lassig, C. 22-23
leadership: influence on creativity 240-243; and school culture 246-251
Leahy, S. 245
learning communities: student 169; teacher 245-246
legacy projects 209-210; in Food and Nutrition 213; questions in setting up 212
lesson unplanning 143-147; AI bot to help with 152; criteria 146-147; problem 144; process 144-145; product 145-146
little-c creativity 6, 20, 21-22, *21*, 56
Lovell, O. 86
Lubart, T. I. 47, 53
Lucas, B. 88, 92, 191, 222, 225, 226, 229, 235, 246, 247

Malthus, T. 50
Maths: comparing questions in 108; goal-free problems 86; introducing uncertainty into 141–142; lesson unplanning 143–144, 146; limited understanding affecting students' transfer 106, *106*; overcoming student preconceptions 86; planning for setbacks 148; and student engagement with constraints 128–130, *129*; views on creativity in *74*, 75, 85, 86
Mayer, R. E. 58, 205
McCartney, P. 154
Mccrea, P. 106
McDaniel, M. A. 121
media, teachers in popular 12, 236
memory: drawing as a memory strategy 43; 'implicit' 161–162; long-term retention 42, 104; making most of 41–43; mind maps to aid 64; retrieval 53, 61–62, 64; schemas 60; structure of knowledge in 58–61
metacognition and strategic creativity 153–172; activating prior learning 165–166; applications to practice 163–169; applying incubation 163–164; conclusion 169–171; control of incubation 159–160; defining metacognition 44–45; demystifying creativity 155–156; discussion questions 171; exploring research 155–163; flashes of insight 153–154, 154–155, 156–158; forgetting 164–165; metacognitive awareness 167–169, 170; the myth 154–155; planning for incubation 160–161; productive delays 161–162; professional learning tasks 171–172; role of incubation 159; sleep and associations 162–163; student learning communities 169; toolkit of strategies 166–167; Wallas' four-stage model of creativity 157, *158*
'micro moments', creative 23–24
Milgram, R. M. 199
mind maps 63–64
mind-wandering 202, 203–204
mini-c creativity 20, 21, *21*, 22, 56; sharing insights 24, 25, 26
motivation and creativity 173–193; Amabile's model of creativity 175, *176*, 240–241; applications to practice 187–191; autonomy 182–183, 191; in business 240–241; competence 180–181, 190; conclusion 192; constraints 191; deadlines and rewards 189–190; discussion questions 192–193; exploring research 174–186; extended projects 186; growth theory of interest 178–179; identity foreclosure 178; intrinsic and extrinsic motivation 184–185, 241; making classes fun and exciting 183–184; motivation as not always fixed 176–178, *177*, 180; the myth 173–174; procrastination, creativity and motivation 187–188, *188*; professional learning tasks 193; relatedness 181–182, 190–191; self-determination theory (SDT) 180–183, 184, 190–191, 241, 250–251; strategies linked to competence, relatedness and autonomy 190–191; timing 187–188, *188*; value of

creative motivation 174-176; where motivations come from 179-183
Mueller, J. S. 135
music 57, 65, 70
myths and misconceptions in education 2-3, 255; assessing creativity 218; breaking from routine 95-96; building blocks 33-34; constraints and creativity 117-118; creative projects 194-195; creativity across all subjects 71; developing teachers' creativity 236-237; flexible knowledge 51-52; metacognition and strategic creativity 154-155; motivation and creativity 173-174; schools and creativity 13-14; structured uncertainty 135

NASA study 13, 14-15
Nathan, M. J. 109, 110
nature-nurture debate 51-52
Nijstad, B. A. 34, 54
note taking 63-64
Noulas, A. 137
novelty: a criteria for creativity 4, 5, *5*; featuring recombinations of existing knowledge 53-54, 57-58; seeking 45-47

O'Keefe, P. A. 179
'optimal adaptability corridor' 243-244
Ormerod, T. C. 159, 160
Osborn, A. F. 197
overconfidence cycle 81-83, *82*

paper aeroplanes study 137-139, *138*
parents: involvement in school culture 251-252; reporting to 232; role in developing students' creative thinking 233
passions 179, 190; finding students' 173-174, 178, 192 see also motivation and creativity
passive procrastination 188
Paulus, P. B. 197, 198
PEEL (point, evidence, evaluation, link) 131
Perkins, D. N. 40, 95, 96, 97, 98, 113, 114
perseverance *88*, 89, 179
philosophical essays 125
Pink, D. 123
PISA Creative Thinking Assessment 223-224, 226
playfulness 26-27, 28
Plucker, J. A. 81, 195
poetry 128
'pre-crastination' 187, 189
'premortem' concept 148
preparation stage 157, *158*
prior learning, activating 165-166
Pro-C creativity 20-21, *21*, 22, 23, 77
problem space 118-119, *120*, 122, 123, 124, 128, 191
problems: comparing SSDD problems 108; cross-curricular days for solving 17; goal-free 86; importance of deep understanding of 105-106, *106*; knowledge as a constraint in solving 122-124, 131; problem solving and creativity 9-10, 156; similarity and transfer 99-100; 'what if?' questions 43-44; wheeled suitcases as a solution to a problem 31-32, *32*
procrastination, creativity and motivation 187-188, *188*

productive focus and creative projects 201-203
promises and perils of creativity 19
prompts and sparks 64-65
Proyer, R. T. 26, 27

questions, wait time after asking 25, 189
quotations, categorising 28

Ramalingam, D. 227, 235
relatedness 181-182, 190-191, 251
reminders 61-62
Remote Associates Test (RAT) 55
repetitive practice 97, 99, 102-103, 104
research tasks, constraints on 125-126
Rethinking Assessment: 3D model of creative thinking 226-227; Learner Profile 232
rethinking cycle 81, *82*
rewards 189-190
Riazat, N. 49
risks: bad 140; and failure 140, 242, 250; good 140; taking beautiful 140-141
Robinson, K. 12, 30
Rogers, C 179-180
Rohm, A. 137
routine, breaking from 94-116; adaptive expertise and curriculum 104-105; applications to practice 107-114; boosting variation 107-108; bridging 113-114; comparing questions in Maths 108; conclusion 114-115; concreteness fading 109-110, 113; deeper understanding 105-106, *106*; defining transfer 96-97; discussion questions 115-116; exploring research 96-106; geographical landforms 113; interleaving 108, 110-112, *111*, 113; the myth 95-96; professional learning tasks 116; routine and adaptive expertise 100-102; routine expertise and curriculum 102-103; sport skill 98; three views of transfer 98-99; why transfer is important (and difficult) 99-100
routine expertise 100-102; and curriculum 102-103; and tackling non-routine problems 123-124, 131
rubrics 126
rules, following the 136-137, 137-138, 139
Runco, M. A. 4, 5, 19, 155
Ryan, R. M. 180, 182, 184, 241, 250

Said-Metwaly, S. 14
Salomon, G. 40, 95, 96, 97, 113, 114
Sawyer, R. K. 7, 196
schemas 60, 99
Schmidt, P. 65
schools and creativity 12-30; adapting curricula and assessment practices 247-249; applications to practice 23-28; categorisation in English 28; children's creative thinking 14-16; conclusion 28-29; creative 'micro moments' 23-24; cross-curricular days 17; discussion questions 29; Ed-c 22-23, *23*; exploring research 14-23; 'four C' model of creativity 20-22, *21*; leadership and school

culture 246-251; leadership influencing creativity 240-243; motivating teachers to embrace uncertainty 250-251; the myth 13-14; negative stereotypes of teaching 12; playfulness 26-27; professional learning tasks 30; promises and perils of creativity 19; revising class schedules 247; schools don't kill creativity 18-19; tackling 'creative mortification' 25-26

Schwartz, D. 243

science: creativity in 71; creativity in school subjects 85; differences between students in arts and 83-84; lesson unplanning process 144-145; lesson unplanning product 146; overcoming student preconceptions 86; planning for setbacks 148; practical Chemistry 147; STE(A)M education 78; teachers' views on creativity in *74*, 75; use of 'formula triangles' 103, 131; using creative learning habits in 90

self-assessment 221-222, 226, 232

self-determination theory (SDT) 180-183, *184*, 241, 250-251; autonomy 182-183, 191, 251; competence 180-181, 190, 250-251; relatedness 181-182, 190-191, 251

self-reflection using creative learning habits 229

self-report measures of creativity 77-78

setbacks, planning for 148-149

Shin, J. 187

Simon, H. 77, 105

Sio, U. N. 159, 160

skill, creativity as a 1, 16, 33; linking knowledge to 57-58; a thinking skill 33, 40-41; a transferable skill 95-96, 255

skills vs. knowledge 38-39, 255-257

sleep and associations 162-163

Soderstrom, N. C. 42

Spencer, E. 88, 92, 191, 225, 226, 235, 246

sport skill 98

STE(A)M education 78

Stefl, M. 137, *138*

Sternberg, R. J. 47, 53, 259

Stoll, L. 246

strategic creativity *see* metacognition and strategic creativity

structured uncertainty 134-152; applicable to teacher learning 244; applications to practice 141-149; chaos and creativity 137-140, *138*, *139*; classroom talk 143; conclusion 150; discussion questions 150-151; drypoint in Art and Design 149; exploring research 136-141; following the rules 136-137; increasing in line with students' competence levels 206; introducing uncertainty into schools 141-142; lesson unplanning 143-147, 152; the myth 135; overreliance on technology 136-137; planning for setbacks 148-149; practical Chemistry 147; professional learning tasks 151-152; speaking in foreign languages 142; taking beautiful risks 140-141; teachers' embracing of 244, 250-251 students: differences across subjects between 83-84; engagement with constraints 128-130, *129*; learning communities 169; overcoming student preconceptions of subjects 86; perceptions of own creativity 119-121, 128

subjects, creativity across all 70-93; applications to practice 85-90; conclusion 91; creative learning habits 87-90, *88*; creativity in school subjects 85; creativity is not just for arts 72; differences between students across subjects 83-84; discussion questions 91-92; domain-general or domain-specific creativity 76-77; domain-general vs. domain-specific debate 79-81, *80*, 83; domains and creativity examples 77-79; exploring research 72-84; the myth 71; overcoming student preconceptions 86; overconfidence cycle 81-83, *82*; personal reflection 70-71; professional learning tasks 92-93; STE(A)M education 78; teachers' views on 72-75, *73*, *74*; Theory of Knowledge (TOK) 87

success, characteristics of creative 259

suitcases, wheeled 31-32, *32*

Superman, a date with 239-240

Syed, M. 98

teachers: attitudes to creativity in students 135; learning communities (TLCs) 245-246; in popular media 12, 236; views on creativity in their subject 72-75, *73*, *74*; views on teaching creatively 3

teachers, developing creative 236-253; adapting curricula and assessment practices 247-249; adaptive expertise 243-245; applications to practice 243-252; challenges to teaching for creativity 238-240; conclusion 252; discussion questions 252-253; embracing uncertainty 244, 250-251; end of year assessments 248-249; exploring research 237-243; influence of leadership on creativity 240-243; involving parents 251-252; leadership and school culture 246-251; the myth 236-237; professional learning tasks 253; revising class schedules 247; teacher learning communities 245-246

TeacherTapp survey 72-75, *73*, *74*

technology 136-137, 232

Theory of Knowledge (TOK) 87

times of day, creativity at different 162, 164

timescale of creativity 157, *158*

timing of tasks 187-188, *188*

Torrance Test of Creative Thinking 220

transfer 96-97; metacognitive awareness and 170-171; three views of 97-99; why it is important 99-100

Tromp, C. 118, 122, 127

true self 179-180

uncertainty *see* structured uncertainty
unconscious processing 161–162
usefulness: a criteria for creativity 4, 5, *5*, 15; seeking 45–47

varied practice 104, 107–108
verification stage 157, *158*
Vohs, K. D. 140
Voltaire 53–54
Vu, T. V. 181

wait time after asking questions 25, 189
Wallas, G. 157, *158*, 159

Wammes, J. D. 43
washback effects 218–219
'what if?' questions 43–44
wicked learning environments 93
Wiliam, D. 189, 227, 245
worked examples, using 127
workplace, creativity in 175, 240–242, 258–260
World Economic Forum (WEF) 258–259
writing, creative *see* creative writing
writing, extended 207

Did you love reading about the research on Creativity?

Want to get **amazing online training for your staff** that can take their understanding even further?

Then

The **Teacher CPD Academy**.

is for you!

Simply scan this QR code

Or head over to
teacherCPDacademy.com

Or email
info@innerdrive.co.uk

to request a free trial.

We **illuminate research** with **inspiring** and **interactive** modules, interviews and keynote talks.

So, do not hesitate. A **brilliant professional development platform** for all your colleagues is only a click away!

For Product Safety Concerns and Information please contact
our EU representative GPSR@taylorandfrancis.com Taylor & Francis
Verlag GmbH, Kaufingerstraße 24, 80331 München, Germany